Extremely Pale Rosé

Extremely Pale Rosé

A Very French Adventure

JAMIE IVEY

St. Martin's Press ❦ New York

www.stmartins.com

Library of Congress Cataloging-in-Publication Data

Ivey, Jamie.
    Extremely pale rosé : a very French adventure / Jamie Ivey.—1st ed.
        p. cm.
    ISBN-13: 978-0-312-34956-1
    ISBN-10: 0-312-34956-4
    1. British—France—Fiction. 2. Wine and wine making—Fiction.
3. France—Fiction. 4. Friendship—Fiction. I. Title.

PR6109.V64E98 2006
823'.92—dc22
                                                           2006040849

First published in Great Britain by Weidenfeld & Nicolson

10 9 8 7 6 5 4 3 2

For Tanya

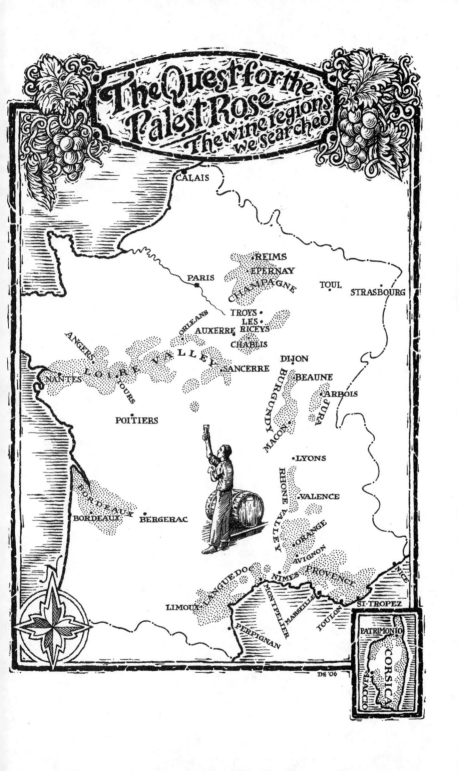

'Peter took great delight in
referring to his rosé as Rosie.
He thought it was harmless fun.'

I

Extremely Pale Rosie

It was a lunch that changed our lives. Just six months later my wife and I and our good friend Peter Tate would set out on a remarkable journey, but at the time our thoughts were culinary not revolutionary – was the foie gras too heavy and rich for lunch? Could we really manage yet another deliciously intense *daube*? And, more worryingly, would we get served at all?

We arrived one hour late for our booking at the Hôtel Sénanque, a squat, faded building set in the flat plains beneath the Provençal village of Gordes. Behind the hotel, amid great bushes of thyme, rosemary and tarragon, was a small restaurant. Five tables, laid in crisp pink linen, nestled under a white awning that flapped gently in the breeze.

We waited at the entrance to the herb garden in the limited shade offered by an old olive tree. A menu rested on an ornate iron stand. *Côte de veau aux morilles, gigot d'agneau aux herbes, gambas au feu de bois* – I mentally devoured each option, attempting to sate my stomach with the mere thought of food, but the likelihood was that we were too late. In France, lunch is taken between midday and 2 p.m. – the optimal hours for digestion. It is not to be rushed or undertaken as a mid-afternoon afterthought.

An elderly waiter served the whole restaurant. He was

formally dressed in black trousers and a white shirt left open at the neck. In the breast pocket of his shirt sat the tools of his trade – a pen, notebook and corkscrew. He moved slowly among the tables, clearing plates, filling glasses and exchanging pleasantries.

Minutes passed. I felt the despair of the foreigner unsure of local custom. Should we just sit ourselves down? Would the waiter treat his fellow countrymen like this? I fidgeted from foot to foot. By now my mind had reached the petits fours and my stomach was threatening open revolt.

Finally, with a dramatic glance at his watch, the waiter acknowledged us. Once appropriately chided for arriving at 2 p.m., we were shown to our table. The other diners were just finishing dessert. As we sat down, reverential conversations about the sweetness of the *tarte aux pommes* ceased. Spoons and forks were dropped heavily on to china plates. We felt like food pagans arriving at a feast of the righteous.

When the waiter returned to take our order he nodded approvingly as we all chose foie gras and then the regional speciality – *daube*, a slow-cooked beef stew flavoured with anchovies and tapenade. But then came the wine.

For us, there was only one wine to choose. We were sitting beneath a wonderful white awning in the middle of a delightful Provençal garden. Leaning back on my chair, I could pick sprigs of rosemary. A resplendent purple carpet of lavender encircled the restaurant, and, above, the sky was a clear blue. In the distance we could see the town of Gordes perched on its rocky promontory. It was high summer in France and the cicadas were beating their afternoon lament before the heat gradually faded from the sun.

As I announced our choice the waiter's pen ceased its frantic scribble. He turned and looked sheepishly away. Thinking I had been misunderstood, I pointed to the wine on the list. He affected to study a small fly that had landed on his shoulder. I pointed to the wine again. He flicked the insect away and suddenly developed an intense interest in a speck of dust on his black shoes. Nobody spoke. What had we done? How long could he ignore us for? Then, with pursed lips and hunched shoulders, the waiter snatched the menus away. He tucked them under his arm and disappeared without a word.

We had asked for rosé. It was the perfect accompaniment to the landscape. Beyond the herb garden stretched fields of vines. Peeping through the green foliage hung an abundance of grapes, already heavy with juice. As each day passed they would swell and slowly change colour. At the end of each row roses bloomed a deep luscious scarlet.

A glass of chilled rosé was our salute to the blissful view that lay before us. We would raise our glasses, wish for a bumper crop and bid our farewells to another wonderful week in Provence. By nightfall we would be on a plane back to London, already dreaming of next summer, of air heady with herbs and the perfumed pale rosé that for us epitomised the whole experience.

Of course, our elderly waiter could not possibly understand this – to him, we had just committed a sacrilege. Never mind that we knew we should have asked for a glass of sweet wine to accompany our foie gras. The best value on the wine list appeared to be a Muscat from a vineyard just outside the Roman town of Béziers. And then a full-bodied red to bring out the intense meaty flavours of the *daube*. By ignoring the pricier Bordeaux and Burgundies, we would doubtless have pleased our host by opting for a '98 from Bandol, a small fishing village to the west of Toulon.

If ignorance was not our excuse, then ordering rosé in the full knowledge of our sins against gastronomy, and hence the French nation, was quite possibly enough to have us evicted from the restaurant. Rosé was fit for peasants, certainly not this restaurant's €40 menu.

But eventually it turned up, pale, crisp and delightfully cold, wearing a white napkin round its neck like a dinner shirt and dipped in a stainless-steel bucket piled high with ice.

'Marvellous,' said Peter.

Peter is sixty years old, wears a pacemaker and lives for the three 'f's – friends, family and France. Late at night it became the four 'f's.

He is a perfect holiday companion. When in France, he believes everything is marvellous. Sometimes wonderful, but more often than not, marvellous. Being woken by the incessant reports of shotguns as the local peasantry tries to annihilate anything with wings or a snout – come to think of it anything that moves – is to most people annoying, but to Peter, it's marvellous.

As is his first glass of rosé at 10.30 in the morning. 'It's twelve o'clock somewhere in the world,' he declares, in a deep gravelly baritone. Later he strolls into a nearby village, buys ham, bread, cheese and of course some rosé. Shopping complete, he sits, a picture of contentment with a cigar, coffee and pastis in the village square.

Typically, he wears sandals, shorts and an unbuttoned shirt. Tufts of hair mushroom from his chest and plumes rise from his eyebrows. A pair of glasses usually rests on the bridge of his rounded nose. Laughter lines play around the corners of his eyes. Take away the hire car and throw in a Deux Chevaux and he would pass as a local artist.

Back at the villa he'll play boules all afternoon, have a game of tennis before supper and still find time to push a few people in the pool. At dusk a transformation takes place – linen trousers, a pressed cotton shirt and hair swept back to reveal a sun-burnished face. He even wears socks with his boat shoes. A notorious rake in his younger days, my wife, Tanya, assures me he could still charm the tail off a *sanglier*.

Joining Peter, Tanya and me for lunch at the Hôtel Sénanque

were my sister-in-law, Claire, and her baby, Rosie. They had recently emigrated to France and lived in Montpellier. Rosie was twelve months old and taking her first few tottering steps. Blessed with kiss-curls and a wide, ever-present grin, she was a magnet to the child-loving French. Unfortunately – or fortunately as it turned out – that day she was not particularly well. It was Rosie's pale face that started this story.

On the adjoining table a French lady was dining alone. We later learnt her name was Madame Etienne. Later still Miriam. We never learnt her age. She dressed like a thirty-year-old – wearing her straight blonde hair at shoulder length and an off-the-shoulder dress cut just above the knee to highlight long brown legs – but her hands were those of an older lady. Her skin bunched over her knuckles and creased around her wrists. She wore two opulent gold rings set with rubies and diamonds. Jackie O sunglasses masked any tell-tale wrinkles around her eyes.

Dining next to Madame Etienne was an experience. Eavesdropping and food were treated with equal seriousness. She operated rather than ate – holding her spoon and fork precisely between thumb and forefinger like surgical tools and dissecting her dessert into tiny morsels. Each mouthful was accompanied by a sip of sweet white wine. As she chewed, her head swivelled to pick up snippets of conversation. Periodically, she paused to wipe the corner of her mouth and to smooth the folds in her black dress.

By the time our starters arrived we were on to our second bottle of rosé and the restaurant had nearly emptied. Madame Etienne remained, stirring the dregs of her coffee and pretending not to notice us. Then a teddy bear landed on her lap.

What followed was the type of chaos that new mothers seem so anaesthetised to. Rosie flung away the book she had been quietly flicking through, knocked over a glass and demonstrated the full power of her year-old tonsils. The waiter gave Rosie a small flower in a fruitless attempt to mollify her and then began sweeping up the shards of glass. The flower was immediately ripped to shreds, and another glass was deposited into the colourful *mélange* under the table. I recoiled in shock at the explosive force of a teddy-bear-less baby. Claire smiled benignly. Rosie forgot her lost cuddly toy and began eating a flower petal.

'*Excusez-moi*. I am sorree. *Parlez-vous français?*' Madame Etienne stood rigid-backed, thin-lipped, overly made-up, apparently intent on garrotting Rosie's teddy.

Claire nodded an affirmative.

'I think this belongs to your baby,' she said, still holding the teddy in a stranglehold as she looked with evident disdain at Peter.

I assumed that she was used to men standing up for her when she arrived at a table, or at the very least acknowledging her. To be fair, Peter usually would, but he was apparently oblivious to the baby-induced bomb-site around him and was staring with rapt satisfaction at the colour of his wine. He was probably still recovering from a traumatic experience earlier in the week when he'd asked for the rosé to be passed to him. Instead of the wine, a relieved Claire had plonked Rosie on his lap and he'd been left wine-less and holding the baby for over an hour. Ever since, as revenge, he'd taken great delight in referring to his rosé as 'Rosie'.

It was harmless fun until, still ignoring Madame Etienne, he held his glass up to the sun and gazed with admiration at the resulting reflection of the pink-tinged landscape. 'I think it's the palest, most beautiful Rosie in France,' he declared.

Something about this upset Madame. She pointed directly at Rosie, who was sitting on Claire's lap apparently intent on adopting our bottle of wine as a surrogate teddy. As Rosie clasped the wine, Madame Etienne released a torrent of words that washed through my wine-addled brain.

Claire speaks fluent French, Tanya passable, and Peter and I struggle to order a loaf of bread in a bakery, even if we can manage a beer in a bar. Guesswork has, however, got me through many a situation and, as Claire – our supposedly fluent French-speaker – was looking more than a little bemused, I interpreted for the rest of the table. Never again. My only excuse was that I am sure Madame Etienne mimicked Peter and used the word 'Rosie' instead of 'rosé'. In any event, lulled by our long lunch, I momentarily confused wine and baby in my head, and so began an unlikely challenge.

Madame Etienne's French went something like this: '*De plus, vous faites une erreur si vous croyez que ce petit Rosie est le plus pâle de toute la France. Si vous voulez nous rendre visite l'année prochaine, on vous le montrera.*'

Tipsily translated by me this became: 'Madame thinks she knows a child paler than Rosie. She's invited us to visit her this time next year and she'll prove it.' At the time I remember thinking that perhaps the French had some strange cultural attachment to pale-skinned babies. But before I could reconsider and before Tanya or Claire could intervene, Peter had plucked Rosie – still seemingly surgically attached to the bottle of rosé – from her seat and, with a big smile, raised her above his head.

'*Excusez-moi, Madame*, but I think you will find that *this* is the palest Rosie in the whole of France. We will see you next August.' Setting Rosie down, Peter took another sip of rosé and declared it to be 'marvellous'.

Madame Etienne took a step backwards and toyed with a stray lock of hair. Now she was looking confused. '*Bon,*' she said, suddenly making a decision. '*Amenez-nous le rosé de votre choix. Celui de mon mari, Bernard, sera sans aucun doute le plus pâle.*'

She handed Rosie her teddy and removed a business card from her purse, which she placed on the table. Using an old fountain pen, she wrote a short message in big florid letters. As she did so, a smile spread across her face, as if she were treasuring some private joke. Handing the business card to Peter, she gave us all a curt nod and left. I could still hear her heels clicking slowly across the stone as Peter flicked over the card. The message simply read, '*Bon courage.*'

Tanya and Claire began to laugh uncontrollably. They wiped away tears with their napkins. They took deep breaths to try to stop, but each time their eyes met, a fresh round of mirth would begin. Eventually, Tanya choked out the words in between giggles. 'Do you realise what you have just done?' More laughter. 'You have just bet that by next August we'll deliver to her the palest rosé in France.'

'And so we shall,' chorused Peter and I, confident that Claire's little cherub would be comfortably cuter than any French baby.

The laughter started again. Tears ran down the girls' cheeks.

'No, not *Rosie*, you bet her that you could find a paler *rosé* than the one her husband makes.'

'Ah,' I said.

'Marvellous,' said Peter, pouring himself another glass of rosé. 'When do we start?'

Soon we were all captivated by the wonderful implausibility of the idea. There were hundreds of sensible reasons to forget the misunderstanding had ever taken place, but instead we were intoxicated by our surroundings.

For the next hour we sat relaxing in the sun, dreaming of a summer spent touring vineyards, tasting wine and exploring France. Peter excitedly planned a lopsided itinerary, according to which we would spend nearly all our time in Provence, and by the time the waiter presented us with the bill, we'd all convinced ourselves that the quest for France's palest rosé was the most natural thing in the world.

We were still chattering animatedly about next summer as we passed the old olive tree that stood at the entrance to the restaurant. It was only when we got into our airless cars and began to drive to the airport that the challenge began to appear an indulgent fantasy. The conversation slowly stopped, and the idea began to slip away.

2

Leaving London

A week later, in London, Tanya was making her usual journey to work. A clogged Northern Line train took her from Balham to Charing Cross. Spewed out with the other commuters, she headed past Saint Martin-in-the-Fields Church towards Shaftesbury Avenue. Stopping at her usual café, she bought a coffee for herself and a pastry for the tramp waiting outside.

She turned into a small side street by the Gielgud Theatre. The detritus from another night in Soho surrounded her. A young lad with peroxide hair, ripped jeans and a tight leather biker jacket lay face down in his own vomit. A prostitute stood and stared, slack-mouthed from chewing too much gum. Tanya rolled the boy over to check he was breathing, and then stepped over him and put her key in the door to her office.

When she was interviewed for a job at Townends TV, her boss-to-be Stephen Eltham, promised a champagne lifestyle. 'We work with some of the biggest names in television, but, above all, this job is about teamwork and having fun. And every Friday we have a glass of champagne to celebrate working together.'

The champagne never materialised, however. Stephen Eltham's definition of fun appeared to consist of allowing his employees to be touched up by lecherous celebrities, and teamwork involved passing the buck rather than the ball.

'Tanya, get that boy off the doorstep and wash the puke away. We can't have it seen by clients.' Stephen was waiting by my wife's desk as she entered the office.

'I'll call an ambulance for the boy, but I'm not your cleaner.'

'Well, do some f★★★ing work, then.' Stephen's face flushed red. He swept his hand through his grey, slightly greasy hair and returned to his office. It was the first time that Tanya had spoken to him since she had returned from holiday.

Midway through the morning Tanya looked up from her work.

Stephen had planted both his hands on her desk. His face was still an ugly blotchy red. '*GMTV* have asked for the press pack. Where is it?'

'You asked me to have it ready for the middle of next week,' Tanya replied as calmly as she could.

'If you jeopardise this f★★★ing deal with your f★★★ing forgetfulness, I'll make your life f★★★ing hell.'

And so it went on. A ten-minute barrage of swear words, during which Tanya calmly collected her belongings and left.

That evening we opened the last bottle of rosé from our summer holiday and sat down to work out what to do next.

At moments of crisis Tanya always argues we should move to France. For her, sitting in a Parisian corner café with a few ramshackle tables, a surly waiter and trails of smoke wafting past is a semi-religious experience. She's so immersed in all things Gallic that it's possible there was some sort of celestial mix-up at birth and she was allocated a French soul by mistake.

Until now I'd always relied on the fact that we couldn't just simply give up our careers. Not after all the hard work. Tanya had paid her way through university with a succession of awful jobs – washing dishes for entire summers, becoming a street-corner cupid signing men up for dating agencies and – my personal favourite – working as a door-to-door saleswoman despite her dog phobia. After graduating, she answered an advert for a marketing assistant at a theatrical PR company and spent the next year making tea and watering the office plants.

Shortly afterwards Tanya started work with Stephen Eltham. Apart from her new boss, it was a real step forward in her career – instead of ensuring the office didn't run out of paper clips, she was in charge of ensuring all the new output of the production company was vigorously and well promoted on TV and in magazines.

My career path was more consistent, if a lot less colourful. After university I spent two years at law school and then became a solicitor. I successfully swapped firms a couple of times, made plenty of money and in the future I stood to make plenty more. But in return the partners had extracted their pound of flesh. I was rarely home before 10 p.m. and worked most weekends. I felt like part of a well-oiled machine. The moment I finished one piece of work, another would roll on to the production line. If I worked hard for the next five years then I had a chance of making partner. The problem was that most of the partners at my latest firm were overworked, haggard and rarely appeared happy.

What should Tanya do next? What should I do next? The simple option was for Tanya to find another job in the entertainment industry and for me to carry on working as a lawyer. Our future would be secure. I would spend a lifetime not seeing my wife, but at least we could pay off the mortgage and afford to start a family. Eventually, we would move to the countryside around London, and twice a year we could spend a week in Provence. It was probably the right thing for us to do.

On the kitchen table lay a pile of bills, mostly relating to our summer holiday. We discussed what temporary work Tanya could get to help us pay for our extravagance. Amid the credit-card slips and hotel receipts I came across a forgotten business card.

Madame Etienne
DIRECTEUR DE PRODUCTION
Château Etienne
St Maximin la Ste Baume

Tanya smiled and took a sip of her wine. 'Why not?'

'Don't be ridiculous,' I said.

'Come on. It will give us a chance to think about our careers.' She flipped the card over, and we both looked once again at the two words written in such distinctive handwriting on the back. '*Bon courage.*'

David Jakes is one of the most feared lawyers in London. He's a ball-breaker, a rainmaker, a twenty-four-hours-a-day, 365-days-a-year ass-kicker, devoted to his clients and making money. He gets through secretaries quicker than most people do Biros and was once seen smiling in 1994. Nobody can ever remember him laughing.

'David, can we have a quick chat? I've got something to tell you.'

David raised his left hand to signal I should wait. For the next five minutes he methodically read various papers, occasionally pausing to make an annotation in red ink. Eventually, he looked up and, with a single glance, conveyed his irritation. 'Yes?' he said.

My mouth was dry. My eyes darted from the floor to the ceiling to the blank walls. Why hadn't I just saved the speech and jotted down my resignation on an email?

'I just wanted to let you know that I am giving notice to terminate my contract.'

'Very well.' David picked another document from his in-tray and resumed his reading.

'It's just that . . . ' Suddenly I wanted him to understand why I was leaving. 'It's just that my wife has lost her job and we have a once-in-a-lifetime opportunity. You see, we met this woman in France and she challenged us to find the palest rosé. And Tanya loves France, and we can rent out the house and pay the mortgage that way . . .'

'Quiet,' said David in his thin reedy voice.

'I just feel it is something that I have to do,' I continued nervously.

'I said quiet.' He glanced back down at his notes and made an annotation with a swift flick of his pen. I winced as the nib grated over the paper. Looking up, he seemed surprised that I was still there. 'I'll expect you to work your full six-month notice period,' he said calmly.

And that was it. I shuffled out of his office and sat back down at my desk. David's reaction had been as blank as my computer screen. I'd been prepared for an angry reprimand but instead there was silence.

For the rest of the day my mind kept returning to those moments in David's office. Almost anything would have been preferable to the emotional void I'd walked into. I knew that before he went home David meticulously filled out a paper timesheet detailing exactly how he'd spent his day. He'd enter details of which clients were to be billed and any time he'd spent mentoring young lawyers. Every second had to be accounted for, and apparently I was now worth less than ten.

Persuading Peter to join us was not a problem.

3
Bernard's Rosé

Dear Madame Etienne,   23 October

*It was so nice to meet you in August at the Hôtel
Sénanque. We have decided to take up your challenge to find
the palest rosé in France and we look forward to seeing you at
Château Etienne next August when we will deliver our
findings.*

*Please could you send us a few bottles of your husband
Bernard's rosé – we need to know what we're up against.*

Kind regards,
Yours sincerely,

Jamie Ivey

While we waited for Madame Etienne's response we decided to
conduct a little research. A brief search of UK off-licences
proved depressing. We hoped to discover a few vineyards to visit
– domaines hidden in the hills known only to industry buyers,
where viticulture is passed from father to son, not learnt at
university, and where grapes are picked by hand, not stripped
from the vine by machines. Instead, we found Mateus.

The round-bottled Portuguese-produced wine was ubiquitous. Even worse was supermarket own-brand Portuguese rosé.

Same round bottle, same nasty fizz, and after two or three glasses I was left feeling distinctly sick. Also common was a wine called white Zinfandel from the Napa Valley in California. It was so dark we could have mistaken it for a red. The few Côtes de Provences we discovered were largely disappointing – or is it just that slate-grey skies and rosés do not mix?

Each morning I checked the post for a reply. Each morning I was disappointed. I took to reading wine books, trawling through them for mentions of rosé. Pages and pages were devoted to Burgundy and Bordeaux. If I wanted to distinguish my Nuits Saint Georges from my Beaune, or my Mercurey from my Rully, then a bevy of experts could assist, but just finding out which vineyards produced rosé, let alone what it tasted like, proved beyond UK wine buffs.

Rosé became an obsession. We drank nothing else with our meals. Friends returning from a skiing trip to the French–Swiss border gushed about a rosé that they swore was local and which was as light as falling snow. I had sleepless nights thinking about this wine until I encountered a bottle of rosé from Savoie in a specialist wine merchant. It was not that pale, but the wine merchant confirmed that vineyards throughout the Haute-Savoie were renowned for rosé.

My father surprised me by producing a bottle of pink Sancerre. It was as crisp as the white Sancerre but delicately coloured. After drinking it, I began to feel that we might succeed.

But there was still no news and the clock was ticking. Before long I would have served my notice period. In France, the labourers would be back in the fields pruning the vines and taking the odd cutting for grafting later in the year. The sap would start to rise and a new growing season would start.

We had made all the preparations to change our life for six months. We'd surrendered our careers, rented out our flat, packed our possessions away and booked a ferry crossing. All to pursue a challenge from a French woman who appeared to be determined to deny our existence.

At the end of February an unusual parcel arrived, accompanied by a letter. The envelope was scented with lavender and lined with silk. The author wrote in luxuriant black ink, and the big circular letters were all too familiar. The letter was signed 'Miriam' and the crest at the top read 'Château Etienne'. At least we were now on first-name terms.

I read and reread the letter to make sure I understood it correctly. Miriam was delighted we had accepted the challenge and suggested we meet one month later than planned, during the September *vendange* festival, which celebrated the grape harvest. She was clearly confident because if we won, she was offering us a lifetime's supply of their rosé, which I thought was a nice gesture.

But then I got to the final paragraph. If we lost the bet, Miriam wanted us to agree to find a UK importer for their rosé. There was no indication of the number of bottles they would want us to buy. Just the ominous phrase 'amounting to a small percentage of our annual production'. And as for the length of the contract, it was to last until we discovered a paler rosé than Château Etienne. The moment I read these words a feeling of nausea gripped my stomach. What would happen if we didn't win? How small was small? And what choice did we now have but to accept?

After months of research, days skim-reading wine encyclopaedias, hours on the phone to obscure wine merchants, endless tastings and some awful hangovers, we reached one key conclusion. It would have horrified those who had so freely given their time to discuss the intricacies of viticulture. We thought it verged on genius in its simplicity. It cut through all the nonsense about nose, volume and fingers and got to the heart of what makes a good rosé.

The key finding was that rosé was best enjoyed pale, cold and in the open air. Masters of wine may spit into their spittoons at the thought, but there are few better working rules. Try it.

It was one o'clock on 20 April. Our ferry sailed at 7 p.m. We sat outside Peter's house, near Sevenoaks in Kent, wearing huge overcoats, our breath blowing plumes into the cold air. On a table in front of us sat the box of Bernard's wine, still unopened. There was no need to chill the wine or the glasses. Peter's wife, Jenny, watched from inside, shaking her head at our folly.

Taking off my gloves, I prepared to cut the seal. We could not have looked more ridiculous. Three supposed adults standing shivering in the countryside, opening a box with the reverence reserved for a religious artefact. Peter and Tanya crowded round, keen to glimpse the colour of Bernard's wine. On the table was a sheet of white A5 paper and a digital camera. The tape gave way and I pulled aside the cardboard flaps and removed a tall thin bottle with an elongated neck. The label read 'Côtes de Provence, Château Etienne, St Maximin la Ste Baume'.

And the colour. Well, perhaps colour is the wrong word. The wine was so transparent that it bore only the memory of a colour – the gentle pink of a cloud lit by a fading sun moments before dusk, or a fleeting reflection of pink coral beneath a still ocean. We held the bottle against the white paper and took a shot with the digital camera. We could now measure all other rosés against this benchmark.

'Don't just stare at it – we might as well drink it,' said Peter.

I poured three glasses. Swilling the liquid around the base of my glass, I took a sniff. 'Gooseberries. Definitely gooseberries.'

'It's zingy, like lemons,' said Tanya.

'Flint with just a hint of crisp apples, I think you'll find.' We looked up, amazed, to find Peter grinning knowingly at us. 'It's just what it says on the label. Or at least I think that's what it says.'

We each took a sip. It was delightfully light and easy to drink. Château Etienne was simply too good. Even standing outside on a bitter day with dark clouds rolling ominously over the North Downs, the wine brought back memories of towns perched precariously on hillsides and copses of umbrella pines planted all the way down to the sea.

'Bloody marvellous,' said Peter.

'Provence in a bottle,' commented my wife.

'It's so pale they should call it something different,' I added, holding my glass up against the white background.

'You've invented a new type of wine,' laughed Peter. 'Extremely pale rosé. They'll have to change wine lists across the world.'

'Extremely pale rosé. It has a certain ring to it,' smiled Tanya.

'Or EPR for short,' I said.

'Wonderful,' said Peter.

As we left Peter's house we felt the delicious freedom that comes from doing something utterly mad. We had given ourselves six months to find the palest rosé in France.

It was time to hunt for EPR. First stop Champagne – or so we thought.

APRIL

'And when do the French drink rosé?'
I asked.
'Maybe with one of your curries.'

4

Juveniles

Peter paced up and down at the stern of the ferry. Seagulls swirled around his wind-whipped hair, and puffs of smoke from his cigar trailed with the wake of the boat back towards Dover. A couple of schoolchildren dodged past him, scattering crisps, and the gulls dived deckwards, uttering harsh cries of thanks for the impromptu feast. Clouds hung in dirty smudges over the coast, but as the boat chugged slowly onward and the sea swallowed the land, the sky cleared.

Looking over the top of his glasses, Peter turned to us and raised one bushy eyebrow. 'We've got a problem. I read last night that there are over two thousand producers in Champagne and over ten thousand vineyards in Bordeaux. God knows how many there are in the whole of France. I've just worked out that we could spend all six months in Champagne and still not get round everybody. If we really want to win this challenge, we're going to have to shorten the odds.'

He was right – our wine books offered us a selection of the best vineyards in France, but even by consulting them and asking for recommendations in local towns, our chances weren't good. We had to assume that Madame Etienne's wine was the palest rosé widely available in France. Why else would she have made the bet? Our chances rested on finding a lost wine hidden in the back of a cave, a rosé that a vigneron just made for his own consumption or only supplied to his closest friends.

Peter paused and looked back out to sea. When he judged we had suffered enough, he gave a little wink and said, 'Fortunately I have a solution. We need to go to Paris.'

'Why?' I asked. 'Paris seems the last place we should go to look for rosé.'

'Who needs a reason to go to Paris?' said a delighted Tanya.

For the last half-hour she'd been taking farewell phone calls from a rich variety of friends. Battle-hardened career women slurping overfilled sandwiches at their desk as they snatched a quick conversation, and young mothers dunking chocolate biscuits in their tea and celebrating getting their baby to sleep. I'd watched as she'd talked and absently wrapped her curly golden hair around her fingers. As Dover shrank from view her mobile lost its signal and she fell silent.

Until, that is, Peter announced we were going to Paris and she began to chatter excitedly about the city where we'd got engaged five years earlier.

Peter's car is a fifteen-year-old BMW convertible. Its bumper hangs loose, its bodywork is rusty, and the hood refuses to fold away properly, but he slaps its bonnet with the type of camaraderie he reserves for good friends. Unfortunately Peter's determination to visit Paris involved me driving it into an insurance black hole. The world's first and worst roundabout – l'Etoile, or 'the Star' – where twelve broad Parisian avenues meet at l'Arc de Triomphe, and where no insurance company will cover you.

Making it as far as l'Etoile was difficult enough. On the outskirts of Paris there were no lanes, no rules, just cars. Drivers cut across each other, hooted at each other and, if all else failed, rammed each other. A cyclist flashed past the front of the car and I swerved sharply to avoid him, but rather than a grateful wave, he dismounted in the middle of the roundabout, removed his mirrored glasses and started shouting at us.

Everything came to a standstill. Cars hemmed me in on my left and right. A battered Renault with an irate female driver filled my rear-view mirror, but there was simply nowhere to go. Not an inch of road to edge into. The hooting became incessant and the hand gestures more graphic. The roundabout I'd failed to negotiate was Porte Maillot, effectively the Arc de Triomphe's kid sister.

I put my head down on the steering wheel and began to laugh. Twenty drivers were now berating me, but I felt in no way threatened – it was simply part of the rich street theatre of the capital. Aside from the fear of crashing Peter's car, I was actually quite enjoying myself. Within hours of leaving England we'd been transported into a different culture, where it was acceptable to stop your car in the middle of a roundabout, gesticulate furiously at other drivers and then continue on your way as if nothing had happened. The whole experience was just so ridiculous.

Eventually, a traffic policeman intervened. A few short shrill blasts of the whistle and some precise white-gloved hand gestures and we were away. In theory it was one of the most beautiful drives in the world, a time to pull on the leather gloves, put the hood of the car down and parade around town.

The Eiffel Tower played hide and seek behind the elegant houses of Avenue de la Grande Armée, and ahead, through the arch of the Arc de Triomphe, I could see the Champs-Elysées – the road on which I'd proposed to Tanya. Everything was bathed in a wonderful reddish-brown light, the sepia of a negative just before the image crystallises.

The city was on the cusp of summer. Some people clung to the comfort of politically incorrect but infinitely snug fur coats, teamed with fine-leather gloves, warm tweed skirts and high boots; others were already in the clutches of the new season – all pastels, sling-back shoes and designer sunglasses. The weather – a warmish spring day – appeared an irrelevance; as always, the Parisians were determined to parade the fashion of the moment. The only problem was that nobody knew whether it was time for mufflers or minis.

The café seats were laid out in long rows along the pavements, and pictures of Parisian life were momentarily framed in the windscreen as we passed. A young woman with shoulder-length blonde hair was eating an ice cream, dipping her long spoon in a glass of iced water after each mouthful. She had chocolate-brown eyes, full red lips and an all-too-natural pout. Her coat was unzipped, revealing a T-shirt with a sequinned plea: 'Mend my broken heart, please.'

Observing the street scenes momentarily distracted us from the Arc de Triomphe, which was looming ever larger ahead of us, until Peter commented, 'Apparently, the secret to driving in Paris is that those on the right have priority.' A second later he added, 'Never understood how it works, though.'

'So, according to you, we don't stop at the next roundabout. Everyone will stop for us because we'll be on their right. Right?'

Tanya leant over from the back. 'Oh, we *are* stopping. There are twelve lanes of fast-moving traffic, we're not insured, and there are more accidents here than anywhere else in the world. And you just want to drive straight across it?'

'We've got about five seconds to make up our minds.'

'Just go for it,' urged Peter.

'It's your car.'

Tanya and Peter closed their eyes. I might as well have closed mine. I pressed the accelerator and seconds later it was over. The cars on the outside lanes of the Etoile parted as we approached, allowing us into the faster-moving centre of the roundabout. As the turning for the Champs-Elysées came closer I'd gathered such pace that I cut easily across the traffic on my outside and made the exit. It was like being sucked into the middle of a whirlpool and somehow spat out just as a life-raft was passing.

'I'm glad that's over,' said Peter. 'Betty won't be doing that again.'

'What did you just say?'

'I said, "Betty—"'

'Your car's got a name?'

'Of course. Betty the BMW. She's a girl, you know.'

François Gilbert was one of Paris's top financiers as well as one of its most respected wine experts. Between brokering deals for the capital's largest companies, he added to his cellar, which contained over three thousand bottles, including 106 vintage wines. What François didn't know about wine was apparently not worth knowing – he had personal relationships with vignerons across France and access to wines that never saw a shop shelf. He was also unlucky enough to be closely acquainted with a friend of Peter's. It was in order to meet him that we'd braved the Parisian traffic. If he didn't know who produced the palest rosé in the country, he would know a man who did.

As the hour of the meeting approached I became increasingly nervous; it was perfectly possible that we would make fools of ourselves. I considered myself to be averagely knowledgeable about wine – I knew Chablis was made from Chardonnay, and Sancerre from Sauvignon, but I couldn't list the grape varieties that made up a typical red Bordeaux, and although I understood that a Burgundy *grand cru* was a superior wine to a Burgundy *premier cru*, I wouldn't fancy my chances of identifying the better wine in a blind tasting. As far as I could see, the next hour was going to involve an elaborate game of bluff as we all attempted to hide our ignorance. It felt like going into a Shakespeare exam having read the wrong *Henry*.

'If you take a seat then François will be with you soon.'

The reception area was bare apart from a low black sofa and a glass coffee table on which the day's financial press was neatly arranged. A flat-screen TV showing share-price movements hung on the wall. Across from us was a long corridor lit up like an emergency exit and punctuated by a row of closed doors. Lafite-Rothschild, Mouton-Rothschild, Latour, I mentally rehearsed the names of some great wines I could drop into the conversation. If we were convincing at the beginning of the meeting, then hopefully François would take over and we could gently guide him on to the topic of rosé.

'Welcome. Please come through to my office.' François had emerged from a door at the end of the corridor. He wore a deep-blue shirt with a contrasting white collar and flame-red tie. Pinstripe trousers were hoisted by braces well above his waist, revealing bright-yellow socks and a pair of immaculately shined shoes. His swept-back hair accentuated the roundness of his face and glasses. In contrast to the minimalist reception area, François had turned his office into a grotto full of antiques. Silver carriage clocks perched on mahogany sideboards, watercolours hung in gold frames, and four ornately upholstered armchairs appropriated the corners of the room. As we entered, a relay race of clocks from around the office chimed the hour.

François sat down behind a Victorian writing table; its feet were shaped like lion's paws, and the polished dark-wooden surface of the desk was inlaid with green leather. There was no computer, just a dog-eared diary, a packet of Gitanes and a silver lighter, which François tapped against the wood as he waited for the clocks to fall silent.

To my great relief, we didn't even need to ask him questions. François leant back in his chair, with a massive smile on his face and a shine to his eyes. He chose his words with the care of an academic – afraid of over-simplifying yet anxious we should understand his points – but spoke with the enthusiasm of a child. Rather than test our knowledge of wine, he excitedly ran through the history of his wine collection. Relaxing into his wonderful armchairs, surrounded by beautiful paintings, we could have been whiling away a lazy Sunday afternoon in a country house, chatting about our host's favourite subject.

The English, he argued, thought too much in terms of good and bad wines and not enough about the food a wine complemented. For example, plenty of people were derogatory about Alsace wines, but, for him, many of them were a perfect accompaniment to foie gras. By contrast, every Frenchman was passionate about wine. It was part of the country's cultural heritage, and it was embarrassing, even a sign of ignorance, not to be able to offer an opinion on a wine and the food it might complement. If a wine was matched with the right food, it should provoke an explosion of easily identifiable flavours in the mouth.

'When I was younger, my father told me, "You taste, you buy, you leave to rest, then you will be a collector, my son." I've heeded his advice ever since.' François continued, running through his collection of very special wines – Pomerol, Margaux, Hermitages – rather than an explosion of flavour, drinking these wines was – and at this point he sat back in his chair with a beatific grin on his face and closed his eyes – 'like having an orgasm in the mouth'.

In retrospect, it was an inappropriate moment to introduce rosé into the conversation. François was almost recumbent in his chair, enjoying the last imaginary sips of a 1966 Pomerol, when I tentatively asked, 'And when do the French drink rosé?'

He opened his eyes and reached for a cigarette. Taking a deep puff, he adjusted to the alarming reality that we were there to discuss rosé. 'Maybe with one of your curries. I once had one and asked for the hottest they could make. Rather than an orgasm in the mouth, my mouth nearly exploded.' He laughed and held his breath until his whole face was red, and then popped his cheeks with both hands.

'Who do you think makes the palest rosé in France?' I asked.

François looked perplexed and then inexplicably left the room. I have to admit that even to me it sounded like an odd question, so what thoughts it must have conjured in François's brain, a man who'd spent his life devoted to discerning the delicate flavours of wine, I can only imagine. I assumed he had either called security or simply left for another meeting, firmly convinced that we were not worth any more of his time.

Instead, he returned clutching a magazine and a bottle of sherry. The grin was back on his face as he handed over a photocopy of an article. 'I've just remembered reading this a couple of months ago.' It was from *Le Point*, a current affairs and lifestyle magazine. The headline read, 'Rosé becomes fashionable – sales of white and red fall. Rosé sales continue to grow.' Beneath the article was a long list of vineyards throughout France.

He shrugged. 'Perhaps the world is changing. I'll mark some producers I think you should visit. They make good red and whites, but who knows about their rosé, and as to whether it's pale or not . . . ' He raised his hands with palms up to the sky in a gesture of supplication – we would have to trust to the gods.

While Tanya and I relaxed back at the hotel, Peter took on the important task of finding us a restaurant for the evening. Letting him loose alone in Paris was a bit of a risk – on previous French holidays Peter had promised to buy lunch and then disappeared for hours. At the butcher's he would discuss which particular innards went into a pâté, then later at the baker's he would debate the merits of oil versus butter croissants. Almost inevitably, he would make a friend in the queue and be whisked away to buy goat's cheese from a farm or mushrooms fresh from the field. Meanwhile we would wait back at the house, getting hungrier and hungrier.

Allowing him to choose a restaurant in Paris meant we might not eat until midnight. Most people when they read a menu look at the prices and check there are a couple of things they'd like to eat. Instead, Peter analyses each dish and pictures the work involved. Is a starter of aubergine caviar, wrapped in smoked ham and accompanied by a salad of rocket and nutmeg sorbet too ambitious for a young chef? Will the combination of flavours work? Since any given menu in France will contain at least ten dishes for Peter to evaluate, it's a time-consuming business. His aim is to find a secret gem, either a locals' local hidden in a forgotten back street or a new restaurant with an up-and-coming chef – a place to enjoy the food and the atmosphere before a Michelin star sullies both. It's a search he takes great delight in.

The earlier meeting with François had left us all a little bit dejected. While he'd been very kind to us and talked at length about his wine collection, he'd provided us with very little information about rosé. And although the list of vineyards he'd given us looked useful, we still had no idea how long we should devote to the various wine-producing areas.

'Here we are,' said Peter, pointing to a tiny bar across the street. Even for Peter it looked an unusual choice – a cramped open kitchen blazed heat into the room, old posters were pinned haphazardly to the wall, and the battered mismatched tables and chairs would have been more appropriate around a swimming pool. The only thing missing from the wooden floor was some sawdust.

But it was packed. The clientele was mixed: a petite brunette sat with a full glass of red wine and a copy of Descartes; labourers, still in their overalls, scooped great mouthfuls of *andouillette* and mash into their mouths; Havana-cigar-smoking, Gucci-loafered, Ralph Lauren-shirted boys brayed in the corner; and at another table a man sat alone, swilling his wine around the glass, seemingly hypnotised by the resulting pattern of heavy glutinous fingers.

The rich aroma of cigar smoke, the steam pouring from the kitchen, the candles flickering on the tables, the hubbub of voices bouncing around the narrow room and the wonderful informality of the place, as customers pulled wine from a rack which covered the whole wall behind them, appealed to us. We managed to squeeze on to the end of a long table and sat down to look at the menu.

It was a little strange. Alongside French classics were dishes such as Spanish omelette, Aberdeen Angus steak and Montgomery's farmhouse cheddar. The wine list was even more surprising. Spanish Cava was offered alongside champagne. Australian Semilion and a German Riesling were the alternatives to a white Burgundy from Marsannay. Italian Montalcino, Spanish Rioja and Californian Zinfandel outnumbered the two French reds.

For a Parisian restaurateur to offer such a choice was heretical. The supremacy of French wine is, like gravity, considered an immutable law. Take it away and you'd have anarchy. Cooperatives would form workers' committees to organise protests across France, tractors would block the *routes nationales*, and the flags of New World wine producers would be ceremoniously burnt.

An unwritten pact exists across the country that bars should sell only local wines. Ask for a glass of Bordeaux in Marseille and you'll be politely directed to a Côtes de Provence. Only in gourmet restaurants and cosmopolitan Paris will you find a choice of wines that is in any way representative of the best France can offer. As for New World wines, the French attitude is about as blinkered as American foreign policy – they are simply not interested.

But we'd apparently stumbled on some sort of philosophers' bar for those who refused to be shackled by centuries of food and wine tradition and could own up to the fact that they rather fancied a glass of German Riesling with their Scottish smoked salmon.

A slightly dishevelled red-faced middle-aged man emerged

from the kitchen. His shirt had escaped from his trousers and his glasses were bent out of shape.

'Welcome to Juveniles. Can I get you a drink?' The French was too comprehensible for him to be French. Taking a chance, I asked in English for some rosé and a broad grin spread across the man's face.

'Of course, *le pink pour le printemps.*' Leaning over us, he plucked a bottle of pale rosé from the rack behind our heads and called to the waitress to bring a wine bucket.

'I was wondering if you could help us,' I continued. 'This might seem a bit strange, but we're trying to win a bet to find the palest rosé in France.'

He pulled up a chair, introduced himself as Tim and signalled to the waitress to bring another glass. 'You could start by visiting this producer – Château de Roquefort, near Marseille,' he said as he poured. 'The owner's fantastic. His name is Raymond de Villeneuve. He'll know most of the good rosés around Bandol and Cassis.'

Rather than leave us to look at the menu, Tim topped up all the glasses and called for his address book. Most of the pages were bent backwards, Post-its protruded at irregular angles, and wine stains smudged the ink at various points, but Tim didn't let this put him off and, while we ordered, he searched for contacts. If a number was lost in a Merlot stain, he reached for his mobile and called three or four friends until one of them was able to produce it.

By the time our food arrived Tim had made a list of about fifteen producers on the back of our menu, drawn a map of France on the front showing the amount of time we should spend in each wine-producing area and summoned Antonio, a sommelier at the George V, to meet us. As he wrote down each new name he gave us advice that months later was to shape our story, but not quite in the way he intended.

'Raymond's a double "*de*". That makes him a bit eccentric,

like our Royal Family, but great fun. It's always worth meeting a
"*de*". The Hôtel Panoramic is a must in Sancerre; the views are
fantastic.' And, 'You've got to go to Collioure. It's the most
romantic town in the whole of France. You can visit Christine
Ontivero; she's a great friend.'

We moved from rosé to white to red as Tim chose a new
wine to go with each course, pouring us all large glasses as he
talked. 'Historically, rosé was a dreadful wine. It used to be made
from red-wine leftovers. It would be put in a forgotten vat in the
corner of the cave and sold for next to nothing to anyone foolish
enough to buy it.

'But that's not true any more. There's not a great winemaker
in France who hasn't learnt his trade by producing a good rosé.
It's the hardest wine to make, much more complex than red or
white. France is making some fantastic rosé now, and it's real
wine that can accompany food. Anyone who is still snobbish
about it is wrong.'

It was like sitting opposite another version of Peter Tate, one
who'd chosen a different path in life and become a restaurateur.
Like Peter, Tim peered over the top of his glasses, his eyes intent,
as he passed on a particularly important piece of knowledge.
Once the wisdom was imparted, his face would crack into a
broad smile and he'd tell us how fantastic he thought our
challenge was. Such was his passion as he leafed through his
contact book that I wished we could have picked him up and
taken him with us.

'Now, Tavel. It might be marketed as France's best rosé but
beware: most of it is oxidised rubbish. I'll put you in touch with
Christophe Delorme at Domaine de la Mordorée; he makes a
superb wine. Have I said how fantastic I think this idea is?'

We nodded. Tim raised his pen to his forehead, glared at us
for a second and then continued. 'Of course, if you're going to
be in Bordeaux, you must meet Cousin Esme. He's one of the

most successful of the Johnston clan. There's little he doesn't know about wine. Give Cousin Esme a call.'

I was beginning to wonder how long Tim could talk about rosé. Every time he seemed to have exhausted his list of contacts another idea would spring into his head. The exasperated waitresses had just about managed to drag him away when a slight man in a linen suit entered.

'Antonio,' cried Tim, 'come over here.'

Antonio was a sommelier at the George V whom Tim had called earlier. He had a shaved head, an impressively hooked nose and sunken eyes that darted around the room. He wasn't, as it turned out, a great conversationalist and he spent the rest of the evening with his nose deep in his glass of red wine. We emptied and refilled our glasses several times, but Antonio seemed to derive great pleasure from just sniffing wine. In the hour we spent in his company he managed only a small glass of red and most of it probably evaporated up his nose.

'So what do you think of this wine?' Tim asked Antonio.

The hooked nose was plunged deep into the glass one more time. 'I can smell sun-baked earth, a tough, arid landscape where the vines have to struggle to push their roots deep into the soil. The grape variety is Mourvèdre mixed with maybe a little Grenache. The fruits are black cherries, blackberries, and there's just a hint of truffle as the wine lingers on the tongue.'

We were amazed that simply by smelling a wine, admittedly for an awfully long time, Antonio could discern all this information.

'Yes, yes,' said Tim, apparently unimpressed, 'but can you tell me where the wine is from?'

Further nose antics followed before Antonio declared, 'I can also detect the freshness of the sea – I think it's a Bandol. It reminds me most of Domaine Tempier.'

Tim called for another bottle to top up our by now empty

glasses. He rocked forward in his chair and gave Antonio an affectionate slap on the back. 'Absolutely right.'

It was a remarkable skill, so remarkable that I wondered whether there was any trickery involved. Had Tim, for example, had a Bandol on his wine list a couple of weeks back that Antonio might have tasted? Or had he, as he appeared to have done, identified the single correct vineyard out of hundreds of thousands?

But Tim hadn't finished. He gave a great bellow of laughter, slapped Antonio on the back again and said, 'Absolutely right, apart from one small thing – it's from California.' Antonio dipped his nose disbelievingly back into the glass and departed shortly afterwards.

I am not entirely sure quite what time we left Juveniles. Tim treated us to some more fantastic wines, and the restaurant emptied around us. Late-night revellers put their heads round the door and bought wine by the bottle. The waitress cleared all the other tables and stacked the chairs, and still we talked.

'Antonio is a fantastic sommelier, he's just a bit young and a bit bold in his opinions. He got nearly everything right about that wine, and ultimately his business is not about being able to identify individual wines but to tell the story of the flavours, and he did that nearly perfectly.'

I confessed that I struggled to identify an individual fruit in a wine, let alone sun-baked earth.

'You'll be surprised – by the end of your trip I think you'll be able to do it,' said Tim as he finally ushered us out through the door. 'But my advice for now is whatever you do, don't follow your noses.'

We walked slowly back to our hotel. 'Do you know,' said Tanya, 'I think we've just been drinking some very special red wine, only none of us realised it. We've got a lot to learn, haven't we?'

'Yes, but isn't it going to be fun?' I smiled. 'And we've now got a good contact in every wine region.'

Peter stopped at the entrance to the hotel, as if uncertain what to do next. 'Do you remember the girl near the Champs-Elysées with the chocolate eyes and the broken heart? Is it too late to give her a call?'

MAY

'You know, Jammie, wine in France is a small family. If you become friends with the family then anything is possible, but, Jammie, you don't want to be an enemy of the family.'

5

Macération, Tipicité and Sexual Confusion

Like a child glimpsing the sea, Peter gave a great cheer when we saw our first vines in Champagne. For the next five months we would exchange the dirty streets of London for a landscape dripping with grapes, and rather than squeeze past angry mothers in oversized four-wheel drives, we would follow small tractors up dirt tracks. Our office would be the back seat of the car, piled high with books on wine and scattered with scraps of paper. We would measure time not by dates but by the gentle swelling of the grapes.

By the time we reached Reims the vines stretched to the horizon, arrayed in immaculate lines like battle-ready soldiers. Tiny markers by the side of the road displayed the owner's name – Moët & Chandon, Bollinger, Krug – and teams of workers criss-crossed the fields, finishing the job of training the new growth to wires. Roadside garages carried more choice of champagne than I'd seen in any off-licence, and in bars, biker boys with oil-flecked beards perched on stools insouciantly sipping from flutes. From an occasional treat, champagne was transformed into an everyday drink. It was available as an aperitif, a digestive, a sundowner, even a sun-upper.

The tiny hamlets that dotted the hills either side of the Marne Valley brought home to us the enormity of our task. There were hundreds of producers competing to sell their bubbly – some simply placed a bottle in the front window of their house, others stencilled their name on roadside walls. Behind the houses were fields and fields of vines, subdivided again and again between generations of families into a patchwork of smallholdings, each hill interlocking with another, the new growth tumbling down to the flood plain of the Marne.

'Come on,' said Peter, 'we've got a lot of tasting to do.'

It was nearly eleven o'clock in the morning in the small Champenois village of Rilly la Montagne, we were about to meet our first vigneron, and I felt more than a little foolish.

'What do you mean you don't know whether he makes a rosé?' asked Tanya.

'Well, I just picked producers with good write-ups in my wine book. He had one, so I arranged a tasting,' I replied calmly.

'And if he doesn't produce a rosé,' continued Tanya, 'what do we talk about then?'

'Ah.'

It was a dismal May day – cold, wet and windy. The buildings around us were slate grey and their doors bolted shut. The staples of a French village – a bar, a butcher's, a baker's – were nowhere to be seen, and it was highly likely that there was no rosé to taste. Yet Peter and Tanya couldn't have looked happier. Heaven might be a small cobbled square with a trickling fountain and an old olive tree for shade, but the line of plane trees bordering the central square in Rilly la Montagne at least hinted at the Provençal paradise to come.

Across the square from us was a dilapidated warehouse. The paint was flaking away and the concrete crumbling on to the pavement. The name of the champagne house was once floridly written above the large double doors, but now the script was faded and illegible. There wasn't a car in sight, and the whole scene was redolent of a past when horses with stamping feet and steaming nostrils were harnessed to carts full of grapes and stood queuing to deliver the harvest.

We were all anxious about our first tasting; if it went badly it could set the tone for the whole trip. Francophile friends back home had advised that the best way of explaining our quest was to attribute it to the English sense of humour. The French apparently loved the quirkiness of the English, and the more eccentric we appeared, the better. The story of poor pale Rosie being confused with a bottle of rosé was likely to garner some sympathy, but what if it didn't? And what if the first vigneron we met didn't even make rosé?

To the side of the warehouse was a more modern construction – a long, low building made from thick wooden beams and reclaimed bricks. A couple of expensive cars were parked outside and baskets laden with flowers ringed the courtyard. The gates were embossed with the words 'Vilmart & Cie' in large gold lettering.

'Well, at least the flowers are pink,' Tanya muttered as we entered.

I was expecting the cliché – an old man in worn overalls wiping the grape stains from his hands and leading us through into a haphazard old cave where crates of wine were piled high and receipts lay discarded in corners of the room – but Laurent Champs resembled a businessman as much as a vigneron. He was smartly dressed in chinos and an ironed shirt, and invited us into his office rather than the cellar. On his desk was a model of a Ferrari and a personal organiser the size of a photograph album. He was warm and friendly and looked at us through small metal-rimmed glasses as he chatted away about the estate. 'It was founded in 1890 and we have eleven hectares of land. We're delighted to supply London restaurants such as Hakkasan . . . '

To my great shame, I only half listened as I desperately looked around the room for any sign of rosé. There were magnums of champagne, baseball caps and keyrings with the Vilmart logo on, but I couldn't see any rosé. His wife, who could have been dressed for a magazine shoot, briefly interrupted, trailing perfume and two immaculately dressed children into the room, and I quickly flicked through some marketing brochures – still no rosé.

'I'd also like to stress how important the environment is to us – we don't use any chemical pesticides and we even get rid of the grass between the vines with a hand-held hoe.' Laurent finished his brief history and looked enquiringly at us.

The moment had come. 'Tell us about your pink champagne.'

Rather than answer, he excused himself. First François and now Laurent. There seemed to be something about quizzing wine experts about rosé that made them leave the room. I crossed my fingers and thought of the pink flowers: a man who had pink flowers must make pink wine.

But instead of a couple of bottles of rosé, Laurent returned with a long test tube, which he handed to me. I could put my whole arm inside it without touching the base. It might make a handy receptacle for decades of spare change, it might also trap the odd unwary arm, but what could it possibly have to do with rosé?

'What do you know about making pink champagne?' asked Laurent.

Instead of answering the question, I said hopefully, 'So you do make a rosé?'

'Of course. Every few years we make a deep ruby-coloured red wine, which we store in the cellar. Each year we work out the mix for the rosé in this test tube. We add maybe ten to fifteen per cent of the red wine to eighty-five to ninety per cent of champagne until we have the desired colour.'

'But that means you can make it any colour you want?' interrupted Tanya.

Laurent looked bemused. Why were we so excited? 'Yes, that's right.'

'Tell me, who would you say made the palest rosé in Champagne?'

Rather than ridicule our quest, Laurent embraced it. Flicking through the leaves of his thick Filofax, he made call after call. I'd fondly imagined that the art of making wine was a skill that coursed through the blood – that the vignerons we'd meet would be born not taught – but I was wrong. Laurent summoned the help of the French equivalent of the old-boy network or the Oxbridge Mafia. Wine universities stretch across France from Beaune to Bordeaux and Montpellier to Marseille, where young winemakers have the chance to spend up to five years studying subjects such as soil type, grape variety and pest control. Conferencing in all his old university friends on speakerphone, Laurent leant back in his chair and cajoled them into meeting us. By the time we left his office our diary was full of tastings, but rather than gnarled old men with faces like dried grapes, we met dark-eyed, immaculately dressed vignerons fresh from college. They were the new generation of winemakers – Champagne's young guns.

We were welcomed as friends and taken to examine the vines, the presses, the *cuves* and the cellars. Our naïvety could not have been more obvious – we gawped like small children when we were told that an area about half the size of a football pitch could produce 8,000 bottles. In the caves we were shown old hand-operated wooden presses, two metres in circumference, that took four men to operate. The presses straddled empty drainage pools deep enough to swim in. From these pools the juice was somehow transferred to enormous vats or *cuves*, where the first fermentation took place.

Yeast, a special liqueur and sugar were then added, and the champagne was allowed to ferment for a second time in the bottle. The whole process was explained to us time and again and yet it was impossible to visualise how it worked, as the equipment was so basic and the output so large – the cellars contained countless bottles stretching in rack after rack and row after row. Making rosé was even more complicated and so, after one particularly disastrous tasting where yet again we'd failed to grasp the basics, Peter called a meeting.

'If we're going to win their trust we need to speak their language, not just French but the technicalities of winemaking.' Unsurprisingly, Peter's new initiative proved a little tricky, even the simplest words were causing me difficulty. London bankers might drop the 't' in 'Moët', but the French certainly didn't, and my phonetic pronunciation of 'Reims' bore no resemblance to the French 'Ranze'.

My confusion reached its peak in the appropriately named town of Dizy. Behind us were two large oak *cuves* about the height of three men. We established that unlike the metal *cuves* used by the larger champagne houses these allowed a little bit of oxidisation to take place, which gave the champagne a more distinct flavour. Then things got complicated.

'This house is looking for great *tipicité* in its wine, so we tend to use sexual confusion rather than pesticides.'

Peter and I nodded knowingly as if it all made perfect sense. I guessed that *tipicité* was a slightly tart or acidic taste, but I was far from sure I'd heard the rest of the sentence properly – what did sexual confusion and pesticides have to do with *tipicité*?

Tanya was more determined and tried to clarify. 'But what is *tipicité*?'

'*Tipicité* is *tipicité*. I find you get more *tipicité* from a *macération*. So if you're after *tipicité* look for a *rosé saignée*.'

My interpretation still made sense – *tipicité* meant tartness – and I was busily congratulating myself when, in the corner of the *dégustation* area, a man identified to us earlier as a wine journalist proceeded to remove all the glasses from a cabinet on the wall. He wore the type of trilby hat favoured by detectives in novels and a baggy violet suit that flapped this way and that like a mainsail waiting to catch the wind. Rather than pour any wine into the glasses, he proceeded to sniff each one individually before replacing them one by one into the cabinet. Peter and I looked at each other, completely bemused — so much for understanding the technicalities of winemaking.

Nobody else seemed to find this behaviour the remotest bit strange so Tanya persevered: 'Is a *saignée* the same as a *macération*?'

'Not at all, but to do a *saignée*, you must have a *macération* and then you get your *tipicité*. The problem is you've been visiting *négociants*. *Tipicité* is very difficult for a *négociant* but not for a *récoltant*.'

My carefully constructed meaning for *tipicité* had been shattered in a second. I knew that *négociants* were allowed to buy grapes from other producers to make their champagne, whereas *récoltants* used only their own grapes, but why was producing a wine with a touch of tartness easier for one than the other?

It was all too much for Peter who took a gulp of the wine. By then I had ceased to be amazed by his tasting technique — he tipped back his head and sucked the liquid to the back of his throat. The noise was akin to a submerged vacuum cleaner. Then, like a boxer limbering up before a fight, he rotated his head in great semicircles in either direction, swilling the wine around. He grinned, thought about spitting it out and then swallowed the lot. 'Marvellous, absolutely marvellous. Wonderful *tipicité*.'

After we left, I looked up *tipicité* in the dictionary. There was no definition.

As we travelled between the different producing regions — the Montagne de Reims, the Côte des Blancs, the Côte de Sézanne and Aube — we discovered we had a secret weapon: Tanya. She was a natural at eliciting information, charming her way around Champagne, touching knees, flicking her hair and, above all, enjoying the whole experience so much that long-forgotten bottles of pink champagne were dusted off and poured. Off-licences, bars, *tabacs*, Tanya asked everywhere: motorists at traffic lights, mayors hard at work in their offices, even accosting little old ladies as they carried their shopping home.

Sometimes it seemed that she was more interested in the French way of life than in finding rosé. In the village of Cumières, near Reims, she walked down the cobbled road with one of Laurent's friends, Jean-Baptiste Geoffroy, discussing his burgeoning family. One of four daughters, she was ideally placed to advise Jean-Baptiste on the impending arrival of his fifth child, and possibly his fifth daughter. They talked about anything but wine – the heartache of a father when his daughter brings home her first boyfriend and the joys of having an extended family in a small village.

In fact, this approach worked wonderfully well: the longer we spent with people, the more they trusted us and the more producers they recommended. At times I worried that I might lose my wife to her love of France and the charming Champenois vignerons with their luxuriant descriptions of wines. Their champagnes were split into families: spirit – vivacious and light; heart – generous and smooth; soul – mature, rich and complex; and body – powerful and intense. As they talked I noticed that they seemed to hold eye contact for indecent periods of time and almost savour the sensuality of their language.

'Never mind,' said Peter gently, 'we'll meet a female vigneron soon. Mind you, she'll probably have biceps and a moustache.'

It didn't help my fast-developing paranoia when Tanya emerged from one meeting with Nicolas Chiquet and declared, 'He was so handsome I lost my power of speech.'

I could see that he was good-looking – he had sandy-coloured curly hair and the nut-brown eyes Tanya seemed so partial to – but what else did my wife see in this twenty-eight-year-old Frenchman and his twenty-two-hectare estate in the heart of

Champagne, and why did she insist on asking whether he was married?

Meanwhile Peter was having a fantastic time, excelling himself by discovering a specialist veal restaurant where my choice of main course was limited to veal's head, veal's brains, veal's testicles or the slightly tamer, but still to my mind stomach-churning, veal's liver. That night he peered over his glasses and fixed us with his most earnest look. 'Did you know that just before the millennium celebrations some champagne houses were accused of buying and re-labelling cheaper champagne and then selling it on as their own? We've got to find out who did it.'

Finding those responsible was the last thing on my mind. We'd already spent over two weeks in Champagne, and attended over twenty tastings, but still had found nothing to compare with Madame Etienne's rosé. Our last chance was a still rosé made in the south of Champagne in a town called Ricey. Our wine books were universally rude about it, claiming that it was an overpriced and unremarkable wine. In Juveniles we'd asked Antonio, the sommelier from the George V, about it and he'd shrugged his shoulders and muttered, 'Who knows?' But among the dismissive comments was one passage in Don Philpott's *The Vineyards of France*: Rosé de Ricey 'has the most incredible colour, often described as red sky at sunset'. We simply had to go.

But, in between mouthfuls of veal's brains, which he protested were delicious, Peter insisted that our priority should be to get to the bottom of the millennium scandal. He argued with such a combination of boyish abandon and rectitude that it was impossible to gainsay him, and in the end we agreed to split up: Tanya and I would head to Ricey, and Peter would stay in Reims.

'Did you know,' said Tanya, changing the subject, 'that Louis XV's mistress, Madame de Pompadour, declared, "Champagne is the only wine that leaves a woman beautiful after drinking it"? Do you think it's true?'

'In your case, yes,' said Peter, winking at me. 'Which reminds me, what's sexual confusion? And why do the French sniff empty glasses?'

During the couple of days we spent without Peter I came to regard him as some sort of lucky talisman whose absence led to bad luck.

Tanya and I stopped in Epernay, a town that we'd visited together before we were married. In my mind's eye, I remembered a quaint, almost Alpine village nestling among fields of vines which snaked, like ski slopes, right into the centre. Instead, Epernay was a town without a heart: roundabout after roundabout diverted traffic in great loops around it, and the much-vaunted Avenue de Champagne – home of great champagne houses such as Mercier and Moët – consisted of a series of new-build glitzy palaces, more suited to the Arab Emirates than France. We were finally driven from the town by the wail of an old air-raid siren that for no apparent reason howled incessantly for fully half an hour.

That night we stayed in Bar-sur-Seine, a small town about an hour's drive from Ricey. We fondly imagined it would command panoramic views over a meander of the river, but instead we found juggernauts streaming down the *route nationale* and a town with little to offer apart from two Citroën dealerships, a fire station and an enormous cemetery. It rained so hard that a bee decided to take shelter in Tanya's trouser leg and stung her twice, and her mood was hardly improved at supper that night by a table full of locals loudly discussing why English women just weren't sexy.

We'd phoned ahead to organise a tasting and I began to feel that our Peter-less trip to Ricey was cursed when the only producer we could get hold of – Pascal Morel – insisted that we see him at 9 a.m. We'd learnt that vignerons were busy people with plenty to do in the fields, but meeting one of them at 9 a.m. was next to catastrophic. However much we protested, it was considered an insult not to try every wine a domaine produced.

We arrived in time to have a coffee and a croissant in the local bar. The beer was already flowing and all sorts of trophies – for shooting, *pétanque*, football and early-morning drinking – were arranged on a shelf around the room. I felt slightly effeminate rejecting the proffered *pression* and asking for an orange juice to accompany my breakfast. If only they understood that a drinking marathon awaited me up the road.

Ricey is the sort of French village you stumble upon and are so delighted by that you stop for a quick drink or some lunch. It's full of old stone squares and hump-back bridges over free-flowing streams. Louis XIV was so enchanted by the stone from the area that he used it to build Versailles. He also developed a taste for Rosé de Ricey, which was introduced to the royal palace by the stonemasons.

We walked up the cobbled streets, with our stomachs still swilling with orange juice, slightly queasy at the prospect of tasting a wine renowned for helping a king raise a bejewelled palace in record time. Would stonemasons really drink a pale rosé? Surely they'd favour a strong, gutsy wine, a restorative to get them going for the day ahead, and one which would probably knock us out.

Pascal Morel greeted us in the conservatory built on to the side of his house. He was a small, pleasant man with a beard, glasses and warm eyes. He explained that Rosé de Ricey was only made in years when the Pinot Noir grape became overripe – the grapes were then piled on top of each other and their combined weight forced the juice out. Unlike other rosés, it was a wine that you could keep. He was just sorry – and I think a hint of an ironic smile crossed his face at this point – that he could only offer us four vintages to taste that morning; during the

Second World War the German officers who'd lived in his house had consumed most of his older stock of wines.

As the deeply viscous liquid coated the *dégustation* glasses, I thought jealously of Peter presumably still tucked up in bed in Reims. I also rued the day that Don Philpott wrote about a rosé with 'the most incredible colour, like red sky at sunset'.

The wine was like no sunset I'd ever seen. Far from the palest rosé in France, we'd found the darkest. Tanya and I each took a sip – it was heavy and slightly sweet, like a port. There was nowhere to spit it out, and we still had three more glasses to go.

Pascal motioned to us to try some more. We should savour the aroma of cherries, and then, as if to offer encouragement, he told us that the next wine tasted of wild strawberries, the third of blackberries, and the fourth of blackcurrants.

He was wrong. They all tasted of port. Inadvertently, those thirsty German soldiers had done us a favour.

We found Peter Tate sitting happily on the terrace of a café in Reims. He was puffing on a cigar and sipping on a glass of furiously bubbling, terribly pale rosé. He had a huge grin on his face as he beckoned us over.

'Try this, my darlings. I think you'll find it's the palest rosé in Champagne.'

'How do you know?'

'It's got the lowest mix of red wine to champagne – just seven per cent, nothing else even comes close. It's called Billecart-Salmon.'

'And what about your millennium mystery?'

'Ah, I got waylaid.' He grinned, happily puffing on a cigar. 'But I did discover that you sniff wine glasses before a tasting to check they haven't picked up an aroma of staleness from the cupboard. Oh, and I know all about sexual confusion.'

'I'm sure you do,' smiled Tanya.

'Get yourself a glass of this, it's marvellous,' said Peter, taking a good slug of bubbly. 'Now, tell me about Rosé de Ricey.'

6

The Psychoanalyst

In our absence Peter had learnt a surprising amount. He explained that sexual confusion was a way of preventing female insects from finding mates. A small capsule taped to the vines at the end of each row released a hormone that effectively prevented the insects from recognising the opposite sex. He'd also discovered that although a *macération* sounded like a form of medieval torture, it was in fact an alternative method of making rosé.

Rather than mixing red and white wines – a method of making rosé exclusive to Champagne – in a *macération*, the pink colour of the champagne was derived from letting the juice of the grapes rest on the skins. This was the most common method of making rosé and was used across the rest of France. According to Peter, the secret in making it pale was to carefully control the amount of time the crushed grapes spent in contact with the skin and stalks. All grape juice is white. Red wines develop their colour from contact with the skin – the deeper the red wine, the longer it has been in contact with the skins. For rosés, even the briefest of period spent in touch with the skin will allow the wine to develop a pink hue.

I'd been learning, too, and I shared with Peter the most useful word in the French language – *donc*. Its equivalent in English is the more ugly 'um' or 'then', but in those dreadful moments when my brain tried to frantically unscramble a tangle of French, I found I could always resort to *donc*. It broke conversations up, it gave me breathing time and, judiciously laced into a phrase, I kidded myself it made me sound like a local. Soon Peter was beginning every sentence with the word.

But there were still problems – linguistically we remained confused by the way vignerons used the words *saignée* and *macération* almost interchangeably but in subtly distinct ways. And while we'd discovered it was complimentary to say a wine had a good *tipicité*, its meaning remained a mystery. Most importantly, although Billecart-Salmon was a beautiful delicate pink, Madame Etienne's rosé was paler still.

We headed south to Burgundy and a region called the Côte d'Or – literally 'the golden slope'. It was the land of Montrachet, recognised as one of the five great wines of the world, and Chambertin, a red so delicious that Napoleon wouldn't touch anything else. Tim Johnston hadn't been able to recommend a good rosé producer anywhere in the region, and our wine guides contained only fleeting references to rosé while devoting pages to reds from Nuits Saint Georges and Beaune, but there was always a chance we might discover a fabulous rosé hidden in the shadow of a famous red.

And after Champagne, I wondered whether I had been mistaken about the dismissive attitude towards rosé in France. Far from being the downtrodden cousin of the more serious white champagnes, rosé was more expensive and more difficult to make. Demand for pink champagne was spiralling across the world, with Britain and Japan the two biggest growth markets. Was the same true in Burgundy? Were vignerons making and selling more rosé? And what would be the reaction if we ordered pink wine to accompany a gourmet meal?

As we entered the town of Gevrey Chambertin, my mobile rang.

'Hello, is that Jammie? Hello, yes, this is Guy de Saint Victor.'

Guy de Saint Victor is a Béziers-based wine merchant recommended to us by a friend of Tanya's. The '*de*' in his surname apparently denoted him as part of the old French nobility. If we wanted the French wine establishment to embrace our quest, I had to get on with Guy. It was to prove a little difficult.

Guy continued talking. 'Yes, you sent me some emails, but I deleted them. I thought they were – how you say? – junk. Jammie, you must change your email address: anything with numbers looks like junk.'

'Uh, I'll try and get it changed, Guy, thanks for—'

'Now, you want some help finding rosé wine, no? You've asked the right person. You know, Jammie, wine in France is a small family. If you become friends with the family then anything is possible, but, Jammie, you don't want to be an enemy of the family.'

Guy burst into laughter and I managed a nervous giggle in response.

'You know, Jammie, when you get further south, I'm going to introduce you to some fabulous winemakers. I know *the* guy in the Rhône.'

I thought I was supposed to sound appreciative so I began to mumble thanks, but Guy was already speaking again. 'And in Bordeaux, too, I know *the* guy. If they don't welcome you with open doors, then you can blow the doors off.' Guy laughed. It took me a second to get the joke, and by the time I had mustered a small chuckle, Guy was talking again. 'Okay, for now, Jammie, you know the best thing you can do? Go to the shops, Jammie, and buy a magazine called *La Revue du Vin de France*; there is a special rosé edition. Call me when you're in the south. Bye bye, Jammie.'

Guy hung up, I hadn't even had time to manage one '*donc*'.

★

At first I really liked Gevrey Chambertin. It was a chocolate-box sweet French village, with pretty pâtisseries, tiny wine shops and plenty of tables and chairs on the narrow high street. There was something wonderful about being able to order delicious wines such as Pouilly Fuissé by the glass and sit and savour the procession of people passing in the street. We decided that so far we'd been taking the search a little too seriously. In Champagne, we ran around like Londoners and treated time as a precious commodity. We felt uncomfortable when we weren't speaking to a vigneron or doing something to further the quest. In Gevrey, it was time to relax and, well, be more French. There was no hurry to hunt for rosé; instead, we marvelled at the view when we cast open the hotel windows – row upon neat row of vines with the local church floating in their midst halfway up the hillside. We took walks and watched parties of Japanese tourists sit on stools and prune vines. Well, why do the work yourself if someone else will pay to do it for you? We enjoyed a new take on *bœuf bourguignon* – rather than the steaming stew we had expected, tender slices of beef arrived in an iron skillet coated in a deliciously rich red-wine sauce.

In the tiny supermarket in the heart of town we became accustomed to the fact that Madame couldn't possibly be expected to do two things at once. Conversations about the weather, the cut of a dress or one ailment or another were far more important than the waiting customers, and items seemed to hover mid-air between basket and bag until a particular topic was finished. After I'd learnt to accept that buying a bar of chocolate could take up to twenty minutes, I began to enjoy the whole experience. Madame noticed my eczema and recommended treating it with a towel soaked in the first press of olive oil and a little lemon. And if I came down with a cold, she advised crushing leaves from the calypso tree into a bowl of steaming water.

But despite the prettiness of the village, the good food and fine wine, and of course Madame, for some reason we all began to feel uneasy. The local tourist office marketed the area as *Le Goût de Vie*, literally 'the tasting of life'. But slowly we began to dislike the taste. Why? Small things annoyed us, like trying to buy some red wine for a picnic but being unable to find a local bottle for under €20, or sitting in a restaurant and listening to a couple, with the placeless accents of the ultra wealthy, drool over which vintage of Gevrey to choose – the price of both wines was well over €500.

The vines that carpeted the landscape were immaculate, too immaculate. Not a leaf was out of place. Each vineyard had a massive iron gate by the roadside identifying their grapes, but they could have been the gates to a theme park. Tourists, not locals, filled the fields and the towns. And as for rosé, there was none to be found. We experienced some short-lived excitement when Peter emerged from the storeroom of a supermarket clutching a bottle of rosé so pale that I mistook it for white wine. It was called El Faragui and it turned out to be Moroccan. We visited huge commercial operations with warehouses full of wine and one-man bands who struggled to fill a corner of their garage, but the response was the same – a shrug of the shoulders and a consolation glass of red or white. Even the magazine that Guy had recommended on the phone didn't list a single Burgundy rosé, and as for ordering rosé in a restaurant, the idea was clearly so preposterous that there wasn't a single one on the wine lists.

On our final night in Gevrey Chambertin we visited the smartest restaurant in the village. We'd purposely avoided it until then, put off by its apparent austerity and the prices, but it was Monday night and every other restaurant was shut or fully booked. We were shown upstairs into a small square room containing four tables immaculately dressed in white linen. The walls were painted a dark purple, and the only light came from a single bulb hanging in a heavy shade in the middle of the room. Attempts at conversation were either drowned by the piped music or trapped by the net curtains. The only other customers were a middle-aged couple and their adult son who managed to endure the whole evening without uttering a word to each other. As little *amuse-bouche* – jellied fish in shot glasses and cold soups in espresso cups – came and went, I found myself longing for the bonhomie of Juveniles or the simplicity of a piece of grilled fish accompanied by the receding hush of the sea and a glass of rosé.

It was still light when the meal finished and we wandered, disheartened, back through the narrow village streets. We'd yet to find any rosé in Burgundy and the atmosphere of oppressive opulence had put us off looking any more. Instead, we agreed to head for the Jura where we knew we would find plenty of pale-pink wine or mountain *gris* as it was described in one of my wine books.

As we turned a corner on the outskirts of town we came to a large square, in the middle of which was a circle of trees with silver lights looped between them. An old ex-US Army Jeep was parked next to a line of Harley Davidson motorbikes and a stage had been erected in one corner of the clearing next to a temporary bar that offered a choice of beer or champagne.

As we arrived a band was cheered on to the stage. The lead singer wore a T-shirt with 'NYC' embossed on it, a skullcap and a pair of Doc Martens. He was the most un-Gevrey thing we'd seen in a week, and his group played a type of Latin-American jazz that filled the square with swaying, snaking hips. We'd stumbled upon a mini fête. It wasn't for the tourists, or even the local vignerons; in fact, I am not quite sure whom it was for. In the middle of the dance floor a man with a tattoo on his ankle, wearing a green miniskirt and matching silk shirt, was dancing with a pashmina-clad woman. 'Welcome to chiquana, sexy marijuana,' encouraged the singer, and women with clothes seemingly grafted to their curves provocatively ran their hands over the nearest body, sometimes a man's, sometimes a woman's, sometimes their own.

Peter grabbed a leather miniskirted, red-stilettoed, red-headed dancer who I hoped was female and stood clapping his hands flamenco style as she (or he) danced around him. I whirled Tanya around, careful to avoid the little boy freewheeling across the dance floor on his scooter. There were hot dogs and trestle tables stained with beer and some of the funniest dancing imaginable, as men in motorbike helmets performed the French version of the 'Birdie Song' at one moment and a waltz the next. Even when the green-miniskirted man was nearly castrated on the handlebars of the boy's scooter the evening remained good spirited. It was let-your-hair-down, frivolous fun, and it was just what we needed.

Across the street Tanya spotted an old man leaning out of the window of his house. He was unshaven, wore a white string vest and looked like this was the first time he'd been out of bed all day, but he had a big grin on his face as he watched the carnival in the square. In France, Tanya has the ability to talk to anybody, anywhere, anytime, and whereas Peter and I had more or less given up on finding rosé in Burgundy, Tanya hadn't.

Twenty minutes later she returned to the fête and ordered herself a glass of champagne from the bar. 'His name was Joseph Roty and, like everybody else here, he makes a fantastic red wine, he sells to Berry Bros & Rudd, who, as he pointed out, supply the Queen, and,' at this point Tanya paused, 'and if you'll have one more dance with me, I'll tell you the rest.'

'Agreed,' I said.

'And he has a couple of fields of vines in the town of Marsannay, just five kilometres up the road. And,' Tanya screwed her face up and let out a little scream as she continued, 'he makes a rosé. So do all the vignerons in Marsannay; in fact, they make one of the best rosés in France.'

★

It was a blustery morning in Marsannay, and, despite it being mid-May, showers hit the village in great squalls, sending everyone scurrying for cover. The Bar du Centre was the only option for lunch. It was right on the main road, the paint was peeling from the walls, the doors were shut and the windows frosted. '*Steak frites*' was scrawled on a battered blackboard that had been knocked to the ground by a gust of wind. From inside we could hear people shouting aggressively. It didn't seem like the type of place where we'd find the creamy white Chaource cheese that Peter had been fixated on since our departure from Champagne.

I nervously pushed the door open and smoke and noise billowed out towards me. A table full of Lycra-clad cyclists were clamouring for more wine while watching a TV that was blasting images of a furiously pedalling *peloton* into the room, a crowd of men stood at the bar drinking pastis, which appeared to have been anointed rather than diluted with water, and in the far corner a mother attempted to rock her baby to sleep while waving a betting slip at another screen showing live chariot racing. We'd planned to find the palest rosé in Marsannay by simply asking the locals, but what would this bar make of our quest and us?

Two hours later we'd had great *steak frites*, met the barmaid, her husband the barrel maker, the local teacher and two firemen, and discovered a universal truth – everybody in France has an opinion on wine and it's usually a strong one. The argument ebbed and flowed round the bar, voices were raised, fists waved and heads shaken in disgust. At times we appeared moments from a consensus, only for a new customer to walk in and reignite the discussion. Although our table was the centre of the debate where all conclusions were finally presented, splinter conversations developed in the betting-shop area and in huddled groups around the bar.

It took a mushroom-picker to settle the matter. He entered

the bar with great clods of mud on his boots and *girolles* fresh from the woods brimming from his upturned hat. Picking twigs from his scraggy beard and accepting a large beer in return for the mushrooms, he immediately declared that Laurent Fournier made the palest rosé in Marsannay. Perhaps he was a respected local vigneron, or even the town's mayor. In any event the answer could not have been more definitive. Everyone nodded in agreement, half glasses of pastis were dispatched in a single swallow and the bar emptied. Foolishly, we didn't write down Laurent Fournier's name.

Perhaps we were distracted – in the corner of the bar, underneath the TV, a pair of gentle eyes had been staring at us. Their owner had quietly sipped a glass of red wine and flicked through *Le Monde*, but I don't think he'd missed a word of the discussion. We invited him to sit down and share our story. He nodded and introduced himself as Philippe. Something about his relaxed demeanour, the smiles he interspersed between questions, the way he made sure we were all included in the conversation despite our varying ability to speak French made us trust him.

For the first time since we'd been in France, Tanya and I thought again about the reasons we'd taken up the challenge. As we talked, Philippe pulled at the grey flecks in his neat beard, gently encouraging us with a mixture of supportive remarks and the odd thoughtful puff on an ever-smouldering cigarette.

'You've done the right thing. We all go a little crazy in life, and what better place to go crazy than France?' He leant conspiratorially over his wine glass. 'Just remember that people on a quest only think they know what they're searching for.'

Seemingly satisfied with his advice, he put on a long mac that nearly stretched to his shoes and a pair of leather gloves. Wrapping a scarf around his neck and placing his paper under his arm, he opened the door. 'Oh, and one more thing: wherever you are, keep in mind that the wine speaks of the people.'

Before we could ask what he meant, the door swung shut. After a couple of minutes we were still nonplussed.

'Right, time to go and see Monsieur Fournier,' said Peter, standing up. 'Does anybody remember his first name?'

'No, but I saw a sign for a Fournier up the road, so we'll find him,' I replied.

As we left the bar, almost as an afterthought, Tanya asked the barmaid, 'Who was that man?'

'The one you've just been talking to? He's a very kind, wise person,' she paused, 'and a psychoanalyst.'

Earl Daniel Fournier stood barring the door to his house. He had a face that looked like it had seen more weather than a deep-sea trawler and broad shoulders as sturdy and heavy as a bulkhead. His bulbous nose was flushed pink, and he wore a moth-eaten woollen jumper underneath a pair of stained blue salopettes. He looked at us with a mixture of disbelief and suspicion as we explained that we'd been advised he made the palest rosé in Marsannay, and his response, when it came, was completely unintelligible – it was fast, it was slurred, and it bore no resemblance to any French I'd ever heard before. Whether we were invited in or whether Tanya just spotted a little crack between Monsieur Fournier and the door, I'm still not sure. In any event we found ourselves sitting at a long oak table in his kitchen, attempting to talk over sizzling food as his sister prepared pork stew.

The conversation continued to flow from one misunderstanding to another, but, eventually, by producing a picture of Rosie holding a bottle of rosé, we were able to make ourselves understood. My grip on what was being discussed was tenuous at best, but I now gather that Monsieur Fournier made it clear that we were welcome in his house anytime, and that next time we visited we should bring our niece, Rosie. Finally, he reached back into the kitchen for a bottle of his rosé. It was time to test how far local knowledge would get us, and whether the two hours in the bar had been well spent. Just as he was pulling the wine from the rack, he paused and said, 'You must visit my brother. He makes a rosé far paler than mine.'

'There's more than one Fournier in Marsannay?'

'Oh, I should think at least six.'

With five Fourniers left, no first name to go by and as yet no pale rosé, we made the error of asking for directions. In England, a passer-by will typically be honest if he doesn't know the way; in France, there's pride at stake. Rather than admit ignorance, your average Frenchman will list a bewildering series of left and right turns, have a stand-up row with the person next to him who is concurrently listing an opposite set of road names, and then repeat the whole conversation again in a different order just to be sure he's been understood.

A small crowd gathered and a flurry of hand gestures directed us this way and that as each person strove to be more helpful than the last by directing us to his or her preferred Fournier. Then, after a while, it was agreed that we'd save time if we went straight to the maker of the palest rosé and so, rather than give directions, the argument from the bar restarted. Disconcertingly, it was agreed that it wasn't a Fournier we needed after all but a Bouvier, and, unsurprisingly, nobody was sure which Bouvier. Just as the discussion threatened to get out of hand, with people coming out of their houses to investigate the noise, we were rescued by the mushroom-picker from the bar. He spotted us from across the street, extricated us from the crowd and led us to Laurent Fournier.

Outside the small cave it was streaming with rain and gusts of wind hurled heavy drops of water through the open door. Laurent was wearing a windcheater, Tanya her winter coat and Peter a mac, but I only had a sodden summer jumper that clung to me as I shivered. It felt like we were a million miles from

Provence. Producing a razor blade from his pocket and brushing his careless mop of brown hair away from his eyes, Laurent cut into one of the boxes of wine stacked high against the wall.

He explained that Marsannay rosé was made from the grapes grown on the poorer slopes at the foot of the valley, predominantly using the pinot-noir grape, but that he had found the resulting rosé too strong and earthy, and so, unlike other winemakers, he used a mixture of Pinot Noir and Chardonnay grapes. 'This,' he said proudly, 'makes my rosé the palest in Marsannay.'

Pouring the liquid into the glass, he held it up against the bare bulb that lit the room. Despite the chill and the flat grey light, we stood rapt. We could see the whole room reflected in the glass – discarded corks, crates of wine and a map of Marsannay, all tinged a faint translucent pink. And the taste? Laurent swilled the wine around his glass, took a deep sniff and then a small sip: '*Fraise du bois et bonbons anglais.*' He looked at us expectantly as we tasted. It was fresh and fruity with a little more depth than the Provençal rosés we'd become so accustomed to, but try as I might, I couldn't discern wild strawberries. And as for English sweets, surely it depended on the colour of the wine gum.

'*Oui, fraise du bois et bonbons anglais.*' I nodded, delighted that, at last, after a month in France, we had a contender.

7

The Mountain *Gris*

For a while the psychoanalyst's advice bothered me: 'People on a quest only think they know what they're searching for.' It was enigmatic psychobabble, scarcely more credible than the weekly predictions of astrologers. But it did make me think.

My prime motivation was undoubtedly the bet. Part of me still felt foolish about agreeing to find an importer for the Etiennes' rosé. Had their late reply to my letter tricked us into a challenge we couldn't win? Could it have been a deliberate ploy? And why had our polite requests to be told just how many bottles 'a small percentage of their annual production' amounted to been met with silence? The solution to all these worries was simple – we had to win. The more I thought about it, the more determined I became. At times the image of Madame Etienne garrotting Rosie's teddy came unbidden to my mind. I even visualised Madame prowling the Provençal countryside, like a latter-day Cruella de Vil, snatching children's toys and dismembering them at her leisure.

But there was a more personal side to the trip. When we'd left, the idea of dropping everything and running away to France for the summer had seemed like a last hurrah. At thirty-two, I was like thousands of other people – doing a job for which I had no real affinity but which I couldn't see myself leaving because it paid the bills. From an early age I had enjoyed words, but as a lawyer, I was responsible for filing them down and forcing them to give up their last kernel of meaning. Then, they stood alone on the page, bare and unencumbered, perfect for a court case, but devoid of any other purpose. I was hoping that our time in France might finally help me to reconcile myself to life as a lawyer. When we returned to England, Tanya and I could settle down, have a family and who knows, one day, as I grew more senior, I might even begin to enjoy my job.

And Tanya? She had clung to her childhood dreams far longer and with more tenacity than I had ever dared to. At university she spent every spare moment rehearsing for musicals and by the age of twenty she was performing lead parts in fringe plays at the Edinburgh Festival, but then her fingers had slipped. Instead of plunging into the abyss of the impoverished Equity-card-seeking actor, she chose to work on the commercial side of theatre and then television.

From being a salve for the soul, the business element of the entertainment industry had left a gaping wound. It was a world populated by failed actors who'd never learnt to let go. Every time Tanya's colleagues looked upon a stage or set, they wanted to be on it. They also wanted the trappings of stardom, the adulation of an audience and the fawning of fans. In an office environment this was never possible, and at times it felt like the whole industry had flown too close to the sun. So I hoped that Tanya was resolving to pursue a different career.

There was also a chance that the experience of travelling around France for six months might soften her conviction that we should one day move here. As a couple we rarely argued, but when we did, it tended to be about the possibility of living in France.

As Tanya frequently pointed out, she was very nearly born French. Her parents had met in the rippling heat of Bermuda on the steps of an aeroplane. Her father, Stuart, was returning to

England at the end of a business trip, and Ashara was arriving on holiday from Canada. Their eyes smiled as they passed, and as Stuart looked from the plane at Ashara's retreating blonde bob of hair, he knew he had to do something. His work could wait but his future couldn't and so, pushing past an astonished air hostess, he went in search of romance.

Within months they were married, but then came the hardest decision – where to live: England, Canada or the fairy-tale choice of France? With so much changing so quickly in their lives, they plumped for England, and Tanya was born in the suburbs of London. But it could so easily have been Paris, and at times it seemed that Tanya asked herself on a weekly basis whether she should correct Fate's mistake and move to France.

But however dearly I loved my wife, and however much we shared the same sense of humour and the same friends, I couldn't bring myself to share her dream. I didn't speak French and I'd spent the last ten years of my life training to be a lawyer. For me, Tanya's idyll foundered on questions such as how would we support a family? I couldn't believe that mere geography was that important to our future happiness. So secretly I wished that our trip would help Tanya see that day-to-day life abroad wasn't like our long sweet holidays in Provence.

In France, it's possible to ignore the map and measure progress by the changing cuisine. Just forty minutes from the rich red-wine stews of Burgundy, we lunched in Chaussons, at the foot of the Jura, on pork in cream sauce with cheesy gratin Dauphinois. As we climbed upwards into the mountains, we left the country we were familiar with behind.

By the time we had reached Arbois the language was still French, but the customs had changed. Waiters expected to be paid when they served our drinks. While it was nice not to have to search dark recesses for bar staff, paying up front felt like an affront. Then there was the launderette. We dropped our clothes in for a service wash and were told that we couldn't possibly have them back until the end of the week. So far, so French. But when we returned to the hotel that evening, our clothes had been delivered and were waiting in a neatly pressed pile.

In most French towns you can't even get a *croque-monsieur* after 2 p.m., but at the bottom of the high street was La Finette, a twenty-four-hour, 365-days-a-year restaurant that had never closed in its twenty-year history. Near the end of our meal we were offered a Jura bag to carry any leftover wine home. 'Since when have the French been unable to finish their wine?' asked Peter. Arbois, it seemed, was a geographic mistake: it should have been in nearby Switzerland.

But after Burgundy and its pristine vines, the Alpine feel of the Jura was a delight. The food was hearty and wholesome: piping hot dishes of chicken cooked in a creamy wild mushroom sauce and plates of mountain salami known as Jésu de Morteau. And the wine? The region's winemakers were called *fruitières* and specialised in some unusual drinks. They dried grapes on straw before vinification to create *vin de paille* or concocted Macvin by adding spirits to non-fermented grape juice. But, amid all these weird and wonderful options, we seemingly had a real chance of finding France's palest rosé. The reference in my wine atlas read, 'Jura wine is not only red, white and rosé but yellow and grey . . . the grey wine is simply a very pale rosé, rather sharp and sometimes extremely appetising.'

The best place to start should have been Château Chalon, Jura's most renowned appellation, but finding the mountain *gris* proved to be a little more complex than we expected. The road from Arbois coiled upwards ducking through tunnels and snaking away from precipitous falls. Fields were stepped into the sides of cliffs and vines grew on thin perpendicular terraces. Each breath of air was fierce, fresh and cold. Wire mesh prevented heavy boulders from blocking the route and bent crash barriers wore scars from cars and rocks. Then, after one last hairpin, the land sloped away into a high fertile plateau, where cows and sheep grazed next to lakes as clear as any Caribbean lagoon. There were more cyclists than cars, and more campsites than villages. People hiked, canoed, and rather than drool over a glass of Gevrey, they deliberated on which spring water to have with their picnic.

Tanya had read that small numbers of wolves and bears still roamed wild in France. She became convinced they lived in the Jura and kept scanning the tree line for signs of movement. The variety of the landscape and weather reminded her of the Eastern Townships in Canada, where her mother grew up, with lush green woods bathed in sunshine or submerged in mist. As Peter stripped off and strode into a small lake fed from a fresh mountain stream, Tanya glanced anxiously back at the trees and told me of the time her mother had been trapped treading water for an hour while a coyote paced the shore. At times living in the Jura did feel like being part of a fairy tale. I could see Peter, but where was the wolf?

Château Chalon did nothing to dispel our feeling that there was something magical about the region. The spire from the church pierced the first layer of cloud and appeared to float freely in the sky, leaving the rest of the village clinging to the mountainside beneath. The houses were dug into the ground so you had to descend two or three steps and bow your head under a heavy oak lintel to enter, and the gardens were cut from the cliffs and ringed by old stone walls.

Peter and Tanya wandered, as if bewitched, through the tiny streets, deriving a vicarious pleasure at the thought of living in a tiny mountain cottage with only the crisp air for company. I was keen to meet some *fruitières*, but just when I'd succeeded in shepherding Peter in the right direction, Tanya would dive into one shop or other. I felt like a schoolmaster with a party of footloose children.

We lost Peter for over half an hour in the back room of a house from which he eventually emerged with three small packages. They were all goat's cheeses. One was ready to eat that day, another in a few days' time, and the third needed to be stored in a cool cupboard for a couple of weeks to mature. 'There's always the glove compartment,' he declared when I asked where he was going to keep it.

Tanya meanwhile was getting into trouble of her own. She'd spotted a house on the crest of an outcrop of rock with floor-to-ceiling windows and a wonderful view of the great basin of vines that surrounded the village. Cupping her hands over her eyes and pressing her nose to the glass, she strained to see into the house and through to the other side where there was a glorious roof terrace. Suddenly she jumped backwards. Her mouth was wide open and she stifled a cry as she held her hand to her heart. Inside I could see a young man in a pair of jeans and a shirt laughing away. He had crawled across the floor from the side of the room and painstakingly pulled himself up to the glass window. According to Tanya, one minute she was straining to see the view and the next all she could see was his massive grinning face pressed cheek to cheek and lip to lip with hers on the other side of the glass.

Further down the road I dragged Peter away from a prolonged study of a restaurant that he assured me would be just perfect for lunch, only to find that Tanya had recovered from her shock and was now interrupting an old man who was chopping wood outside his house. Joseph Votava's hair was white as snow, his skin cracked and creased like old leather, and hundreds of little wrinkles played around his eyes like tributaries feeding a stream. With his little half-moon glasses, his twinkling eyes and woodcutter's axe, he reminded me of Pinocchio's father, Gepetto.

But rather than a craftsman, he turned out to be a vigneron. We ducked our heads as we followed him past piles of neatly stacked wood and into his cave. In Champagne and Burgundy, the cellars we'd visited tended to either be in the basements of old houses or in warehouses with state-of-the-art temperature control, but Joseph Votava's was hewn out of the side of the mountain. It was dimly lit and cool, and I had to stand with a permanent stoop to avoid being impaled on various rocky spikes that hung like stalactites from the ceiling.

Before we tasted his rosé, Joseph insisted on pouring us small glasses of his *vin jaune* or 'yellow wine'. Château Chalon, he explained, was famous for it. The wine was sealed in oak barrels for five years and a layer of yeast was allowed to form across the top; when bottled, it could keep for hundreds of years. It smelt of roasting chestnuts and looked and tasted of luxury – rich and viscous in the glass like liquid gold and as smooth as brandy butter. Beside an open fire at Christmas time it would be perfect as an indulgent aperitif or a decadent digestive.

He then produced a light-red wine made from the Poulsard grape. We politely tasted it, wondering when the rosé would turn up, but fully aware that we'd probably have to taste all his different wines anyway. Another red and then a white emerged but still no rosé and we eventually left, slightly confused, with two bottles of *vin jaune* tucked under our arms – one to give to Rosie on her twenty-first birthday and one as a present for Claire's unborn second baby, due during the summer.

Later, at lunch, Peter discovered a dish which he didn't stop talking about for months – *coq au vin jaune aux morilles*. It arrived in a casserole pot brimming with a thick bubbling liquid – not the deep red of a normal *coq au vin* but a gentle dark cream laced with thin slices of morels. The taste was so rich and indulgent that I thought the overall effect might be like eating too much chocolate. I was wrong, and an hour later we had to ask for more bread to mop up the last drops of the sauce from the casserole.

'I told you it was the best restaurant in the village,' said Peter as we left.

We walked along the main street and ducked into the houses

of some more *fruitières*. Some said they didn't make rosé. Others produced a light-red wine very similar to the second wine Joseph had offered us and insisted that it was a rosé. But with each visit and each exotic new wine we encountered, the mystery of the missing mountain *gris* deepened.

Peter had heard about the Firemen's Ball while paying one of many visits to the little chocolate shop on the corner of the main square in Arbois, and later that evening we walked up a tree-lined avenue towards the outskirts of town, where the ball was taking place. The ball was held every year in aid of the families of firemen who had lost their lives, and in the distance we could hear the loud beat of disco music.

We'd only been in France for six weeks but already we'd appreciated the important role the Fire Service played in French life. Each town had its own fire alarm and we'd been hounded from Epernay holding our ears when the town decided to test its system. It seemed senseless – why did the whole town have to be able to hear the alert? What was wrong with a bell in the fire station?

In bars there was always idle gossip about the Fire Service. Why did the firemen not cope with last year's fires? Was it because pyromaniacs had joined the service and enjoyed setting light to the countryside? Had part-time firemen started fires to create work? Perhaps we would find some answers at the ball, and we might even find some more information about our missing *gris*.

As the light faded and we walked through the shadows of the trees, I smiled at Tanya. This was exactly the type of experience I wanted to pack our trip with. Rather than popping down to our local on a Friday night and seeing the same group of friends harrowed from a week at work, we were going to a ball, and not just any ball – a *pompiers'* ball. I was delighted. It sounded so quintessentially French, like being invited to watch Morris dancing on May Day but a lot more fun.

The sliding doors of the fire station had been pushed back to reveal a garage the size of an aircraft hangar. Multicoloured spotlights danced between the five concrete stanchions which supported the weight of the building. At one end a DJ on a podium gyrated to the music and, despite the nearly deserted hall, made small talk between the songs.

Behind the DJ a bar had been set up. Fairy lights were draped from the wall and hundreds of plastic beakers were set out on temporary tables. Lined up behind the tables were the firemen in dark-blue uniform with reflective bands across their chests and on their wrists. Their boots were freshly polished and the creases in their trousers newly pressed. They were mostly young men, with close haircuts and eager smiles, and they chatted happily away to Tanya as she bought the drinks.

At about ten o'clock the residents of Arbois remembered the ball. The elderly arrived first, leaning on their canes and gingerly positioning themselves around the edge of the dance floor. Next came the new generation of parents, who, grateful for a moment alone, hugged the bar and set their young children loose in the hall. Small girls in party dresses with their hair in pigtails screamed as they were chased by packs of little boys, and gradually the area around the bar became busier and busier as teenagers with dyed jeans and various piercings joined the press.

But nobody seemed willing to dance. I couldn't blame them: that night French pop music more than earnt its reputation for being among the worst in the world, and if any further inducement was needed to stay by the bar, there was the army of grandmothers surrounding the dance floor scrutinising every move. An inappropriately placed hand would probably be the talk of the town for weeks, a stolen kiss might mean the chapel at dawn, which meant that Tanya and I were almost alone in enjoying a dance in the open doors of the fire station, looking out at the peaks of the mountains as the moon emerged from behind the clouds. It would have been romantic, but for the fact that the song was 'YMCA' and the whole town was watching.

Driven from the floor by embarrassment, I joined Peter near the bar. He was sitting with his arm around a great bear of a man who had a big woolly beard and gaps in his teeth and was called Frederick. The Jura, Frederick explained, was a region in crisis; lack of jobs meant more and more young people were deserting the area and moving to Dijon or Lyon. He was unemployed himself and had considered moving, but he didn't want to give up his role as a volunteer fireman.

One of Peter's great qualities in life is his ability to make strangers feel like lifelong friends. I've not encountered a more passionate and sympathetic listener. He kept the conversation going with a mixture of '*donc*'s and extravagant gestures and even began a rant about problems in rural areas in the UK. Frederick was suitably encouraged and continued to talk. 'It's sad to watch – bars which were once full are now empty or given over to people who gamble their benefits away on lottery draws such as Rapido.' He pointed to the dance floor and argued that the police's new zero-tolerance approach to drink-driving had destroyed traditional events such as this. 'People have to drink rosé now if they want to drive,' he said indignantly. 'It's one of the reasons the vignerons are selling so much of it.'

Quite why it was possible to drink rosé and drive we didn't discover because a siren wail silenced the disco. Frederick jumped up and quickly joined the rest of the firemen who were dragging the tables away and scattering drinks to the floor in the process. We were herded with the other guests back against the wall in order to clear a corridor to the exit. But instead of screeching off to deal with a fire, a single engine edged into the road and sat there idling, its blue siren revolving with the disco lights. The tables were righted and everyone's drinks replaced. Still the fire engine waited; it seemingly had nowhere to go.

It was at this point that I noticed Tanya was missing. Peter eventually discovered her draped among ten firemen beaming for the camera. She explained – without a hint of guilt – that she'd taken an educational tour of the fire station. It was about furthering our quest rather than any fondness for French men in uniform, she assured me.

As if to prove her point, she began lecturing us on how a town's fire alarm had to be loud enough to summon the volunteers from their day jobs – butchers and bakers had to be able to hear it in their shops, accountants and lawyers in their offices, even labourers in the field. She'd also asked about rosé and, according to the firemen, Jacques Tissot was the best wine shop in town. If the mountain *gris* existed – which they doubted – we'd find it in this shop.

As we left our ivy-covered hotel the next morning we were still debating whether we'd witnessed a drill or whether there'd been an actual emergency. The fire engine did eventually drive off towards the centre of Arbois, but after twenty minutes it returned and parked up the road. Perhaps the firemen did it every year as a way of reminding people they were always on duty. At least the alert had been serious enough to make them desert Tanya, leaving her stranded high in the cabin of a fire engine. 'I can't believe I didn't get to slide down the pole,' she teased as we entered Place de la Liberté.

Around the edges of the square, narrow four-storey buildings stretched towards the mountains. From each roof long ropes decked with multicoloured flags were draped on to the central fountain, so that standing at street level and looking upwards was like being in the middle of a giant kaleidoscope. A little boy in a bright-red jumper whirled around the fountain chasing a dog that wheeled away in the opposite direction.

Exclusive shops nestled under a covered arcade, their windows visible through a row of arches. We passed Peter's favourite – the *chocolatier* Monsieur Hirsinger. Immaculate chocolates and pastries lined trays in the window and miniature blackboards identified each delectable – *fours aux amandes, fours aux noix, florentin au lait noir, baba rhum* and the fantastically named *religieuse au chocolat*. 'He's even made a special chocolate to go with each of the region's wines,' explained Peter, 'but I've checked; he's got nothing to go with rosé.'

Next door was the wine shop, Jacques Tissot. It was clearly no ordinary off-licence – the sign was written in ornate lettering and the window was surrounded by carved wood more suitable for a picture frame than a shop front. Squat hundred-year-old bottles of *vin jaune* were displayed next to tidy rows of elongated and thin-necked *vin de paille*. Underneath the window a wooden trap door was propped open and steps led underground. A faint light glowed in the darkness.

'Shouldn't we go into the shop?' I asked.

'Come on,' said Peter, 'this will be more fun.'

We climbed down into the dank cellar. The sound of water dripping rippled around the high ceiling, and each breath I took was heavy with moisture. Gradually my eyes became accustomed to the darkness and I could make out the nearest walls of the cave, which were covered in green moss and, in places, an almost fluorescent yellow fungus. Rows and rows of wine bottles stretched into the darkness and each rack was labelled with a year. The oldest wine, just behind Tanya, appeared to date back to 1734.

'*Bonjour*,' I called in my friendliest voice, which echoed around the cellar.

As the word bounced back to me for the third time, there was an enormous bang and the whole cellar reverberated. I looked accusingly at Tanya, had she knocked some ancient bottles to the floor? Instead of guilty she looked terrified as a smartly dressed middle-aged man emerged from the shadows and sprang right past her face and up the steps.

We waited, slightly shame-faced and with only the dripping water for company, for the man to return. When he did, he was out of breath and even in the dark of the cellar I could see that his cheeks were flushed red. 'Kids with firecrackers.' He took a breath and rested his hands on his knees. As if to explain his exhausted state, he continued, 'Louis Pasteur used to carry out experiments in this cave and now kids chuck firecrackers in for a joke. It makes me so angry that I have to give chase.'

Resting one hand on the slimy wall, he finally recovered his breath. 'My name's Philippe. Can I help you?'

'We are looking for pale rosé, a mountain *gris*,' I said confidently.

Philippe looked at me as if I was as mad as the kid who had just let off the firecracker, and then shook his head in disbelief. He led us up the uneven stone steps and guided us from the bright morning light into the shop. On the walls were various certificates of excellence, awarded in wine competitions from Poligny to Paris, and on upturned barrels stood bottles of wine wearing silver and golden chains around their necks like medals.

Pouring us a glass of the light-red wine we'd become so familiar with in Château Chalon, Philippe explained that he'd been born and bred in the Jura and that he'd been making wine all his life and there was one thing he knew beyond all doubt: 'There's no *gris* in the Jura.'

Silence. I looked along the shelves of the shop. There wasn't a single bottle of pale rosé in sight. 'But what about my wine book?' I asked.

'I'm sorry, your book is wrong. Some of the winemakers label their light-red wines made from the Poulsard grape rosé, but they're vinified like a red wine. You'll not find any real rosé here and certainly no *gris*.'

Peter scratched his head in confusion, took one more look at the shelves full of wine, and announced his conclusion to the whole shop with a broad grin: 'Double *donc*.'

[78]

★

It was now nearly June and the vines were flowering. For almost two months it seemed it had not stopped raining. If the grapes were to mature properly, it was essential we had some sunshine. A change in the weather would also help our spirits. Green rot had started to grow on the fabric hood of Peter's car, and on our final day in the Jura water began to drip through an ever-widening hole in the roof. The argument to head south and continue our quest in Provence could not have been stronger, and yet we still had the Loire to explore – Touraine rosé, Chinon rosé, Rosé d'Anjou and of course Sancerre.

Tanya sat in the back of the car with her feet in a puddle. She wore a fleece and a woolly hat. Peter and I turned to her. 'It's time to go south and find the sun,' I said.

Tanya shivered. 'What about Sancerre? If it's still raining after Sancerre, we'll head south.'

JUNE

'Why is pale rosé so popular?'
asked Tanya.
'Because people like you don't
know a good wine from a
bad one.'

8

Nicolas Reverdy

Peter and I accepted Tanya's decision and arranged an early-evening tasting near Sancerre with a vigneron called François Crochet from the village of Bué. From the map it looked to be a three-hour drive; we could have a leisurely lunch somewhere near Dijon and then head across the Morvan National Park to the Loire in the afternoon. At least that was the plan, and it didn't seem too unrealistic given that in France you can travel from Calais to Nice in one day.

Unfortunately travelling west was considerably more difficult than plunging south on the Autoroute du Soleil, particularly with one travel-phobic companion. Tanya's love of everything French mysteriously vanishes when it comes to their motorways and *routes nationales* – according to her, the lanes are too narrow and the juggernauts too plentiful.

Each time a lorry passed us she would clutch at the seats, dig her nails into the leather and suck the air so violently between her teeth that she almost hissed with fear. Even I had to admit that some French driving habits were a little unusual. The caricature of the continental driver overtaking on the crest of a hill or around a blind bend was so accurate that I'd become immune to the ill effects of being tailgated at 100 km.p.h., but each hour in the car was still a learning experience.

The respect shown to cyclists was a revelation. It seemed a French driver would rather lay down his own life than cause a cyclist a moment's inconvenience. Lorries swerved into the opposing lane of traffic to avoid buffeting them, and cars idled behind them rather than risk squeezing them against the hard shoulder. In the land of the Tour de France, anyone riding a bike was idolised, and anyone else was simply fair prey.

Two hours of hissing later Tanya took over the driving and, ignoring the *route nationale*, we headed into the countryside. Minor roads in France are shown as D-roads on maps, but what the maps don't show is that any one D-road can be subdivided into ten other roads. Thus you have the D10A, the D10B, the D10C and so on, and out of all the various letters it's really pot luck which road happens to be heading in the right direction. And that explains how, besides a few major map-reading arguments, we came to spend an idyllic afternoon snaking round the deserted hills of the Morvan National Park, discovering that the D10E, the D10F and the D10G were in fact loop roads that took us back to exactly where we started.

While I became ever more anxious about our six o'clock meeting, Peter reclined his seat and enjoyed the view. 'Come on,' he encouraged me, 'it's simply wonderful, much better than all those juggernauts.' And he was right. Our stomachs leapt into our mouths as we pitched over rolling hills into a landscape full of basking sunflowers and lorries stacked with hay bales trailing blizzards of straw. Hawks hovered silently, hiding their shadow in the high hedges, and horses stood tail to face obligingly swishing the flies from each other's eyes. Wild poppies sprouted by the roadside, and fields of delicate multicoloured flowers were woven together in patterns as beautiful as any Persian rug.

Out in the middle of nowhere we suddenly encountered an old woman in widow's black hobbling away with only a cane for company and then moments later a shirtless jogger pounding the road, with the sweat shimmering like a mirage on his back so that seconds later we questioned whether he'd existed. Railway tracks with grass growing between the lines preceded isolated villages decked with flowers, and finally glimpses of a wide stony flood plain flicked into view between the foliage. We'd picked up the first broad sweeps of the Loire. All we had to do was steer clear of juggernauts, contend with a strange smell that was beginning to develop in the car and follow the river to Sancerre.

The village of Bué wasn't at all what I'd expected – the houses tended to be relatively modern bungalows with picket fences, tarmac drives and even garages. In France, cars were usually abandoned straddling the kerb or blocking the road, but here they were all neatly stowed away, allowing tractors to weave unhindered through the streets – which was lucky because when we arrived at 6.30 p.m., it was the middle of the rush hour. Tractors queued at each junction, with their tiny orange warning light revolving on the end of a pole and the driver's seat raised artificially high into the sky to allow it to pass over the vines. Hosepipes sprawled from tanks at the rear like spider's limbs, and the vignerons in flat caps and faded shirts resembled small boys attempting to tame great mechanical monsters.

I needn't have worried about being late because François Crochet was having a bad day. The previous night a thunderstorm had hit his fields and he'd spent the whole day meticulously checking for any damage to the vines. Then, just as the hour of our tasting approached, his tractor had broken down. So, after dashing across the country and negotiating the tractor traffic jams, we stood waiting on the porch of the Crochets' house.

As each vigneron passed, our hopes were raised – surely it would be François this time. Finally a barrel of a man waved at us as he drove by. He looked like he'd been at the wrong end of too many rugby scrums, with his hair shaved short and his nose flattened against his face. His thick arms swung the wheel of the great tractor around as it turned behind the house, and moments later François emerged with a bottle of rosé in his hand and a big toothy grin on his face.

For the next hour we sat on the terrace and watched vignerons chug by as François chatted away. 'Five years ago Sancerre would have been the perfect place for your quest,' he explained, as he poured us all a glass of his none-too-pale rosé. 'Vignerons were making rosé in real quantity then and dotted among the hills you'd have found some fantastic *gris*. But now rosé is in decline – producers can make more money from producing a red wine from Pinot Noir grapes. It's a lot less difficult to make well and a lot less time-intensive.

'You might even have some difficulty buying rosé in Sancerre. Demand from London and Tokyo is huge, and in restaurants the price of a bottle can be marked up five times,' he continued, topping up our glasses as he spoke. 'Last month an established client of my reds and whites put in an order for a couple of cases of rosé and I had to turn him away.'

Given the scarcity of his wine, it seemed a little churlish that François persisted in spitting it all out. He sucked the liquid to the back of his throat, swilled it between his gums like mouthwash and then jettisoned the liquid into a spittoon. He explained that the idea was to awake all the different flavours of the wine and that our most sensitive taste buds were located in the roof of the mouth and in our gums.

As we listened we sipped on probably the nicest rosé we'd tasted since we arrived in France. But at the time it seemed like small consolation. We'd ignored the lure of Provence and driven six hours out of our way. By now we could be sitting in the shade of an olive tree, listening to the song of the cicadas and soaking up the heady aroma of lavender.

Realistically, I had to admit that our quest to date had been a failure. Seen in sunlight rather than in the confines of a poorly lit cave, Laurent Fournier's Marsannay rosé wasn't as pale as Madame Etienne's. We'd also wasted nearly two weeks driving around Champagne with nothing to show for our efforts, not to mention making complete fools of ourselves in the Jura.

We'd all been really excited about Sancerre – the area's reputation for fine wine had drawn us across France – but we'd made a mistake. It was, we all agreed, time to head south.

Then, just as our car was pulling out of the drive, François called to us, 'You may want to visit Nicolas Reverdy in Maimbray. I don't think I know anyone as enthusiastic about rosé as Nicolas.'

Maimbray is known as the 'village of the vignerons'. A large wooden signpost sits on a grass verge in the heart of the central square and houses a hand-drawn map depicting the estates of each of the winemakers. The map showed the road through the village splitting like the lifeline on the palm of a hand towards the various domaines. Little bushes of rosemary and lavender were sketched in next to the houses and a deep-blue sky hung in the background. It was like a picture of an enchanted kingdom. We just had to hope that 'X' would mark the spot where we would finally find a *gris*.

The size of the map made the journey to the Reverdys look like a five-minute hike. Instead, it was just a few metres up the road. Set behind several rows of flower beds and a small herb garden was a large open courtyard with a squat red-brick house in one corner and a large warehouse opposite. A battered white Land Rover was parked next to the house, and underneath its bumper a child's go-cart lay scuffed and deserted.

We pressed on the doorbell and moments later we were greeted by Nicolas Reverdy. There was something about his slightly lopsided smile that immediately inspired affection. He was about thirty years old, had a scraggy, almost ginger beard, and his limbs were loose and gangly. There was still a little of the adolescent about him – as if he was only just becoming accustomed to the size of his body and the demands of his life.

Best of all, he had a slightly goofy sense of humour. Never has a vigneron been more delighted by the tale of mad English people hunting for France's palest rosé.

Within minutes of opening the door Nicolas had packed us into the back of his Land Rover. He wanted to show us his vines and so we pitched and rolled as the car climbed higher up a dirt track into the fields. At one point the gradient was so steep that we had to wedge ourselves against the wheel arches to avoid being tossed to the back of the boot with miscellaneous hoes, spades and secateurs. 'I hope this is worth it,' said Tanya as she cannoned against the handle of a shovel.

Finally Nicolas threw open the rear doors and we came tumbling out. He led us into a field of closely planted vines, occasionally stopping and pulling back the leaves to reveal small green clusters of grapes clinging to the plants. We kept climbing on foot. Vines covered every inch of the land. In contrast to Burgundy's gentle slopes this was a far harsher landscape. The hills were steep and inaccessible, and in some of the vineyards grass was allowed to grow between the lines of the grapes to stop the soil eroding away. Perched on a steep escarpment in the middle of a valley of interlocking fields was the town of Sancerre. Legend has it that the technique of pruning was discovered here when Saint Martin left a hungry donkey tethered to some vines. The donkey ate half the grapes, but the remaining crop produced wine of such outstanding quality that local vignerons adopted the method.

Nicolas pointed to the town and then made a sweeping gesture: 'All this is Sancerre appellation, but you mustn't think it is all excellent wine. There are only pockets of good land: Bué, Maimbray and a couple of other villages.' He stopped and picked some brown leaves from a vine and as he did so his mood changed. 'I think this plant is dying. It will last one more harvest and then we'll have to replant the whole field.'

To me, one vine looked very much like another, a gnarled

brown wishbone-shaped piece of wood sprouting from the ground, covered in a swathe of hand-sized dark-green leaves shading grapes which were as yet no bigger than peas. But Nicolas seemed to identify personally with each plant, caressing the leaves, as if remembering the day when it first sprouted. He told us the age of each particular vine we happened upon and explained that the grapes from the older plants were particularly prized. The older the vine, the deeper the roots, the greater the *tipicité* of the resulting wine.

Standing with the loose soil beneath my feet and seeing the heavy earth, sticky from the previous night's rainfall, clumped at the base of the vines, I finally began to understand the meaning of *tipicité*. By growing the vines close together, the vigneron was effectively forcing the plants to work harder to produce their crop and ensuring that each grape was full of the flavour of the land. The resulting wine would then have excellent *tipicité* and on the first sip a sommelier such as Antonio from the George V would be able to visualise the land it was from, whether it was the vast open plains of Champagne, the sweeping valleys of Burgundy, the rocky terraces of the Jura or the criss-crossing hills of Sancerre. *Tipicité* simply meant typical of an area.

I didn't have time to get too elated by my new discovery. Leading us back to the car, Nicolas gave a big broad grin and said, 'Come, let's go and taste some rosé.'

Going down the hill in the Land Rover was far worse than the ascent. Each successive bump threatened to throw us through the front window. One particularly bad pothole pitched Tanya on to the floor, and as she sat up, a prong from a rake stuck in her hair like a curling iron. 'I repeat, this had better be worth it,' she said, pulling at her hair, strand by strand, trying to untangle it.

We sat in a row on one side of a long wooden table in the corner of the *dégustation* area looking out across the room into the cave, where the ubiquitous stainless-steel vats were lined up against the wall. At their base they had small metal doors secured by a circular handle, which worked in a similar fashion to the release cap on the conning tower of a submarine. Next to them were a couple of enormous oak barrels that presumably held the red wine.

Nicolas took our glasses and crossed to one of the metal *cuves*. He flicked a tap, clearly expecting some wine to froth into the glasses, but instead the door swung open and he jumped backwards, arms outstretched with shock. As far as we could see the vat was empty, but, shifting my position, I caught sight of a small boy, perhaps four years old, who lay curled inside the *cuve* like a cat in a warm corner.

'Benjamin,' chided Nicolas, finding it difficult not to laugh.

The boy leapt out with a great grin spreading from cheek to cheek across his cherubic face. Brushing his blond hair away from his eyes, he rubbed his stomach in a broad circular motion, and licked his lips. '*J'aime beaucoup le rosé*,' he impishly declared before running off trailing high-pitched giggles.

Benjamin was his nephew, Nicolas explained, and they'd just started giving him a little rosé diluted with water at meal times. It was his favourite new drink and we'd also just witnessed his favourite new game – switching the signs on the *cuves*, hiding inside and springing out to surprise visitors. As he talked Nicolas removed four dark-green bottles of wine from the fridge. It was impossible to see their contents and I assumed there would be one rosé, a red and a couple of whites. I watched Nicolas slowly prise the cork from the first bottle of wine. The tour of the vineyard had been one of the most enjoyable experiences of our trip, but it would all have been for nothing unless we finally discovered a genuinely pale rosé.

Nicolas poured us all some of his 2003 rosé, giving each glass a vigorous circular swish to awaken the flavour. He watched us, closely gauging our reaction to the wine. As much as I wanted to please Nicolas, I couldn't look that happy – the wine was a light violet colour and on tasting had the same crispy brittleness of a white Sancerre. I'd become accustomed to the disappointment of finding another rosé which yet again didn't match up to Madame Etienne's, but I'd been expecting more from this visit. Tanya was looking out of the window towards the car, but before we could leave I knew we'd have to taste each of the other wines Nicolas had lined up for us.

To my surprise, the next glass we were offered was another rosé. 'Try this, it's a 1995,' said Nicolas with evident delight as he poured the wine. This time it was a deep orange colour, which Peter, in an attempt to be poetic, later compared to the setting African sun. 'Unlike other rosés, you can keep Sancerre, it improves with age. We usually drink this with *magret de canard*,' said Nicolas.

Like François, Nicolas sampled each of the wines he poured us, swishing the liquid around his mouth and then spitting it out in a jet. With each successive wine he appeared to become happier and happier, making little jokes and encouraging us to drink up so quickly it was difficult to keep pace.

Nicolas seemed to be moving with great delight to some pre-planned denouement, but all I wanted to do was to savour the wine. Unlike other rosés I'd tasted, the flavour of the wine lingered and grew with each sip. It was surprisingly rich and full, and I closed my eyes and tried to associate the structure of the wine with the landscape. Although it wasn't quite like François Gilbert's 'orgasm in the mouth', I kidded myself I could taste the *tipicité*.

We moved on to the penultimate wine, a 2000, and Nicolas gave a little wink as we realised it was yet another rosé. But once again the colour was disappointing. It was a similar violet to the first wine, and the feeling of disappointment crept back into my stomach. Nicolas took a deep sniff, swilled the wine around and watched the fingers of liquid trail down the straight sides of the glass. The aroma, he declared, was '*bonbon anglais*'.

'The final wine will interest you the most,' he continued. 'It's a 2001. The weather was really wet and there was hardly any sun. We did a small *macération* and a *saignée*. It's very full on the mouth and has the most remarkable colour.' The lopsided grin that he'd first greeted us with was back, and his eyes were alight with enjoyment as he lifted the bottle and prepared to pour. It was as if he was just about to share the punchline of a terribly funny joke.

Just as the first drops of liquid hit the rim of one of the glasses, the door to the *dégustation* area opened and a dark-haired, dark-skinned version of Nicolas entered. It was his older brother, Pascal. They had similar features, but Pascal was bigger boned with broad shoulders and a presence that filled the room. His eyes were dark brown, as opposed to Nicolas's which alternated between blue and green. Pascal acknowledged us with a nod and fixed his gaze on the bottle Nicolas was about to pour. Quite what passed between them, I'm still not sure, but Nicolas lowered the bottle and picked up the cork as if to replace it. We sat waiting, shifting our eyes between the two brothers.

Then, in what appeared an act of defiance, Nicolas raised the bottle once again and poured four glasses, only glancing away from his brother to check he didn't spill the wine. The colour was the delicate, ever so slightly luminous orange used by painters to evoke the light of the south of France when it is cast on pastel houses or reflected in ripples from the sea, and which, just for a second, can make people's breath stick in their throats. Undoubtedly it was the palest rosé any of us had ever seen. We felt like screaming with joy but we managed to contain ourselves and just grinned at each other. Surely we'd won. We couldn't wait to get a bottle back to the hotel and compare it with Madame Etienne's.

'Could we buy six bottles?' I asked.

Nicolas looked at us, then at his brother, then out of the window. He poured a fresh glass from each of the bottles and then replaced the bottles in the fridge. Lining up the glasses against the white wall so that we could take a photo of the contrasting shades of pink, he opened the door to allow us to measure the effect of sunlight on the colours.

'I'm afraid I can't even sell you one. We've only got two bottles of the 2001 left,' he said, looking somewhat sheepishly at his brother. 'Well, one now, actually.'

We spent the next hour touring the cave with Nicolas and, looking back now, I think he was fighting with a dilemma – could he sell us the 2001 rosé after all? Rather than let his mind churn the problem over, he was full of energy, clambering up the side of the large wooden barrels and extracting red wine with a large pipette. When Benjamin whizzed past him on a go-cart, he swung him into the air and engulfed him in an enormous bear hug. He tried each wine with us, spitting every sip down the drains that ran the length of the cave, but every now and again he returned to the subject that was clearly troubling him. 'Wine is to be drunk not kept,' he assured us, 'but I just can't let you have the final bottle.'

As we were preparing to leave, Nicolas came out of the house carrying two plastic bags. Holding them out to us, he thanked us for spending the morning with him and taking such an interest in the vineyard's wines. 'It was a wonderful way to pass a couple of hours,' he said, 'and I'd like to offer you these as a small thank-you.'

As soon as we left I hurriedly looked into the bag, checking the label on each bottle. Had he given us his final bottle of 2001 rosé?

'Well?' asked Tanya.

'Just six bottles of 2003, I'm afraid.'

'I'm not sure whether we should be despondent or elated,' said Peter as we turned out of Maimbray. 'To be taken up into the fields, to taste such fantastic wines, to open such a rare bottle, to be given such a generous gift. It was marvellous, absolutely marvellous. But to come so close ... ' He left the thought trailing in the air.

Behind me, I could hear Tanya sniffing. I was appalled to think she might be crying. Had rosé become that important to her? Instead, I turned around and saw that she had a look of utter distaste on her face. 'What's that awful smell?' she asked.

'No idea,' said Peter, making a great show of concentrating on the road.

Tanya wrinkled her nose one final time, wound down the window and stuck her head out into the clean air.

There was only one thing that could make such an abominable smell.

'Left here?' asked Peter, trying to stop himself from smiling.

I opened the glove compartment and winced as a warm, sweaty smell engulfed the car. There, sitting innocently in its wrapper, was the third goat's cheese Peter had purchased in Château Chalon.

'Seems to be maturing nicely,' said Peter as we turned south towards the sun.

9

Too Much *Vrac*

It's quite possible to arrive in Saint Rémy de Provence, stay for an hour or so and dismiss it as a lot of overblown hype. Nostradamus was born in the town, Van Gogh painted the surrounding countryside, and, in France, it's renowned as one of the Parisians' favourite summer boltholes. But initially all that struck me was the noose of traffic that threatened to choke the place – Saint Rémy, it seemed, like Epernay, was little more than a glorified roundabout.

Maybe the Parisians were used to the traffic, they were certainly everywhere. Young men in designer blue jeans and pressed white shirts jabbering into their mobiles as they stirred their espresso. Women wearing so much gold they'd sink if they went for a swim, and old men with Gucci belts, coiffured hair and pet poodles, parading up and down.

There was a designer hotel where the chef proposed a culinary journey leading from the subtleties of Japanese cooking to the rediscovery of French cuisine. The hotel had a suite with a tree house and a bar in an old cinema where film credits were continually projected on to the glass entrance. Next to the hotel was an artisan who promised to create a garden in your living room using only natural materials. It seemed the only thing not on offer in Saint Rémy was a chance to soak up the traditional slow-paced Provençal life.

But, after spending a couple of days in the town, I began to understand the attraction. Saint Rémy basked in the heart of the south amid fields of melons, plum orchards and olive groves, just a short distance from the boar-filled forests of the Luberon and the wild expanses of the Camargue. We stayed in an apartment that was part of a large subdivided villa. It was surrounded by umbrella pines and bougainvillea blooming a deep luscious pink. From our balcony we could look across sloping terracotta roofs to the jagged peaks of Les Alpilles – literally 'the little Alps' – which seemed bathed in a permanent haze of colour. The deep azure blue of the sky, the rich yellow of the sun and the brittle Mediterranean green were all reflected in these rocks and hung shimmering in the heat as a resplendent backdrop to Saint Rémy. On particularly hot days it was like watching a southern aurora.

Once inside the old town it was possible to stroll, oblivious to the traffic, along interlocking cobbled streets through squares filled with forgotten pâtisseries and *rôtisseries*, only pausing to pet panting dogs in the shade of olive trees. The locals lounged in cafés idly drinking pastis or clutching carafes of chilled red wine as they devoured the roasted carcasses of small birds, freshly shot that morning. Dried lavender hung in bunches outside shops selling honey, olive oil and pottery the colour of the sun.

In the evenings we'd have a drink in the shadow of Les Alpilles and watch Ferraris and 2CVs compete for parking spaces. Shopkeepers chatted idly, waiting to see if the day would bring one final client, and families emerged on to doorsteps. Grandparents were reverentially positioned on chairs just outside houses, while the men played cards at tables in the street, the women chatted and the children frolicked in the town's fountains. On our way back to the apartment we might pass a father cradling a baby on the steps of the church, or a mother leaning from a window pleading with her son to come to bed. The town was so friendly that we gradually got to know our neighbours – a couple from Normandy with an incontinent dog that needed walking three or four times every night, a beer-swilling Belgian and his demure wife, and two pensioners from Paris who spent all day in their pyjamas sitting in deck chairs watching the world go by.

The Normans – as Peter called the couple from Normandy – attempted at every opportunity to educate us in the French way of doing things. They were horrified when they spotted us finishing a meal with an espresso followed by a glass of red wine. A coffee, they patiently explained, was the culmination of the meal, only to be taken after all the wine was finished. And when they then caught Tanya mixing cassis with some cheap white wine, they shook their heads in despair. What would the other neighbours think? The next day there was a firm rap on the door and the Normans presented us with a bottle of Bourgogne Aligoté, which they assured us was the correct wine to mix with cassis to make a kir.

While the Normans were our social watchdogs, the pensioners became our safety advisers. Every morning as we left to hunt for wine, the old man would put on his slippers – complete with anchor motif – comb a thin strand of his next-to-non-existent grey hair away from his eyes and emerge on to the balcony, slowly followed by his wife. The ritual of warning us of the dangers of driving in France would then begin.

We stood like naughty schoolchildren trying to keep a straight face as these two septuagenarians in pyjamas waggled their fingers at us. 'Your car could be flipped on its side at any moment. Its hood should be kept up at all costs, no matter how hot the day,' they admonished. And then there was the mistral, the fearsome wind that swept down the Rhône Valley. 'You shouldn't even consider driving when the mistral is blowing. It's strong enough to blow a juggernaut off the road, and when it howls between the trees it plays with the minds of the locals.' They looked complicitly at each other, nodding their heads in unison. 'Some of the worst accidents happen when the mistral blows,' they agreed.

Much as we were grateful for the advice, and despite Tanya's travel phobia, the lure of open-topped driving proved too great. And so, each day as we left with the hood down and the threat of the mistral whispering in the trees, our pensioner neighbours made the sign of the cross. It wasn't a comforting way to hunt for rosé.

For us, Provence was the home of pale rosé. We expected to be able to order it in restaurants, find whole aisles of supermarkets heaving with it and drive from vineyard to vineyard discovering ever-paler bottles. Instead we found a battleground. Some vignerons maintained that pale rosé was flavourless water, produced as a sop for the tourists who knew no better. Others argued that pale-pink wines had just as much flavour as darker rosés and challenged us to name the vignerons who'd been rubbishing their product.

I thought Guy de Saint Victor might be the person to offer some impartial advice. He'd told me to get back in touch when we arrived in the south, but despite the new sunny backdrop to our conversations, my phone relationship with Guy only deteriorated. In my head I kept hearing his first ominous words to me: 'You know, Jammie, wine in France is a small family; if you become friends with the family then anything is possible, but, Jammie, you don't want to be an enemy of the family.' The more I spoke to Guy, the more I felt I was going to fall into the latter category. He kept on making jokes and I kept on laughing at inappropriate moments, but eventually he agreed to fax me a list of his contacts in the wine trade. Two days later nothing had appeared, so I phoned again and an exasperated Guy put me in my place: 'You know, Jammie, this is not like England; in France, we enjoy ourselves. Relax, have a good meal, and when you find another fax machine, give me a call.'

We were on our own and so we headed off into the Provençal countryside, with the small Virgin Mary the pensioners had given us sellotaped to the dashboard. Tanya sat in the back of the car, sunglasses on, her blonde curly hair blowing in the wind, with a massive smile on her face. But rather than hunting in wine books for suitable vineyards to visit, she had other ideas. Open on her lap was a coffee-table book containing pictures of the most beautiful villages in France. Try as I might to head up the Rhône Valley to search for obscure wines, we ended up in the wooded slopes of the Luberon. I suspect it had something to do with the fact that Tanya was also map-reading.

She directed me to take a left just before Gordes – a village with a view so spectacular that it had once made her cry – on to a narrow road that fed through a canyon of rock and climbed higher and higher towards the giant Mont Ventoux. The surrounding landscape might have inspired Cézanne, but it was the type of road that would normally induce panic in my wife. There was a sheer drop to our right, and a dented low brick wall illustrated how plenty of cars had careered out of control, carrying their passengers close to certain death. Instead, the more we climbed and the narrower the road became, the more her smile grew.

Finally, we rounded a rocky turn and the landscape fell away into a deep valley. 'Pull over, pull over,' cried Tanya and Peter in unison.

There before us was the image used to promote Provence the world over. I had seen it in guidebooks, calendars and of course in the book on Tanya's lap. In straight lines filling the slopes beneath us were fields and fields of lavender. The land blazed purple. A rich, luxurious, warming colour. Even from our vantage point high above the fields, the unmistakable smell of the south wrapped itself around us. Wild thyme and rosemary, sticky sun-baked pines and the soothingly aromatic lavender mixed together into a balm for the senses. And at the head of the valley, with the lavender lapping around its walls, was the twelfth-century Cistercian Abbeye de Sénanque.

'Well, if I had to be a monk,' said Peter, 'I'd be one here.'

The tour of Provence's most beautiful sights continued with lunch in Roussillon. To begin with, I thought the village was going to be a disappointment. I'd read about its ochre-coloured streets in the guidebooks, but so, it seemed, had hundreds of other tourists, who'd then told their family and their family's friends. The village had more traffic wardens than the London Borough of Westminster. It needed them – double- and triple-parking were the norm and trails of overweight, panting sightseers, unaware of local practice, wound around the mountainside tracing their way to and from cars parked on distant kerbs.

But as we climbed through the narrow streets, the crowd thinned and Roussillon began to work its charm. I pictured the village at dusk, free from teeming tourists, sitting majestically between seams of orange rock, its luminous red bricks and ochre-stained pavements glowing like beacons in the half-light. Needless to say, as we sat down for lunch, the grins on Tanya and Peter's faces stretched from ear to ear. They were almost too excited to talk as they gazed out over a view so full of fierce blazing colours it resembled an Impressionist painting.

A couple of kilometres to the south of the town, I finally persuaded Tanya and Peter to meet a vigneron. Monsieur Formentin's château was screened from the road by a line of cypress trees, and the faded shutters were firmly shut when we arrived. Our car stirred a cloud of dust that hung heavy in the air, as he gruffly greeted us, 'What do you want?' His English was faultless, there wasn't a hint of a French accent, and my immediate assumption, despite the surname, was that he was a London lawyer or banker who'd made his millions and decided to retire to France. Reinforcing this impression was an old Rolls Royce parked in the shade of some plane trees. In his demeanour and looks he resembled Michael Winner, fresh from a month at the Sandy Lane Hotel. He had skin the colour and texture of dark-brown leather, a bulbous nose, a rounded over-indulged paunch and a full head of silver-grey hair swept back and parted in the centre.

'Where are you from in England?' I asked, shrinking back in the face of his fierce unblinking blue eyes.

'I'm French. Now, what do you want?' the same cut-glass English accent, the same sense that he didn't want to be disturbed.

And so, foolishly, we explained our quest. To date we'd managed to win over every vigneron we'd met. A combination of Tanya coquettishly fluttering her eyelashes, Peter's conviviality and our determination to understand words such as *tipicité* had somehow broken down all barriers. If all else failed, the story of Rosie being confused with a bottle of rosé had mellowed even the fiercest Anglophobe. But as we talked, Monsieur Formentin's face became darker.

'Come,' he said and led us into his cave. Opening a fridge, he poured us each a glass of a deep-pink rosé. 'This is a proper rosé. Instead, you're spending your summer chasing after a fad.' As we took small steps backwards towards our car, Monsieur Formentin continued on what was clearly a favourite subject. Didn't we know that the paler a rosé was, the lesser the flavour of the wine? All we had to do was use our taste buds and it would become obvious. 'Failing that, just think about it,' he challenged us. 'Rosé gains its flavour from the skin of the grapes, so the juice needs to macerate as long as possible.'

'But why is pale rosé so popular, then?' Tanya asked bravely.

'Because people like you don't know a good wine from a bad one.'

Despite two months travelling around France, it was becoming only too apparent how little we'd learnt. Our battered confidence was scarcely improved when later, in the local co-operative, we tried to win over a pretty salesgirl with a display of our knowledge.

The co-op was the size of a large factory and housed rows of *cuves* that were so large they could hold enough wine to fill a petrol tanker. A metal stairwell stretched almost out of sight into the eaves of the vaulted ceiling, and there were screws and presses as big as jet engines. The salesgirl patiently explained how the co-operative system worked. Rather than make their own wine, the vignerons brought their grapes to the co-op, where they were weighed and then mixed with the grapes of all the other growers. The vignerons were paid according to the volume and quality of the grapes they supplied, and then the co-op sold the resulting 30,000 hectolitres of wine.

Something about her charming smile and gentle manner made me want to show off.

'That's over thirty million bottles a year,' I calculated. Standing as I was next to a scale, which could weigh a couple of elephants, the figure didn't seem so preposterous.

'Does the world really drink that much wine?' asked Tanya.

'Of course it does,' said Peter, holding aloft what appeared to be a petrol pump. 'Look, isn't this marvellous?' he cried, as wine gushed into a large plastic barrel which he was cradling like a newborn baby against his chest.

The sales assistant cleared her throat. 'You're twenty-seven million too high.'

I flushed. How stupid could I be?

But Peter was totally unflustered. He screwed the cap on his container and grinned. 'All this for five euros. It doesn't matter how many bottles they produce, it's still marvellous, absolutely marvellous.' And, in an attempt to recover some credibility, he rested his elbow on the counter. 'Now, tell me,' he asked the sales assistant, puffing out his chest and tapping his barrel of wine, 'why do you call it *vrac*?'

Back in Saint Rémy, after our busy, sticky and, from a rosé perspective, somewhat disheartening day, we decided to go for a swim at the municipal pool. Tanya made her way there before us and I was left with Peter who, delighted at the cost of wine from the co-operative, had vowed to drink nothing else while in Saint Rémy. He'd even bought himself a new pair of swimming trunks as a reward for the money he'd saved.

The pool was located in the outskirts of the town, far away from the traffic-clogged streets. It was surrounded by shady trees, which were full of cicadas humming their soothing thanks for another wonderfully hot day. Directly behind the pool the sun was slowly falling behind the hills, but it still bathed the green banks by the side of the water in golden orange light. Perspiration dripped from our brows as we looked at this promised land through the wire fence. We paid €2 for our tickets and were just pushing our way through the turnstiles when a large woman, covered in sweat, came running towards us. Cool droplets of water were blown from the pool on to our faces by the gentle evening wind, but the attendant jabbed a podgy finger at Peter's new shorts and then pointed to a sign pinned to the fence. It showed a pair of Speedo swimming trunks with a tick next to them, a pair of Bermuda shorts with a cross drawn over them, and the following sentence, 'By-law 222, by order of the Mayor.'

Peter pulled the elastic round his waist tighter as the woman clutched at the fabric of his shorts and rubbed it between her fingers in an effort to demonstrate what was wrong. The harder she yanked, the more desperately Peter clung to them. Despite this nearly all-too-graphic demonstration, our limited attempts to understand her heavily accented Provençal French failed. From the woman's frantic swipes at Peter's shorts we assumed it was a nudist pool. But why was Tanya inside? And why did the sign show a tick next to the Speedos? What could it possibly matter to the Mayor what swimming trunks we wore?

That evening, back at the apartment, we were still trying to work out the answer. Tanya sat smiling, a little too smugly for my liking, rubbing after-sun on her face. 'I think no Bermuda shorts is a fantastic rule,' she teased.

Peter and I looked quizzically at her.

'Well, no Provençal town is complete without an eccentric mayor. The best bit was when they announced my name over the loudspeaker and I had to come and collect you.' She put on her best French accent: 'Madame Ivey, Madame Ivey, Jammie and Peterrr are waiting for you at reception.

'All the mothers looked at me as if I'd lost my children,' she continued. 'I thought there was something seriously wrong.' Tanya paused and then grinned wickedly. 'I guess there would have been if they'd forced you two to wear thongs.'

Peter had yet to change for dinner and was bare-chested and still wearing his new trunks. He'd already made his way through half of the barrel of co-operative rosé and, in one of his sudden fits of enthusiasm, he leapt on to a chair in the middle of the balcony and raised his glass to the stars. 'Welcome to Provence,' he beamed. 'A toast to her eccentric mayors.'

'To eccentric mayors,' we echoed.

'Do you think the Normans know what's wrong with my shorts?' asked Peter. He was still standing on the chair and his glass of rosé was held frozen aloft. The hair on his chest appeared silver in the moonlight and in profile his silhouette resembled the Statue of Liberty. But instead of a torch of freedom, he clasped a goblet full of *vrac*.

'Why?'

'It's just that they seem to be looking rather curiously at me.' He grinned, taking another slug of rosé.

Peter wasn't still grinning the next day. We were due to visit Tavel, the only wine-growing area in France that concentrated exclusively on rosé and didn't make any red or white wine. If one village in France were to wholly embrace us, and our quest, it should, we all felt, be Tavel, but Peter's brow was sweaty, his stomach unsettled and he had a hammering headache that prevented him from getting out of bed. 'I think I understand why they call it *vrac*,' he stuttered, giving a weak smile. 'It describes how you feel the next morning.'

Tanya and I headed off to the southern end of the Rhône Valley, just to the west of Avignon. We'd arranged a visit with Christophe Delorme of Domaine de la Mordorée. On our travels we'd heard a lot about Tavel. It was renowned for producing France's best rosé and was the second-oldest appellation in the country. The wine had been a favourite of the Avignon popes, and news of Tavel even reached Russian Tsars, who ordered cases for the Imperial Court. From enthusiastic amateur to professional vigneron, everybody we'd met on our trip had insisted we visit the village.

A kilometre away we spotted a hoarding that read, 'Welcome to Tavel, home of France's first rosé.' Standing next to the sign was an exhilarating and slightly alien experience. Beneath our feet were large grey pebbles, which had been washed down from the Alps and eroded to a smooth sheen before being cast on to the flood plain. We'd seen grapes flourishing in unlikely places before, but the terrain beneath our feet resembled a stony beach at low tide. By rights there should have been children flying kites and pools full of stranded crabs. Instead, all around us vines grew in long rows stretching across the valley towards an overhanging crop of limestone. But even in the shadow of this cliff, where the rocks were thin and brittle like shards of glass, the vines still grew, their roots searching for moisture amid what we later learnt were the remains of an ancient coral reef.

Christophe was waiting for us in the courtyard as we arrived at Domaine de la Mordorée. He was a young man, perhaps thirty, with jet-black hair that fell over his forehead, hiding chocolate-brown eyes reminiscent of the Champenois vignerons. His hands were covered in dust and he was wearing a scruffy T-shirt and a rugged pair of jeans that made him look like he'd just left a building site rather than a field full of vines.

'We have a saying here,' he explained as he offered us a glass of wine, 'that there are red wines, white wines and rosés. Then there is Tavel.' He glanced at us as we tasted his dark-pink rosé, before continuing: 'Tavel is vinified like a rosé, but the resulting wine is much more than a rosé. In a blind tasting you would think that Tavel is a light-red wine. It is a perfect accompaniment to Spanish and Italian food. You should try it with African couscous or grilled lobster.'

Until this point I hadn't questioned that the palest rosé we'd find would rank among the best rosés in France. Before we left on the trip, we'd all unanimously agreed that rosé was best enjoyed pale, cold and in the open air. At the time it had seemed a simple truth. But far from reinforcing this belief, our first week in Provence had led me to question the very basis of our quest. Christophe's wine had a delicious peppery taste that lingered in the mouth, yet it was still light and easy to drink. I began to feel uneasy – *was* pale rosé only for tourists who didn't know any better?

'You must understand,' continued Christophe, 'that the French are always looking for pleasure. Our wines reflect centuries of research into it, and I think you'll agree,' he said, flicking a big smile at Tanya, 'that a darker rosé gives more pleasure.'

10

The *Fête du Vin*

We were lucky enough to be staying in Saint Rémy for the town's *fête du vin*. It began the day after our meeting with Christophe with the vignerons inviting everybody for a *verre de l'amitié* or 'a drink to friendship'. So at noon on another gloriously hot sunny day we stood in front of the town hall. Three tricolores fluttered on flagpoles that extended from the Mairie right into the heart of the square. Plane trees with mottled grey trunks the size of ancient oaks stretched skywards, casting a green canopy over the festival. The intricate pattern of their interlocking leaves was mirrored a hundred feet below by the dappled interplay of sunlight and shade on the cobbles. And everywhere there were stalls bedecked in bright colours. A red-and-yellow awning sheltered a winemaker from the Pays Basque, and enormous white and pink umbrellas shaded the local vignerons. From a vantage point on the steps of the Mairie it looked as if a multicoloured patchwork quilt had been draped between the trees. In the corner of the square I could see a Swiss flag fluttering next to a *fruitière* from the Jura. 'Well, we know where not to look for rosé,' joked Tanya.

Amid the vignerons were stalls full of all sorts of local produce and crafts. Bars of soap made from lavender and olives were stacked in purple and green towers, vacuum-packed jars of *confit de canard* and *coq au vin* jostled for the attention of the gourmands amid trestle tables full of aubergine caviar, foie gras, honey and nougat. In the far corner of the square, trays of *coquillage* lay on huge beds of dripping ice, and six oysters and a glass of champagne were on offer at the ludicrously friendly price of €5.

Weaving their way through the stalls were Guy Bertrand and the Tonton Swingers – a five-piece jazz band. The sun glinted off the polished brass of the trombone and sweat poured down the Tontons' faces as they played a succession of upbeat numbers. Everybody was smiling, chatting, tasting wine and enjoying little titbits of food.

Whenever the Tonton Swingers fell silent the festival's compère would take over. Armed with a microphone which was wired to the town's PA system, his voice could be heard all over Saint Rémy. He had dark hair, a thin moustache and wore a Hawaiian shirt covered in motifs of flowering orchids. I think he was supposed to interview each of the vignerons about their wine, but instead he spent his time lounging by the champagne tent, snaring a succession of pretty women on the end of his microphone.

After we'd been at the festival for an hour, the compère dragged himself away from the bar to announce that the arrival of Bacchus, the god of wine, was imminent. Four policemen, looking immaculate in their dress uniforms, took up position at one corner of the square. They joined hands and formed a barrier, gradually pushing the crowds back against the shopfronts. At the end of the street about twenty young boys had gathered, dressed in black trousers and white shirts with red sashes across their chests. They began to form into a neat column, four abreast, and slowly made their way towards us. Behind them a similar number of men attired in the same fashion joined the procession. As they neared the square, the boys produced horsewhips and whirled them viciously in the air, creating a chorus of synchronised cracks. The men behind did likewise, only their whips were longer and snapped in front of the faces of onlookers.

Behind them a chariot, pulled by a large chestnut carthorse, swung into view, carrying a figure that could only be Bacchus. The god had a heavy fur cape around his shoulders and was weighed down by a chunky gold chain. He wore a red velvet robe encrusted with silver stars and around his forehead was a wreath made from bunches of grapes. Falling from his chin was a long fake white beard which would have made any department-store Santa envious. It covered his face in wild curls of hair, hiding all his features apart from his clear blue eyes. His chariot was piled so high with flowers that only the upper half of his body was visible, and in each hand he held a bottle of wine. As the chariot swayed into the centre of the square, Bacchus tipped back his head and upended both bottles, sending their contents gushing down his throat and over his beard and gown.

'At least the gods drink rosé,' commented Tanya.

'Probably stains less than red wine,' smiled Peter.

As Bacchus passed us, we noticed that sitting in front of the Mairie was an old lady, apparently asleep, with a bright-yellow sunhat pulled down to the bridge of her nose. Next to her was a mahogany sideboard, which appeared to have been directly transplanted from her living room. Its doors were flung open, revealing a collection of chipped crystal glasses frosted with age or scratched from overuse. Years ago one of a set of glasses Peter had been given as a wedding present by his best man had been broken. He'd never given up hope of finding a replacement and so he tapped the lady on the shoulder and, with her permission, began rummaging through the sideboard.

'Just remember anything can happen when Bacchus is around,' he muttered, as we left him haggling with the old woman.

Wandering around the square, we tried a tart, slightly fizzy white from the Alsace border, an orangey rosé from Chinon in

the Loire that brought back memories of Nicolas Reverdy's
Sancerre and some pale rosé from Bandol, just to the east of
Marseille. It was like doing a whole week of our trip in a single
afternoon, but disappointingly there were no rosés that even
compared with the colour of Madame Etienne's. There was also
nobody prepared to contradict Christophe Delorme's view that
darker rosés gave more pleasure, so rather than get to the bottom
of this problem, we became distracted by the sights and sounds of
the fête.

'Is this for the cover of *Paris Match*?' joked an enormous man
with a handlebar moustache when Tanya insisted on taking a
photo.

'If it is they'll airbrush you out,' cried his friend as I put my
arm around the shoulders of Tanya's prospective subject and
guided him to the side of his stall, but when he was in position,
rather than release me, he trapped me in a friendly headlock and
then jokingly marched me around in circles. My head poked out
from under his armpit and my arms only just linked together
around his potbelly as I struggled to keep my balance.

'This is how I guide the sheep through the town,' he laughed,
somewhat inexplicably, as I began to run out of breath.

'Or your wife,' his friend added, taking a big gulp of wine.

Once I was released from the headlock and the blood had
returned to my cheeks, we discovered the significance of the
sheep joke. One of Saint Rémy's other big festivals is the *fête de
transhumance*, held on Whit Monday, during which sheep, goats
and donkeys, rather than cars, clog the streets as a 2,000-strong
herd is driven through the town to a chorus of mountain bells.
Errant animals are rescued by the townsfolk before the herd is
packed off to the high pastures for the summer.

Across the square Tanya discovered another seemingly lost
animal – Bacchus's horse, whose head was twitching this way
and that as the god handed out free drink, pouring wine into
plastic beakers and sometimes over people. Tanya approached

and held out her hand. The horse's nose and eyes had been dabbed with olive oil to make them shine and his tail was beautifully plaited and tied with purple ribbons. As she stroked his mane she didn't notice the handlers continually reassuring him, talking gently into his ears.

'What's his name?' asked Tanya.

'Crazy,' came the answer.

'Why's that?' Tanya almost bit off the end of the question as she realised the answer was probably self-evident.

All around us the crowd was pushing closer, proffering empty cups, and over the loudspeaker the compère encouraged everyone to enjoy the god's munificence. More people crammed into the square and the space between the stalls began to feel quite claustrophobic. Elbows jarred against elbows as people struggled to raise their glasses. In an attempt to make space, Bacchus tried to edge Crazy backwards, but the horse stood still, stubbornly shaking his head and champing on the bit. Outstretched hands pleaded for more wine and Bacchus obligingly emptied another bottle while pitching this way and that as Crazy pawed the ground until finally his newly shod hooves slipped on the shiny cobbles and he lurched to his knees. His nostrils flared and he blew heavily as he surged upwards, rearing on his hind legs and kicking forward like a clawing cat, sending Bacchus tumbling to the floor amid a pool of red wine.

'Peter was right,' I said, pulling Tanya away, 'anything can happen when Bacchus is around.'

She grinned back at me. 'The French are potty. First they lead you round the square like a sheep, then they bring a horse called Crazy into the middle of a busy crowd. *C'est fou.*'

As I was about to reply I looked up and saw Peter standing on the steps of the town hall. In his hand he was holding four tiny cocktail glasses that had each been hand-painted with little motifs – a sprig of lavender, a field of sunflowers, an olive hanging from a tree and a field full of vines.

'Any luck?' I asked.

'No, but I found something else to hunt for. These are part of a set of six, each with a different painting on the glass, and guess what's missing?' Peter didn't wait for my answer but continued triumphantly, 'A setting sun and a bottle of rosé. Now isn't that wonderful?' He beamed.

Before leaving Saint Rémy we made one final attempt to discover some pale rosé in the surrounding countryside. For the first time during our stay the mistral really began to blow. Despite the clear blue sky, it howled down the long avenues of trees that surrounded the town and rattled the shutters of our apartment. As we ate our breakfast it fell silent, and we breathed a sigh of relief, enjoyed the warm sun on our faces and gave thanks that the wind had deserted the town for the day, but just when those hopes seemed realised, the mistral came chasing back down the Rhône, sending the cold air from the Alps tumbling through the narrow streets. As we clambered into our car, the pensioners, with eyes as doleful as spaniels, implored us not to go. Glancing in the rear-view mirror, I saw them make the all-too-familiar sign of the cross as we pulled on to the road.

As on previous trips, we spent over half the day attempting to satisfy Tanya and Peter's desire to visit every village in the Luberon. In Goult we amost lost Peter among the regulars of Café de la Poste. We'd left him having a cup of coffee and wandered up through the streets of the village to enjoy the sweeping views over the valley. On our return, Peter seemed to have disappeared. The rows of chairs facing the pretty central square were empty, save for a couple of American tourists complaining to each other about the service, or lack of it.

Inside the bar pungent smoke hung heavy in the air, stinging the backs of my lungs within seconds. There were a couple of battered sets of tables and chairs, a long counter, a *tabac* and a kiosk in the far corner selling newspapers and magazines. The barman was smoking the remains of a rolled cigarette, with his free hand resting next to a long thin glass of pastis. Facing him, four men stood, with their elbows on the bar and their backs to the door staring up at a screen showing the Tour de France. They all had unruly hair, stubble like sandpaper and beers that appeared anatomically attached to their hands. One of them, I noticed, had a cigar. 'If you hadn't found me,' said Peter. 'I could happily have stayed all day.'

Back on the road we encountered a wedding party driving through the town of Apt accompanied by a cacophony of hooting and cheering. The bride wore an old-fashioned floral dress, the groom a cream linen suit, and they rode together on an antique Triumph motorbike at the head of a cavalcade of cars. 'Can we follow them?' begged Tanya. Peter obligingly swung in behind the final wedding guests and we snaked into the hills above the town. As we entered each turn we looked up and saw the motorbike flashing in and out of the shadows of the trees. The bride's veil trailed from the top of her helmet and danced like a medieval pennant in the wind. Periodically she reached into a small purse and threw confetti, which hung in the air and then settled like snow on the bonnets of the following cars. Halfway up the hillside I glanced across and saw a tear falling slowly down Tanya's cheek. 'It's just so romantic,' she sobbed into my shoulder.

The bride and groom turned off the road on to a dirt track just after the mountain hamlet of Buoux and led the wedding party down a potholed track. Cliffs reared up on either side of us. They were too vertical for any trees to grow on and in places bent back towards the road creating overhangs to terrify even the most experienced climber. The road led us down to the base of a deep green valley fed by a mountain stream and surrounded on all sides by vertiginous rocks stained by deep orange seams. A small auberge was built into the hill, and the stream had been trapped to form a freshwater pool, next to which tables full of food and drink were laid out.

'Do you think they'd mind if we joined them?' asked Peter, as we pulled into the car park.

'We could always donate some rosé to the party,' I suggested.

For the next hour we mingled with the wedding guests, ducking between the beams of the auberge, which had been dressed with fresh flowers and bunches of lavender, and standing by the pool with our necks craned straining to appreciate the beauty of the cliffs, as hawks floated on thermals hundreds of feet above us. Peter, of course, managed to kiss the bride, a petite girl with jet-black hair and luscious green eyes. 'Don't you think her dress is very Marilyn Monroe?' Peter asked on his return. 'She said it's a nineteen fifties tea dress,' he continued, 'and that the party is supposed to be like a country picnic. They call it a *fête champêtre*.'

'And you discovered all this speaking French?' I shook my head, wondering how he'd managed it.

'Well, she knew a few words in English. Anyway, we're welcome to stay as long as we want.'

The buffet proved hard to resist – tomatoes baked in Provençal herbs, field mushrooms filled with local cheeses, *moules* cooked in white wine and cream, squid grilled and laced with lemon juice, and slices of smoked duck and ham. I like to think we were indistinguishable from the other casually dressed guests as we stood with full plates and glasses of rosé chattering happily away. We met the Mayor, who was also the local electrician – he'd rigged up the lights for the evening's disco and then performed the wedding ceremony – and we discovered that all the lamp-posts in the local village of Gargas had been painted orange in honour of the groom's grandfather, a respected ochre miner.

Just as we were ready to leave, the groom came tearing out of a room next to the pool. He'd changed into a pair of swimming trunks and leapt into the air before plunging with a scream into the icy-cold waters.

'I think he's cooling down after consummating his marriage,' said Peter with a grin.

Looking around, I saw that the bride had disappeared.

'Well, this is France,' smiled Tanya.

After our impromptu lunch we continued down the other side of the valley, past the village of Bonnieux, which perched on the side of a cliff in the hot afternoon sunshine, towards Lourmarin. Tanya and Peter were once again so immersed in the sights and sounds of the Luberon that I thought it was going to be difficult to persuade them to visit another vigneron. In Tanya's case I was wrong.

'Look at that house, isn't it gorgeous?' she cried. The house in question was actually a château. A long gravel drive bordered by angular cypress trees wound up the hillside towards it. To the left was a paddock where two horses idly swished flies away from each other's faces. To the right was a swimming pool, bordered by old flagstones, and directly in front of us was the château, with walls the colour of sand almost camouflaging the building against the landscape. It was three storeys high with rows of duck-egg-blue shutters opening on to a courtyard full of mature trees heavy with foliage. 'It's also a vineyard,' I said with delight as we drove up towards it past neatly trimmed lavender bushes and flower beds overflowing with colour.

'Do you mind if I pick you up later?' asked Peter as he pulled the car to a stop. 'I need to pop into Lourmarin for a few things.'

At the time we thought nothing more of it and happily waved goodbye. What followed, for us, was a tour of a lifestyle as much as a vineyard. The owner, Bauduin Parmentier, was a Belgian banker who'd decided to change his life. He'd been holidaying in the area since the 1970s and remembered the days when the locals were so hostile to foreigners they'd refused him croissants in the local *boulangerie*. It didn't stop him from falling in love with the area, and two decades later he bought the château. As a foreign wine producer he had to do everything precisely by the book. If the alcohol percentage on his wine was out by as much as a fraction the appellation committee forced him to throw the whole batch away. Then there were the tax inspectors who raked through his books with a strange zealousness and the idiosyncrasies of French bureaucracy which meant that one year he might be given a subsidy to chop down some vines, and the next year the same sum of money to replant them.

As he took us around his property it became clear that all the hassles were more than worth it. His two dogs – Mong and Montible – with their long lolling tongues and loping gait, followed the Jeep as we bounced up into the Provençal countryside. On the brow of the highest hill in the vineyard Bauduin stopped the car and led us into the vines. The mistral whipped sand into our faces, but the view was still majestic. We gazed from the verdant green of the vineyard, across fields of heat-baked pines to the hills of the Luberon where the sun was so intense that the landscape melted into a dark-green shadow. And behind everything towered the peak of Mont Ventoux, one of the legendary ascents of the Tour de France.

Glancing across at Tanya, I began to realise how difficult it would be returning to London at the end of our summer. She stood next to Bauduin, entranced by the view. The dogs lay panting underneath the vines, occasionally nibbling on a grape, and in the distance I could see the corner of the swimming pool and the terracotta tiles on the roof of the château. 'I've been here for five years now and we've started making jam, honey and olive oils as well as the wine,' explained Bauduin, unknowingly bewitching Tanya with thoughts of a simple self-sufficient lifestyle in the middle of the beautiful countryside.

Attempting to break the spell, I asked about his rosé. And, to my surprise, this diminutive Belgian, wearing the beige khaki shorts of a tourist and the rounded glasses of a number cruncher, precisely answered a question that had confused a succession of French vignerons – was pale rosé an inferior wine?

'Of course not. So many factors affect the taste of a rosé. Here, we're so high that the harvest is one of the latest in Provence. It means the grapes are taking on the characteristics of the land right into October and that our rosé although pale, is still full of flavour.'

Later, after we'd juddered back down the hill in the Jeep with the two dogs weaving between the tyres like dolphins playing with a boat, Bauduin poured us some rosé. It was so cold that little droplets of water had condensed on the outside of the bottle and were forming on our glasses. To taste, it was light and dry, and the colour was a delicate, gentle pink.

As we strolled in the gardens of his house, Bauduin continued his explanation: 'Using Cabernet or Syrah to make a rosé is like driving a Ferrari and not using the engine. Yes, you'll have a deep-pink, punchy rosé, but essentially it is just a poor imitation of a red wine.'

Tanya wasn't listening. She was staring dreamily at the château. 'You must have all sorts of long-lost friends phoning up and wanting to stay.'

Bauduin smiled. 'Of course. For the first two years it was like a hotel, but now we just tell people the house is full or that we're away.'

They stood together in the shade of an old tree and Bauduin explained how he wanted the house and its grounds to completely blend with the landscape. To renovate the place, they'd only used local materials, even the pool had been sunk into an old water-holding basin, and the steps had been hidden under the water. 'The last thing you want to do is to look across this landscape and see people clambering up metal steps.' Tanya nodded sympathetically and began stroking the dogs. 'I found Mong one morning on my doorstep,' smiled Bauduin. 'She's a rare Provençal breed; if you look at her eyes you'll see one is blue and the other black. And a couple of years after she arrived, Montible, her daughter, was born.'

While Tanya dropped to her knees to examine Mong's eyes, Bauduin returned to the subject of his wine: 'You'll find a lot of French vignerons are trying to copy the New World. But they can never compete. Thirty per cent of the cost of a New World wine is represented by marketing; in France thirty per cent is bureaucracy. To survive, French wine must concentrate on quality and being loyal to the *terroir*.

'We use Grenache and Cinsault for our rosé. They're grapes with thin skins, which prosper in sandy soils. We can leave them macerating for up to six hours in the *cuve* and still produce a pale rosé.'

Taking us into his small cave, he removed a magnum of rosé from one of the boxes piled high against the wall. 'People give their car the best petrol, and yet they drink bad wine. To me, it's inexplicable,' he said, shaking his head. 'Try this bottle and let me know what you think. It's unusual for a rosé because it's been oaked.'

We tried the rosé and nodded our appreciation.

'Now, I hope you'll excuse me, I have another meeting.' He smiled as he showed us the door. 'Don't despair: if you're looking for a rosé paler than mine, you'll find it in Provence. Try the sand wines of the Camargue, the rosés of the central Var, and don't miss Bandol and the Côte d'Azur.'

It was all I could do to get Tanya to leave. After Bauduin had said goodbye, she hung around in the courtyard, gazing up at the house and the rows of vines, which fed gently down to the doorstep. She picked lavender and crushed it between her fingers and ran her hand along the grain of the blue shutters.

I put my arm around her shoulders. 'It's just a dream.'

'Couldn't we do it on a smaller scale?'

'We couldn't afford it,' I confessed, 'and, anyway, I don't think we're ready for this type of life.'

What I didn't reveal was that the longer we spent in France, the more worried I felt about our trip. I'd come to the conclusion that I was a somewhat peculiar person because as day after day dawned bright and sunny, and Provence lulled us with its charms, I'd begun to feel guilty. The further we travelled from London, the more it felt like running away. My life was as a lawyer not a vigneron. Only determination to win the quest and the financial consequences of losing were keeping me going.

As we prepared to leave Saint Rémy, Peter's car – Betty – was piled high with our luggage and miscellaneous bottles of rosé which we'd collected in vineyards from Burgundy to Bonnieux. There was scarcely any room for Peter to clamber into the back, and rather than get in the car, he was making a great fuss about not being able to shut his suitcase.

'Where are you going next?' asked the pensioners.

Little did they know it was a loaded question. We'd been torn between continuing the hunt in Provence and chasing down an obscure rosé called clairet. In the end we'd decided that to win the bet we had to take the odd chance, and so we'd agreed – or at least I thought we had agreed – that for the next couple of weeks the rest of Provence could wait.

'Bordeaux and then the Dordogne,' Tanya replied.

The pensioners looked suddenly worried. 'Ah. You must be careful there. The rich food can make you very fat.' They puffed out their cheeks and began waddling like ducks across the drive. 'You mustn't eat too much foie gras. They serve it with everything and too much is very bad for you.' They were, of course, still wearing their pyjamas, which proudly showed off their more than healthy stomachs.

'Don't worry,' I reassured them, 'we'll be careful.'

'Did you know my favourite rosé is made by François Crochet

in Bué?' said the old man, combing back the remaining strands of his hair that seemed to give him so much trouble.

'Wait a second, I think I have some in my bag,' said Peter, rummaging in his case and presenting a bottle of wine to the old man who immediately engulfed Peter in a massive hug and began to chatter excitedly: 'We haven't tasted any of François's rosé for years . . . Our local wine merchant in Paris has stopped stocking it because it's so hard to get hold of . . . And, well, here it is in the middle of Saint Rémy . . . '

They could have continued for hours and so I gently hooted the horn to encourage Peter to get into the car, but instead of bidding farewell to our neighbours, he leant on the windscreen of the car and addressed us both in his gruff voice. 'You go on ahead. I've decided to take a little detour via Saint Maximin. Somebody has to work out just how important this bet is to the Etiennes.'

Peter loved a bit of intrigue and he'd clearly convinced himself that we needed to know a little more about our opponents. If we were to follow up obscure leads such as clairet, there simply wasn't time for us all to go to Saint Maximin. But it felt wrong to break up the group, and I was on the point of trying to persuade him to come with us when Tanya leapt from the car and gave him a goodbye kiss.

'You just want to stay in Provence,' she laughed.

'Don't worry,' he smiled, 'I'll be back before you've missed me. Make sure you look after Betty.'

'How are you going to get there?' I asked.

'I'll figure something out,' said Peter as he put his arm around both of the septuagenarians and suggested a glass of rosé. All we could hear as we drove away was a lamentable attempt to explain in French that it was twelve o'clock somewhere in the world.

JULY

'I know just the wine for you.
It's made on the coast near
Saint Tropez and the vineyard
is the most beautiful in the
whole of France.'

II

Clairet de Quinsac and
Les Deux Repas

Having said goodbye to Peter and the pensioners, we headed north-west to Bordeaux, lured by the story of an unusual rosé called clairet. We'd first heard about it at a small party we'd arranged in April two days before we left for France. Most of our guests had arrived with an assortment of sweet, sticky Portuguese and Californian rosés, but our French neighbours, Brice and Sophie, turned up with a bottle of champagne, a naval sword and an intriguing story about a wine called clairet made in Sophie's home village of Quinsac, near Bordeaux. Before they told us about the clairet, Sophie and Brice insisted on opening the champagne. For most people, this means gently easing the cork from the bottle, taking care it doesn't explode in somebody's face, but Brice is far from a conventional neighbour.

Every day the guttural throb of his Harley Davidson punches through the silence of our suburban road, and when Tanya is at home she runs to the window and watches him depart. It's quite a show. Brice leaves like a film star before the final credits run. He wears old-fashioned motorcycle leathers, with knee-length jackboots and a helmet with a small peak but no visor. He revs the bike a couple of times, swings it into the road, lights a long thin hand-rolled cigarette, takes a couple of puffs and then disappears, trailing noise and the aroma of French tobacco.

Inexplicably, Brice leaves the house and returns at least ten times in a day. Either he suffers from chronic amnesia and is always running out of cigarettes or, as Sophie likes to joke, he's a spy, forever heading off on secret missions, with the noise that accompanies him an elaborate form of camouflage. If you believe this – and Tanya and I like to – then Brice's cover story is that he works as a French naval officer seconded to the United Nations in London.

And, as I learnt that evening in April, a French naval officer – or a spy – opens champagne by taking his sword and rubbing it vigorously under the neck of the bottle – as if sharpening a knife on a piece of granite. Then, with a firm upward strike, he decapitates the bottle. It's unclear whether it's also part of the French naval tradition to let an Englishman ineffectively and rather effeminately wave the sword across the champagne bottle first, but Brice kindly let me have a go. And only when I'd failed three times to dislodge the cork did he intervene, with one firm stroke sending the cork and the neck of the bottle spiralling into the air. Not a drop of champagne was spilt and, with a little nod of his head, Brice sheathed his sword.

Towards the end of the party Tanya and I sat talking with Sophie about Clairet de Quinsac. Like Brice, she's far from a typical suburban parent, dressing as if the streets of Paris, not Balham, await outside her door. Her long dark hair falls to her waist, her nails are invariably freshly manicured, and she wears a touch of sultry purple lipstick that manages to hint at whispered candlelit confidences even when she's struggling with the Sainsbury's shopping. Every conversation with Sophie is accompanied by a series of her extravagant hand gestures – her arms punctuate the conversation in a manner which is uniquely French, accentuating specific sentences by almost inscribing them in the air.

The story of clairet involved pretty much all of her extensive repertoire: raising her hands to the heavens in supplication, holding her palms plaintively towards us, screwing her fingers into a ball and drumming them against the table, and casually resting her long fingers on our knees. Once I'd managed to concentrate on the words, rather than Sophie's whirling hands, I became fascinated.

Clairet, Sophie explained, was a little-known rosé which would have ceased to exist but for the intervention of the Mayor of Quinsac. Following the end of the Second World War, he decided that the village needed to be renowned for something and so he encouraged the vignerons to resume production of a forgotten wine called clairet. The Mayor was so excited with his new creation that rumour has it he erected a sign on the *périphérique* to direct thirsty Parisians the five hundred or so kilometres to the town. Understandably the Parisians had other things to do and clairet remained an obscure wine, largely drunk by the Bordelais.

'If you're interested in the rosés of France, then your trip would not be complete without a visit to Quinsac,' Sophie had concluded, with a final flourish of her arms, as she'd said goodbye at the end of the rosé party.

I remember being quite delighted as I went to bed that night. The rampant regionalism of France meant that Madame Etienne had probably never heard of clairet, and that meant we had a possible winner on our hands.

Three months and several thousand kilometres later we were just an hour's drive from Quinsac. But before calling on Brice and Sophie, who were visiting Sophie's family, I'd decided to make use of Guy de Saint Victor's list of contacts within the French wine trade, which had just arrived, and arranged to visit one of his close friends, Thibault Despagne.

During our conversations Guy had given the impression that he was well connected within the French wine industry, but I hadn't quite appreciated how well connected until we arrived at the Despagnes'. The family owned five châteaux and over two hundred hectares in the Entre Deux Mers area of Bordeaux and had just been awarded the accolade of Supplier of the Year by British Airways. Thibault's father, Jean Louis, was due to spend the next six months in Brazil negotiating supply contracts, and the Despagnes turned out to make wine on such a large scale that they were unable to offer it for sale by the bottle.

Considering Guy had advised us to 'blow the doors off' if our reception wasn't suitably welcoming, Thibault made a sensible decision by inviting us to lunch. The experience should have been like a little dose of heaven for Tanya, or a honey day, as she describes opportunities to spend long sweet hours in the sun in convivial company; instead, it represented the beginning of the now notorious '*Jour des Deux Repas*' or 'Day of the Two Meals'.

The Despagnes' house was a low-key, sprawling villa. On a terrace to one side of the building a long table was dressed in a white tablecloth and laid with silver cutlery and red lace napkins folded carefully on bone-china plates. Two carafes of white wine lay on beds of crushed ice at either end of the table, with beads of cool water dripping down their crystal necks. Each place setting sheltered under the branches of an ancient tree. Its leaves were draped like ivy across the trellis by the side of the house, but its trunk was thick and withered in the fashion of an old olive tree. On hot sticky rainy nights when it was uncomfortable inside, the family could eat with confidence underneath its branches, knowing that it would take at least an hour for the first drop of rain to percolate through its tightly woven leaves.

Thibault's mother, Madame Despagne, emerged from the kitchen wearing a sundress, red sunglasses and a matching red belt, carrying tray after tray of food. It was then that Tanya's problems began. We started with a langoustines and smoked-salmon salad dressed in a light vinaigrette on a bed of rocket. The salad was large enough for a main course, layer upon layer of salmon had been carefully arranged on the plate, its woody flavour complemented by the lightly chargrilled langoustines and what I believed to be a heavy Entre Deux Mers Chardonnay. It was absolutely delicious, unless you are Tanya. She's been allergic to seafood ever since she contracted salmonella from a Corsican king prawn.

It's embarrassing enough in any country to leave food, but this was France, a nation in love with gastronomy. Rejecting carefully prepared home-cooked food was just not done. Then again, by attempting to please our hosts and clearing her plate, Tanya ran the risk of reactivating the salmonella that was latent in her system.

Meanwhile I had another problem. Not since our meeting with François in Paris had I been so conscious about my lack of knowledge of wine. Thibault's father, Jean-Louis, sat at the head of the table, wearing a faded yellow shirt that was buttoned halfway up his chest. He was bald, apart from little fringes of grey hair above either ear and, despite being a small man, he reminded me of an old Shakespearean thespian such was the ease with which he held the attention of the table.

'I think Jacob's Creek is a fabulous wine,' he teased.

'But it's Australian,' I replied, as Tanya slipped a langoustine unnoticed on to the corner of my plate.

'How do you know you're not drinking it now?' said Jean-Louis, hanging out the bait.

I took a deep sniff from my glass and then sucked the liquid around my mouth. At recent tastings I'd convinced myself I could accurately identify flavours and so I shouldn't have been intimidated by the question. Jean-Louis's white tasted aromatically woody as a good Bordeaux should, but he had such a naughty twinkle in his eye that I was far from convinced it wasn't Jacob's Creek.

'Just an educated guess,' I said, as another langoustine landed covertly in my salad.

Jean-Louis rapped the table in delight. 'You're right.'

As we chatted away about New World wines, Tanya managed to transfer most of her langoustines to me, but then came the main course – a roast lamb spiked with garlic and rosemary, served with a rich cranberry jus, fresh garden peas and, of course, a heavy red Bordeaux. Again, it was absolutely delicious, unless you are Tanya.

We all have our childhood food phobias. The smell of Smash at school has put me off mashed potato for life, and Tanya's personal pet hate is peas. At the age of six she stubbornly stayed at the table rather than finish the remaining peas on her plate, and, chuckling at her determination, her father eventually had to finish the plate himself. Tanya hadn't eaten a pea since that day. Until, that is, our lunch with the Despagnes when she found her plate covered in them.

'In Bordeaux, you need to know whether you like left- or right-bank red wine,' explained Thibault, oblivious to Tanya's problems, as he poured from a new carafe. 'The more famous reds were traditionally located on the left bank of the Gironde – the Médocs, Château Margaux – these are reds where the mixture of grape varieties is dominated by Cabernet Sauvignon. On the right bank you have the newer appellations such as Saint Emilion where the Merlot predominates.'

'Why don't they just put the grape varieties on the label?' asked Tanya, grimacing as she forked peas one by one into her mouth.

'Because the appellation committee won't allow it and, anyway, everybody knows which bank the towns are on.'

Seeing that I was struggling to keep up with the conversation, the Despagnes kindly switched to English. They apologised for not being able to provide us with a clairet to taste and advised us to head back to Provence to look for pale rosé. Madame Despagne waited until Tanya had scooped the last pea into her mouth before clearing the plates and then served cheese and coffee. As the clock struck two the family immediately rose from the table. Unlike Tanya and I, they weren't apparently tempted to move their chairs into the sun and enjoy another glass of wine. They'd started lunch at twelve on the dot and finished at two on the dot, fitting their love of fine wine and food expertly into a working week. 'It's been lovely meeting you, but we have a busy afternoon ahead,' explained Jean-Louis. 'I am building a hell at the bottom of the garden.'

Tanya and I exchanged glances.

'Yes, you know, a hell, so we can have fresh water.'

We met Sophie two hours later just outside the village of Quinsac and she took us to see a local producer of clairet, Hervé Grandeau. We were both a little jittery with excitement – had the 300-kilometre drive been worth it? To begin with, it seemed promising. Hervé spent the first twenty minutes explaining how important colour was in a wine. He did so in a level of technical detail that exceeded anything we'd heard to date. Before harvesting, vignerons apparently measured the anthocyane in the skin of the grapes. This chemical and its extractability directly affect the colour of the resulting wine and therefore help to determine the length of the *macération*.

It was paramount that the vignerons got their calculations right because a delegation from the Bordeaux appellation committee actually inspected the wine at the vineyard. If the colour wasn't right, it couldn't be called a clairet. Everything seemed auspicious. I couldn't help but think that the word 'clairet' must describe a nearly clear wine. I was also excited that a committee of wine experts was prepared to judge a wine solely by its colour.

'On tasting you should detect wild strawberries and raspberries and a very slight bubble because we allowed a little carbonic acid to develop during the fermentation,' said Hervé as he crossed to the fridge. Tanya and I looked at each other with a smile on our faces.

'Clairet is a unique wine, it can accompany all different types of food. At meals there is no need to order separate bottles of red and white to accompany fish and meat: clairet fulfils both purposes. It is much more than a rosé,' continued Hervé. At this stage my first doubts began to creep in. The language Hervé was using to describe clairet was similar to that employed by Christophe Delorme at Domaine de la Mordorée, and Tavel had been one of the darkest rosés we'd encountered to date.

As Hervé poured us each a glass of clairet I had a real sense of déjà vu. It was Rosé de Ricey all over again – when Peter had tried to establish which champagne houses had put their own labels on inferior wines and we'd ended up tasting a rosé that could have been sold as a port. This time, rather than drive fifty kilometres south from Reims to Ricey, we'd travelled over five times that distance, but the result was the same. We were Peter-less, luckless and had undoubtedly discovered France's darkest rosé.

At least there were two consolations: Clairet turned out to be a delicious rosé and, by the time we left Hervé, Tanya was in a much better mood. The clairet, she admitted, had all but banished the taste of peas.

Little did she know that the second of *Les Deux Repas* awaited her at Sophie's parents' house.

Once again, that evening should have been a little slice of French heaven for Tanya. Quinsac is a small village located on top of a hill with panoramic views of the Bordeaux countryside. We sat on a wonderful terrace overlooking a flower-filled garden that swept away into the distance, dragging our eyes towards the sun as it dipped beyond the horizon. On the corner of the patio, glowing in the half-light, we could see the coals of a vine-wood – or *sarment* – barbecue and smell the heady woody aroma of the smoke.

Most of Sophie's family were there to meet us: her two sons, her petite sister, Céline, who had hair as short and blonde as

Sophie's was long and dark, Céline's husband, Loic, Sophie's parents and even a neighbour with a hot tip about a pale rosé. But unfortunately Brice had been called away on what we supposed was a secret spying mission and wasn't able to join us.

Sophie's father turned out to share a love of photography with Tanya and the two of them closeted themselves away in his study to look at pictures, while Sophie's mother did her best to make me feel at home. My glass was never empty, and little plates of roasted peppers and marinated anchovies were slipped continuously in front of me as unintelligible French conversation buzzed furiously around the table.

After an aperitif and a tour of the garden we sat down to eat. To start, we had an enormous tray of oysters plucked fresh from the Atlantic and then sold in a little *coquillage* stall in central Bordeaux. Interlaced among the oysters were chipolatas cooked over the *sarment* barbecue. For Sophie and her family, the meal before us was a Bordelaise speciality, which they served to visitors as an introduction to the region's gastronomy. For Tanya, it was like being served salmonella on a plate.

With the oysters we tried two different white wines. One from the town of Graves, just a couple of kilometres down the road, and an Entre Deux Mers. Sophie's father sat spearing chipolatas with a serrated knife that was kept for his sole use in a little drawer at the head of the table. 'Which wine do you think goes best?' he asked.

It was an innocuous enough question, but I had no idea of the correct answer and, unlike Tanya, who'd been happily chatting about wildlife photography, I was fast becoming a little nervous of our host. Earlier in the kitchen he'd rejected an electric oyster knife and showed me the scars on his hand from years of shelling them 'in the old fashioned way'. He'd told tales of shooting lions in Africa and drinking Guinness for breakfast during hunting trips in Ireland. I felt that men were supposed to be men in his house and, in Bordeaux, that meant knowing your wines. Nodding my head and saying that both wines were slipping down didn't seem sufficient, and I didn't want to let Sophie down by appearing ignorant. So instead, I plucked another oyster from Tanya's plate and popped it in my mouth in an all-too-transparent attempt to avoid the question.

Fortunately Sophie and her sister, Céline, came to the rescue. They debated the compatibility of each wine like politicians on opposing benches disagreeing over policy, oscillating between waving their hands angrily in the air and then rocking back in their chairs in mock disgust. Sophie's father periodically tried and failed to impose order, and the only thing that ended the argument was the bell, which Sophie's mother rang from the barbecue area to signify that the next course was ready. Son-in-law Loic leapt up and ferried the food from the barbecue.

For me, the vine-wood-grilled T-bone steaks were the culmination of a day of culinary delights. They'd been dusted with sea salt and flashed over the charcoal, searing the meat to a wonderful crispness on the outside while sealing all the juices within. Sophie's mother proudly produced a red wine and shallot sauce and spooned it over the beef as she told us the cuts were Aquitaine blonde, which she considered to be France's finest breed. She then began to carve. In France, steak is nearly always served *saignant*, which literally translated means 'bloody'. And after nearly three months in the country I'd grown to love it, even occasionally graduating to the totally raw *steak tartare*. And, as slice after mouth-watering slice of the blue steak was carved from the T-bones, I couldn't wait to get started.

Poor Tanya, of course, felt somewhat differently. In restaurants across France she'd always asked for her steak to be *bien cuit*, taking the risk of upsetting the chef and receiving a frazzled lump to avoid her meat arriving in a pool of blood. Having accepted only a small plate of oysters, she now had little choice but to eat up. As she cut into the meat Sophie's whole family looked at her expectantly, anxious that the food was to her satisfaction. Little did they know that during the course of the day Tanya had risked the recurrence of a horrific stomach bug through picking at plates of seafood, that she'd faced and overcome her childhood food nemesis of peas and that the reason she was looking pleased, if a little white, as she forked the bloody meat into her mouth, was the knowledge that in culinary terms things couldn't get any worse.

At least the wine was delicious. The T-bones were accompanied by a red from a fine château in a bad year and, as an alternative, a red from a mediocre château in a good year, and once again the conversation centred on their respective merits. I began to wonder whether they taught wine-appreciation classes in the local *lycées*. Sophie and Céline had presumably been weaned on the Bordelaise equivalent of the balloon debate – instead of deciding which famous person to throw out first, they must have vacillated between a Margaux and a Pomerol.

As the guests Tanya and I were cast in the role of judges, and, as each aroma and taste was successfully identified, the family looked to us for approval. We dutifully nodded, doing our best to appear knowledgeable. As the cheese arrived Sophie's father produced another red and explained that the trick to wine-buying in Bordeaux was to visit small producers down the road from the major châteaux. 'The grapes are the same, the soil is the same and the weather is the same, but the wine costs half as much.'

By the end of the evening I was exhausted. I'd spoken more French during the course of the day than the rest of my life put together. Both my jaw and my brain ached from the effort. At times I'd felt totally alienated from the conversation as people laughed and joked around me and I'd tried to unscramble words that, by the time I understood them, would relate to a discussion everyone else had finished ten minutes ago. The experience of eating two consecutive meals with French families must have had some effect, though. As we left I quite naturally bent and kissed

Sophie's son goodbye on both cheeks. Somewhere during the day I'd lost my natural English reserve.

As we walked back to our hotel through the quiet streets of Quinsac, I gave Tanya a sympathetic hug.

'Wait till I tell your father you ate peas, he'll be so proud of you.'

'Actually, I didn't eat many,' laughed Tanya, producing a napkin from her handbag and showing me her collection of langoustines, oysters and peas. 'I thought I'd make you a paella.'

Before we left Bordeaux I was determined to understand why the appellation insisted in calling what appeared to me to be a perfectly decent, if a little dark, rosé, clairet. As I'd understood Hervé's explanation, clairet was made in exactly the same way as any other rosé, so it seemed nonsensical to call it something different.

And so the next morning, after writing a thank-you letter to Sophie's parents, we arranged to visit Esme Johnstone, a distant cousin of Juveniles owner Tim.

The Johnstone clan had been renowned throughout Bordeaux for years. During the French Revolution David Johnstone had stolen a vital part of the guillotine and, in a show of gratitude, the residents of Bordeaux named a street after him. If anyone was going to be able to explain the mystery of clairet to us, it was a Johnstone, and Esme appeared more than qualified. He was a founder of one of the UK's largest and best wine merchants – Majestic Wine – and owner of Château de Sours, located in the heart of Bordeaux, near Saint Emilion.

Unfortunately he was also exceptionally grumpy because he'd just given up smoking. Tanya received an incredibly terse set of directions, and I had to phone three times to clarify them, before we finally arrived over an hour late. From these conversations I'd built up a mental picture of Esme as a corpulent, over-confident man, with a public-school background and a flashing temper.

Instead, in person he was tall and thin with a full head of silver-grey hair and a charming, if sometimes abrupt, manner.

He showed us round the ancient limestone caves where he cellared his wine, passed on some sound advice about how to travel comfortably on economy flights – buy yourself a bottle of Petrus from the Berry Bros at the airport; it's much cheaper than the upgrade and after the first sip you cease being envious of the people in business class – and then finally got around to the subject of clairet.

Esme explained that the word 'clairet' was historically used to distinguish the light-red wines of Bordeaux from the heavier reds made in other wine-producing areas. Over time Bordeaux produced more robust reds and clairet became a forgotten wine, but the English continued to use the word to describe all red wines made from the Bordeaux region. The pronunciation gradually changed to 'claret'. Then, with the reinvention of Clairet de Quinsac, the problems started.

For example, his rosé was tipped in all the UK wine guides as one of the best rosés available and his annual production was around 10,000 bottles, of which he'd already sold the majority. Producing a bottle, he showed me the label, with Château de Sours inscribed in bold lettering above a crest of arms. Then Esme pointed to the bottom right-hand corner where, in writing as invisible as the small print on a contract, was the word 'clairet'. Only the most observant UK consumer would have any idea that they were drinking anything other than a rosé, but the appellation rules required him to put it on the label.

'So is clairet a rosé or not?' we asked.

'Of course it's a f★★★ing rosé. It's just one more almighty bureaucratic f★★★-up by the Bordeaux AOC,' clarified Esme, looking for his cigarettes.

12

A Timely Arrival

After spending weeks in hotels and small apartments, we supposedly had a real treat ahead. A friend of Peter's owned a newly built house in the grounds of a château in the Dordogne and, in return for supervising the completion of the final small bits of building work, he'd offered us the opportunity to stay for a week. We were exactly halfway through our trip and the plan was to rest, relax and take some time out from visiting vignerons. There was even a swimming pool where I could presumably wear whatever trunks I wanted, regardless of the thong fetish of any local mayor.

From Saint Emilion we drove east and counted the kilometres, and the tiny villages, until we arrived at Sainte Foy la Grande and entered the rolling green countryside of the Dordogne. We'd heard that the surrounding area was the most English part of France, but we were far from prepared for the culture shock which hit us when we stopped in the nearby village of Eymet. The shelves of the local shop were full of jars of Marmite, baked beans and Patak's curry sauce. There was a list on the wall where I could sign up for the local cricket team, a rack of English DVDs and a queue at the check-out full of enough braying Home Counties accents to fill a gymkhana.

To escape a traffic jam full of Range Rovers, we turned on to a minor country road and wiggled towards our destination past copses of trees anointing the brows of hills, fields of sunflowers wilting in the heat and, as we rounded the final bend, golfers. Electric buggies criss-crossed the land and middle-aged women in overly tight shorts and pop socks mopped sweat from their brow as they swiped wildly at balls. The course was laid out in the grounds of a sprawling château, in front of which was a long terrace running the length of the eighteenth green. Cast-iron tables and chairs sheltered under white umbrellas and, in the shadow of the building's triangular peaked turrets, fields of plum orchards nudged against the walls. An old dovecote was stranded in the middle of a fairway overlooking a lake and further down the valley, about a kilometre from the château, was a row of new houses.

'This must be it,' I said as we pulled up next to the largest of these houses, which fronted on to the golf course. It was built in local stone with the painted wooden shutters Tanya adored and a turret that mimicked the style of the main château. Beyond the bunkers and greens we could see a field full of vines tumbling over the crest of the hill.

'If we could only get rid of the golfers, it would be perfect,' said Tanya.

As I began unloading the bags I heard a small cough coming from the pool area. We descended and discovered a woman swimming immaculate breaststroke, casting barely a ripple and holding her head high above the water with the grace of a swan. She moved to the side, gave a controlled smile and addressed us in a finishing-school accent. 'You must be Mr Stevens's guests. You'll find his house over there.' She paused and, keeping her legs firmly pressed against the side and out of sight, said, 'I'm so glad you met me before my cellulite.'

Suitably dismissed, Tanya and I made our way to the house next door, and more or less immediately wished we were lodging with our apparently cellulite-ridden neighbour. The drive was blocked by a cement mixer and dotted with piles of sand, paving slabs and breezeblocks. Pipes snaked across a mud-covered field in front of the house, and three builders sat smoking, idly dangling their legs over the void that should have been the swimming pool. Seeing our English number plate, they jumped to their feet and turned on the cement mixer.

'Even Peter wouldn't think this was marvellous,' I said as I avoided a dive-bombing wasp and opened the door.

For the next few days we tried to settle into the house and the area. The French builders realised that a display of extra effort was necessary and their numbers, if not their productivity, doubled. Living on a building site didn't prove easy – as if to make a point, the cement mixer was chugging away by 7.30 every morning and deliveries of sand and paving slabs were deposited outside our bedroom window. The house itself was barely habitable. The cowl had yet to be fixed on the chimney and on our first night a thunderstorm flooded the floor. The moment we went outside we were attacked by wasps, which were having a fabulous time nesting in the eaves where the builders had neglected to point the brickwork.

In the evenings a plague of miniature jumping cockroaches emerged from unplastered cracks in the wall and crawled across all the surfaces. Our first footfalls every morning triggered hundreds of these insects to leap waist high across the room searching for cover. One day we awoke to find a toad snuggling up to our toes and a family of swallows, with overly proprietorial parents, nesting above the sun terrace. For the next week whenever we had a drink outside, a chorus of unhappy chirping from the newly hatched chicks provoked the mother into a series of low-flying swoops. And, as hot sunny day followed hot sunny day, the sight of the empty concrete shell that was to be the swimming pool and the inaccessible swallow-filled terrace became more and more depressing.

To make matters worse, for the first time on the trip the odd conversation between Tanya and me was becoming a little fractious. We'd had a couple of messages from Peter saying that things were going well in Saint Maximin and that he hoped to join us again soon, but, in the meantime, we both missed him and without his jovial presence I found it harder to grapple, on a daily basis, with a foreign language and culture. Although the meals with Sophie and the Despagne family had been great fun, they'd reinforced the sense of alienation I always felt in France – yes, I could order a beer in a bar or ask for directions, but, as I'd learnt, I couldn't even participate in the most basic family conversations.

Tanya, on the other hand, was becoming nervous about returning home. In three short months we'd be back in England and our lives would return to normal. We'd both be looking for jobs, worrying about whether we'd ever have enough money to start a family and facing the interminably grey British winter. The more time Tanya spent in France, and the more she thought about what awaited us on our return, the more anxious she became.

Peter's detour also meant we were spending every hour of every day in each other's company, and one late afternoon, when the air was heavy and oppressive, we had our biggest row for years. Since morning the clouds had chased across the sky driven by a gusty wind. They'd gathered dark and ominous above the forest at the head of the valley seemingly snared in the branches of the trees. The odd bulbous drop of water fell with a weighty splash and lightning flashed across the distant hills. We sat and waited, with the odd itinerant jumping cockroach for company, desperate for the storm to break and wash clean the air.

But, as the rain started to fall, we began to argue. As always, the discussion went further than either of us intended. I was frustrated by our inability to find a rosé to compete with Madame Etienne's and by my own foolishness for entering into the bet. If a paler rosé than Madame Etienne's existed, which I doubted, then our chances of finding it were realistically pretty limited. If there were nearly 15,000 vineyards in the Dordogne alone, how many were there in the whole of France?

I was only too conscious that every day we spent in France was draining our bank balance back in the UK. If we were going to lose anyway, why not go home now? Especially since on our return I wanted to be able to pick a law firm which suited me, rather than just gratefully accept the first offer. And Tanya needed time to select an appropriate new career, rather than fall into another job. Spurred on by an unusually argumentative Tanya, for the first time I began to contemplate giving up. To date we'd had a fantastic time, but at some stage reality always had to catch up with the fantasy we'd created. Perhaps this was the time.

But Tanya, with tears flowing into the pool of water that was forming under the cowl-less chimney, was adamant we should continue with the quest. How could I even think about going home when we still had nearly the whole of Provence to search? And, anyway, what would Peter say?

In the end sense prevailed and, with flushed cheeks and puffy eyes, we agreed to enjoy the rest of the week and then make up our minds.

Market day at the nearby town of Sainte Foy la Grande proved a welcome distraction. The roads were so busy that we had to park on the flood plain of the Dordogne and walk through the outlying streets, full of medieval wattle-and-daub housing, with warped beams buckling under centuries of weight, and narrow alleyways seemingly collapsing in on themselves. We passed stalls laden with designer trainers and tracksuits, baskets full of tablecloths, and furniture shops overflowing on to the road. The streets all gathered towards the centre, funnelling everyone into an ever-tighter crush as we neared the heart of the market.

We entered a square full of vegetables vibrant with colour. Individual growers with grubby nails seemed to specialise in just one crop and offered infinite varieties – fat plump tomatoes, thin heart-shaped ones, tomatoes still clinging to the vine and ugly contorted green ones splitting at the seams. There were piles of garlic, shallots and onions, green beans, white beans, peaches and nectarines, and rosy-red apples sold by chattering girls.

In the adjoining square the fruit and vegetables gave way to meat – great spit roasts with chicken, hams and pork tumbling around in front of the fire, cages of live ducks, doves and rabbits, fresh for the table, pensioners queuing at the *chevalier* for their fix of horse meat, and foie gras producers offering vacuum-packed livers and blocks of pâté. There were *coquillage* stalls with oysters and mussels open and ready to taste, and bare-chested men heaving buckets of ice. In front of the town hall, surrounded by people stooping under the weight of their shopping, was an intriguing pageant. A short old man, with circular glasses and a round cherubic face, bowed his head to receive a medal and then gratefully slipped into a multicoloured gown. It was similar to a university graduation ceremony; there were men shrouding stern looks under misshapen hats and a hierarchy of different robes – the yellow, green and blue one, as modelled by the beaming old man, and others made from fur or interwoven with gold and silver thread.

The crowd fell silent as the new acolytes solemnly read from a scroll of paper. I assumed they'd all just been made freemen of the town or given some similar honour. In fact, they were being inaugurated into the Confrérie des Vins de Sainte Foy la Grande. And, like proud cub scouts newly awarded their toggles and vowing to do their best for Akela, they had to swear allegiance to the wines of the area and promise to do their best to promote them for the rest of their lives.

At 12.30, when the market began to empty and the stallholders retired to the bars, Tanya tucked the food we'd purchased under a spare table and we shared a bottle of wine. We watched as live chickens and pigeons were packed up around us and the square gradually became bare. Young girls with indecently tight leggings and farm boys with burnished skin and gold chains lounged around the central fountain, while men with sideburns as long as Elvis's and bangles on their wrists sipped beers in the sun. As we sat drinking our wine, watching other people's lives unfold before us, the over-friendly toads, jumping cockroaches and wasp infestations all seemed quite inconsequential.

And on our return to the house we heard the most delightful sound – water trickling from a hosepipe. Tanya and I both rushed into the garden to see how long it would be until we could swim. We were greeted by the shaved head of Nibby Paul, who was clambering waist-deep in water, dragging what appeared to be a hoover behind him. Nibby, as we soon found out, was the swimming-pool builder and, unsurprisingly for the Dordogne, he was English. 'You know, you're very lucky,' he said with a grin, as he emerged from the water. 'This is the last pool lining available in the whole of France. If I hadn't got this one, you wouldn't be swimming till Christmas.'

Tanya offered Nibby a beer, which was dispatched within seconds into his barrel-like frame. He put on a baseball cap to shade his round red face and twitched from foot to foot as water dripped from his Bermuda shorts, forming a puddle around his feet. 'I've been living here for fifteen years now,' continued Nibby, 'and I've watched English people with houses come and go. They've either got too much money or they're escaping from something or someone.' He finished his second beer and gave a small burp. 'Me, I'm running from my mother, and I'm too scared to go back after all these years.' As he said this, his lips remained pursed and serious, momentarily fooling Tanya and me into visualising a great ogre of a woman, but under the baseball cap his bright little eyes were shining with mirth.

Over the next two days the water level on the pool gradually crept upwards and Nibby was ever present in and around the house. Every few hours he'd plunge into the pool and make sure the lining was being sucked back against the side walls. He'd then climb out into the sunshine and gratefully accept another beer, hiding it surreptitiously behind his back whenever his French wife, Natalie, was around.

There turned out to be very little that Nibby didn't know about the surrounding wildlife, from the rutting habits of wild boars, to the name of the beaver-like animal – a *coypu* – that lived in the lake on the golf course. Taking one look at our wasp-infested eaves, he clambered up a ladder armed with an aerosol so toxic only the *pompiers* were supposed to use it. After just one squirt he disappeared into a billowing noxious cloud from which nothing could emerge unscathed. The wasps plummeted to the ground and when the smoke cleared and the coughing stopped, Nibby climbed down with a new toxically enhanced sense of humour. The fact that the water in the pool had turned green overnight was now apparently hilarious. He stood with a beer in one hand, scratching his head. 'I don't know why it does this. I had one pool which didn't change back to blue for a month.'

'Can we still swim in it?' asked Tanya.

'Well, people did in the last one and they were fine.' Nibby finished his beer and grinned at me. 'Apart from the green hair.'

'If we can't use the pool, where can we buy some fans?'

'You don't need them,' said Nibby, jumping in the air and clapping his hands together as he began repeatedly chanting, 'Tanya, Tanya.'

Seeing our bemused faces, he shared the joke: 'Don't you get it? I'm your biggest fan.' He clapped his hands and started chanting again, 'There's only one Tanya Ivey, one Tanya Ivey. I am walking along, singing my song, walking in a Tanya wonderland . . . '

To escape Nibby's sense of humour, Tanya insisted on visiting some more vignerons. I think she was hoping to reawaken my interest in the quest – if we could find a pale rosé to compete with Madame Etienne's then perhaps, just perhaps, I could be persuaded to go on. Unfortunately the Dordogne was awash with affluent Home Counties emigrants determined to live the dream, and rather than a forgotten rosé made by a Gauloises-smoking, garlic-growing, beret-wearing Frenchman, we found Olivia Donnan, who'd ceased to make rosé to concentrate on her award-winning reds.

She wore a pair of Chanel wraparound shades, a Gucci blouse, a denim miniskirt and a pair of high heels. To say she wasn't dressed for a day in the fields would be an understatement. But this didn't matter, she explained, pointing to a lone figure out in the vines, because her oenologist took care of that side of things. Eric was in his late twenties, with a mane of dark curly hair which flowed over his shoulders and bobbed in and out of sight as he examined the grapes. According to Olivia, he was an artist who created the most stunning wine.

Tanya and I were initially terrified – the power-dressing, the price of the wine and the *Sunday Telegraph* article pinned to the wall detailing how Olivia had lovingly restored the vineyard on a shoestring budget were all intimidating. But by the time we left Château Masburel, Tanya had adopted Olivia as a role model. While her husband had stayed in his job in London, Olivia had stripped concrete from the exterior walls of the château to reveal the old brick and transformed piles of rotting timbers and collapsed walls into an interior which wouldn't look out of place in *Hello!* magazine. She might have tottered on her high heels as she led us through the rows of vines, but she chatted happily away, spicing her conversation with pieces of wisdom for the aspiring emigrant: 'As I said to my husband, you don't build Château Margaux in a day,' and '*Rien*, that's what you get without hard work, *rien*.'

For an afternoon it seemed we couldn't get away from the English. There was a château founded by the Rymans stationery family and another run by an author who helped subsidise her dream life producing wine with royalties from her books on the subject. And with each new meeting with one of our countrymen making a successful life abroad Tanya's determination to finish the quest deepened. But the visits had the opposite effect on me, reinforcing my conclusion that we were on a fruitless journey. When asked about pale rosé, one vigneron simply shrugged and said that everybody knew that Château Etienne was famous for producing France's palest rosé.

But our perseverance eventually paid off. Just to the south of Sainte Foy we met a vigneron who gave us one of the most tempting tips of the trip – a location of the most beautiful vineyard in France. Jean Gazaniol was in his mid-fifties, had short dark hair and wore a pair of dark sunglasses propped on top of the most enormous nose I'd ever encountered. It was larger even than Antonio's, the sommelier from the George V, and lent support to one of Peter's pet theories – Darwin could have saved a trip to the Galapagos and learnt all about evolution from vignerons' noses.

Jean wore a linen suit and walked with a slight limp as he showed us around Château de Parenchère. The building had been largely destroyed during the French Revolution and only the gatehouse survived from the original construction, but it was still magnificent, with rows of shuttered windows and a tower fit for a fairy-tale princess at one end of the façade. At the rear was an ingenious art deco conservatory which in winter functioned as the central heating by trapping the sun's rays and transmitting the heat through the rest of the building.

We passed through the lobby and into the dining room where

a tasting had been prepared for us. A chandelier hung over a long mahogany table, tapestries were draped from the walls, and freshly cut flowers were positioned in china vases around the room. A set of French doors opened on to a large terrace, beneath which rows of vines dropped away into a deep valley. Jean's daughter, Julia, brought plates of smoked ham, cheese, tapenade and olives into the room and laid them out on the table, and we were both given an ornate silver bowl for any discarded wine.

'If the taste of the wine stays in the mouth for ten seconds, then it is an interesting wine. If it stays for fifteen seconds, it is a fantastic wine,' instructed Jean.

The next half-hour was blissful. We picked at the food and sampled each of the château's wines, occasionally glancing out of the doors and watching as clouds of spray rose up from between the vines. As we tasted, Jean told us about his grandparents, who'd fled France in the middle of the previous century after the cholera epidemic broke out in Carcassonne. They'd established a vineyard in Morocco and then Algeria before the family returned to France at the outbreak of the Algerian War of Independence in 1954.

Fortunately for us Jean was a rosé fan who was genuinely excited by our quest. He explained that the prime purpose of many vignerons when making a rosé was to improve the quality of their red wine – by bleeding off a little of the juice and creating a rosé, they concentrated the remaining flavours in the grapes, enabling them to make better red. But this method of making wine didn't interest Jean. Château de Parenchère was in fact just inside the borders of Bordeaux, so Jean's rosé was classed as a clairet. This, he admitted, caused him all sorts of problems in the export market, particularly since the current trend was for pale rosés.

At this point he went silent, as if trying to grasp a fleeting thought, and began drumming his fingers on the table in irritation. 'You must forgive me, my memory is going these days, but I know just the wine for you. It's made in a vineyard that sits on a hill above the Mediterranean, right opposite the Îles d'Hyères between Saint Tropez and Toulon. It's surrounded by tropical plants, and the vines almost fall into the sea.' He paused and looked at us intently with his dark eyes. 'For me, it's the most beautiful vineyard in the whole of France. If only I could remember its name.'

As he started to drum his fingers again, Jean's daughter, Julia, re-entered the room. Tanya and I were just as twitchy as Jean, willing him to remember the name.

'Papa,' said Julia smiling, 'you're thinking of Château Sainte Marguerite.'

When I awoke the next morning, Tanya was crying. Piles of discarded tissues lay on the floor and tears flowed from her eyes as she ineffectually dabbed at her blotchy face. It was time to make a decision about whether to continue.

I gave her a big hug and pulled strands of her curly blonde hair away from her eyes. 'Come on, let's talk about it. We've had a fantastic trip, but the quest is probably hopeless. And we could always see Château Sainte Marguerite another time.'

She turned to face me, blinking tears from her blue eyes. 'It's not that.'

'What is it, then?'

'Neil just called – Claire gave birth to a baby boy in Montpellier last night. He's called Tristan,' she sobbed. 'I can't believe we've got a Frenchman in the family.'

Outside, Nibby was standing proudly by his newly blue pool and young swallows tumbled through the air swooping to scoop up the water. The last paving stone had been laid on the terrace, and the builders had even returned to point the wall where the wasps had been nesting. Across the valley I could see teams of workers among the vines snipping the excess growth away.

It was known as the *vendange verte* or 'green harvest' – if we were still in France in a couple of months' time we'd see the real version. On the floor of the bedroom our suitcases were lying open with our clothes neatly folded inside. Next to them was our wine collection – the Billecart-Salmon, Rosé de Ricey, Marsannay, six bottles of Nicolas Reverdy's Sancerre, miscellaneous other bottles and the *vin jaune* from the Jura that we'd bought to give to Rosie and her new brother. As hard-hearted and hard-headed as I could sometimes be, it was a four-hour drive to Montpellier and there was only one direction we could possibly head.

'Call it serendipity,' said Tanya, dabbing at her eyes, as one hour later we turned the car once more to head for the sun.

'Come on, let's meet baby Tristan, and then,' I said, ruffling Tanya's hair, 'then we work out how to win this bet.'

13

Extremely Angry Rosie

Montpellier is a city permanently in festival. There's the book festival, the dance festival and the everyday festival that the Mayor encourages on its streets. His policy of turning nobody away from the city has resulted in the most cosmopolitan society in France. On every street corner there's a performer – acrobats doing backflips, fire-eaters tossing flaming torches into the air, dance groups moon-walking outside cafés, and magicians producing rabbits from hats and budgies from people's ears. The pavements are permanently busy, filled with students clasping satchels under their arms, office workers hurrying to hi-tech business parks, and bright-blue trams criss-crossing between neighbourhoods.

It's easy to understand the attraction. Montpellier suns itself on the Languedoc coast, just a three-hour drive from Barcelona and only twenty minutes from the Camargue and the Provençal border. There's an historic old town full of secluded squares and forgotten churches, an ancient aqueduct that threatens on a daily basis to collapse into the valley below, and peaceful botanic gardens in which to escape the crowds. And, in the heart of the city, in the vast open space of Place de la Comédie, the new blends imperceptibly with the old as one sweep of the eye takes you from the glinting glass and stainless steel of the Polygone shopping centre to the gilded statues and vaulted ceilings of the opera house. In between the two buildings are rows and rows of cafés with huge awnings and fans blowing droplets of cold water into the baking air. It's people-watching on a grand scale.

At times it seems like the whole of Montpellier passes through the Comédie – or l'Oeuf as it's colloquially known – and buying a beer, sitting back and watching for an hour is the best ticket in town. Mothers try and spirit their children past the dancing horses and whirling lights of the fairground carousel. There's the usual legion of the elderly, immaculately dressed and gleaming with jewels, parading their poodles. Shoppers with wicker baskets queue to buy melons from Cavaillon and oysters from the salt-water *étangs* of nearby Sète, while travellers with ragged green clothing, piercings in every orifice and tattoos climbing up their arms sit on street corners tossing balls to their Dobermanns and boxers. The whole show is set to music – Spanish guitarists sing love songs to canoodling students, hip-hop blasts from the stereos of dance troupes, and an Irish busker sings the Pogues.

Tanya, of course, was far too desperate to see Tristan to take any notice of the rich street theatre around her. She sprinted across Place de la Comédie, dodging trams and buskers and showing not the slightest interest in the lively market. The joys of Montpellier could wait, her nephew couldn't.

Claire and Neil live in a second-floor flat overlooking a palm-tree-lined avenue just off the Comédie. There's a heavy glass door inlaid with wrought iron and behind it a cool marble lobby filled with tropical plants. Up on the second floor their flat opens on to an enclosed roof terrace with an orange tree in one corner and a baby palm tree in a pot in the centre. We were buzzed into the building, and in a single step we left the noise of the passing trams and the bustle of the congested pavements behind. For a second there was peace, and then the unmistakable wail of a newborn child filled the lobby.

Claire stood at the top of a flight of marble stairs with tears streaming down her face clutching Tristan. Wrapped in great blankets, Tristan had a blotchy red face and skin as wrinkled as a Saint Bernard's chin. His tiny fingers and toes were screwed up tight, and he waved his little limbs in bemusement, but Tanya's immediate, doubtless impartial assertion was that he was very handsome. And when the crying stopped and Tristan opened his eyes and gave a toothless grin, even I, to whom all babies look the same, saw a natural charm.

Rosie was at Claire's side, her head barely as high as my knee, clutching a doll in one hand and her mother's leg with the other. She wore a pretty pink dress and striped multicoloured tights. When I'd last seen her, a couple of ringlets of hair had corkscrewed in front of Rosie's eyes, but now a full head of tight blonde curls was kept in check by matching pink ribbons.

Nearly lost in the commotion of congratulations, kisses and compliments, Rosie muttered a scarcely audible '*Bonjour*'. It was the first French word I'd heard her speak. In little over a year she'd become a true French toddler, and, as I entered the flat, she complimented me, '*Oui, comme ça.*' In Rosie-speak this meant yes, I would have opened the door in the same way. Later, when we were sitting on the terrace enjoying a furiously bubbling glass of pink champagne, she offered me an impromptu olive. Aware that she had the attention of all the adults, she smiled, tipped her head coyly to one side and said in her sweetest voice, '*Voilà.*'

In France, a prospective father's leisure, pleasure and comfort are considered in as much detail as the needs of the mother-to-be. A couple of months before Claire gave birth, Neil received a letter from the local health service. He assumed the brochure inside related to the practicalities of getting Claire to the hospital. He was wrong. He'd been sent a wine list. The hospital had reserved a room next to Claire for him and wanted to know whether he preferred Burgundy or Bordeaux with his evening meal. And after Tristan's birth Neil was entitled to three weeks' paid paternity leave. The French government clearly believed that the responsibilities of fatherhood were more important than work.

And so, as the proud parents got to know their new baby, we put aside our quest and tried to help as best we could around the house. Our first task was the weekly shop. In England, this chore was my personal pet hate. To try to avoid it, I would offer to stay at home and clean the bathrooms or do the hoovering. But despite my sudden enthusiasm for housework, I somehow still ended up straining to push a lopsided trolley down narrow aisles at an annoyingly packed supermarket. At least we'd usually be home within the hour, whereas in Montpellier, the weekly shop took us nearly a day to complete.

The problem was too much choice and it all began with breakfast. To me, one croissant is very much like another, but Tanya and Claire both insist that tiny differences in the amount of butter used in the pastry add up to a big difference in texture and taste. The ideal croissant was apparently butter-based. It should have a crumbly flaky exterior and a soft moist interior. Unfortunately the sisters disagreed about where these heavenly croissants were to be found. Complicating matters still further, Rosie had become partial to the *pains au chocolat* made in a bakery on the far side of town. By the time we'd visited three different shops just to buy breakfast I realised I had a very long day ahead.

Even after the croissant experience, I wouldn't have thought it possible to spend an hour in the butcher's. While we waited in line I studied the meat laid out behind the glass counter. There were skinned rabbits with their legs spreadeagled and bright-yellow chickens with sinuous necks and beady-eyed heads. The butcher grabbed great piles of innards and fed them into a skin to fashion *andouillette* sausages. People greedily ordered things I wouldn't consider eating – slimy red livers, dry pink hearts and, most popular of all, pig's trotters.

The walls around the shop were covered in rosettes awarded

for first or second places in various *inter-boucherie* competitions. And on a shelf behind the counter was an enormous silver cup for first place in the Bovine Concours de France. Above this cup the severed head of a cow was mounted on a wooden plaque. As we queued, its doleful eyes stared at the salivating customers.

Finally it was our turn. Oblivious to the ever-lengthening queue, Tanya asked about the different breeds of French cows. This was a big mistake. The butcher returned with a poster-sized board displaying pictures of over twenty cows. He stood like an old man at a bar with his elbows resting on the glass counter and his head conspiratorially close to Tanya's. Each cow, he explained, had different qualities that made them suitable for particular cooking methods. By cow ten I was getting a little bored and began to tap my feet and look around the shop. The butcher noticed and immediately admonished me: 'It's good that your wife likes cows.'

Some agitated customers gave up and left, and my arms started to ache from the bags of shopping. Perhaps I wouldn't have minded had they been discussing sport or politics, but their mutual fascination with cows began to make me appreciate the benefits of an English supermarket, where if I asked for some Aquitaine blonde, I'd probably be pointed to the beer aisle.

The latest topic was Jersey cows – the butcher had never heard of them and wanted to know what they looked like. There were two ways of answering this question: the simple way, by pointing to the head on the wall which looked remarkably similar to a Jersey, and the more complicated alternative. Tanya, of course, opted for the latter and started to explain her family history. The butcher was treated to a lesson in her mother's Lithuanian lineage, a description of the Canadian holiday retreat she used to go to as a little girl and finally the point of the story – how her grandmother used to keep a cow at the bottom of the garden. It had gentle soft eyes and as a result it was called Stirna, which in

Lithuanian meant deer. 'Stirna,' said Tanya, triumphantly, 'was a Jersey cow.'

I hadn't thought it possible to outdo the French when talking about food, but Tanya had managed it. The butcher looked totally confused, and the remaining customers refused to make eye contact. We gathered our shopping and left as quickly as possible, leaving them all to ponder the potty English and a cow called Deer.

In the following shops we managed slightly shorter stays, but rather than a simple commercial transaction, shopping became a conversation about the delights of France. We bought white wine from an off-licence, a local Picpoul and a Chardonnay. The assistant, a young man in his mid-twenties, was most concerned that we drink the Picpoul before the Chardonnay, otherwise our palates would not detect the delicate flavours of the first wine. He also recommended some *coquillage* from nearby Sète to accompany the Picpoul. As we left, he cautioned us not to put the wine in the freezer to cool; if we did we risked shocking the wine.

And so it went on. We visited another butcher, this time specialising in fowl. We asked for duck breasts, a simple enough request considering the pile of them pressed against the glass. But rather than select the first two, the butcher rooted through his whole stock. Behind us people happily chatted away, apparently unperturbed that such a simple task should take so long. The butcher was only satisfied when he'd identified two pieces of meat of identical weight – that way, he assured us, the cooking time would be the same.

By the time we got to the pharmacy I'd had enough, but not for nothing are the French renowned as a nation of hypochondriacs. Tanya had a small blister on her foot and we needed a pack of plasters. First the pharmacist insisted on examining the affected area, then he selected a packet of hideously expensive cushioned plasters which had been impregnated with both an anti-inflammatory and a disinfectant. All we'd wanted was some Band Aid, but instead we left with a product capable of fighting off every known bacteria in the Amazon. 'You can never be too careful,' smiled the pharmacist as he accepted €20, and clicked the till shut.

The next day I thought I'd made an excellent deal when I agreed to look after Rosie. Neil and Tristan had gone to buy a travel cot, and Tanya and Claire wanted to do some clothes shopping. Rather than be dragged around the shops, I agreed to babysit. After all, how hard could it be to chaperone a two-year-old? As a reward, the girls had agreed to have the children for the whole afternoon while Neil and I went to watch the Tour de France which was due to pass through the outskirts of Montpellier.

Before leaving, Claire patiently laid out all of Rosie's belongings: a rag known as Dou Dou, a beaker for her water, some biscuits, her sunglasses and, most importantly of all, her toy doll, Bébé. Claire handed me some nappies, gave Rosie a kiss and me a reassuring smile. 'If she gets bored, you could always take her to the playground.'

For the first hour I couldn't understand what all the fuss was about. I'd met plenty of weary mothers with clothes stained by jam and hair splayed in all directions who insisted that bringing up children was harder work than going to an office, but Rosie was quite content sitting happily on the floor unlacing and then lacing a pair of Neil's shoes. When she tired of this game, I put one of her DVDs on and we danced around the room to *Mary Poppins*. Childcare, Mary and I seemed to agree, was a magical experience.

I was so confident I risked a trip outside. I buckled on Rosie's shoes, helped her into her jumper and handed her Bébé and Dou Dou. There was a minor tantrum because I forgot her sunglasses, but we held hands all the way to the playground. It was built in the shade of an old church right next to a convenient café. There was a seesaw, a slide and a climbing frame, which thankfully were all completely empty. I sat on a bench and watched as Rosie lovingly positioned Bébé and Dou Dou at prominent points around the playground. While I read a book she happily chatted to her toys. I remember thinking that parenting really wasn't that difficult.

It wasn't until more children arrived that I began to learn otherwise. Toddlers, it seemed, were rather proprietorial about their toys and they were also vicious when provoked. Bébé was blocking the slide and Dou Dou was monopolising the climbing frame, but Rosie expected the other children to wait their turn. A girl with dark tightly curled hair and a sweet button nose thought differently.

I'd never seen a toddler wrestling match before. There was plenty of kicking, gouging and hair pulling as Rosie squared up to the girl, shoving her tiny fists into her face, and instigating a tug-of-war as they both grabbed Bébé's legs. The two of them tumbled to the ground, neither willing to relax their fierce grip, and while they were busy hurting each other, I plucked Bébé from the mêlée. Within minutes there was peace. I relaxed back into my seat and considered ordering a beer from the nearby café.

Some people were naturals with children. I might not be able to sing like Mary Poppins, but as long as I periodically rescued her toys then Rosie would be happy. I put Bébé next to me on the bench and quickly crossed the square to get a beer, confident that there were other mothers around to watch Rosie. My back was only turned for a second. But it was enough.

An Alsatian trotted across the pavement and snapped Bébé's head between its jaws. Standing facing the playground, it vigorously shook the doll from side to side, using its paws to try to separate the head from the body. Rosie let out the most enormous scream and stamped her little feet. Momentarily I thought she was angry enough to fight the dog, but fortunately she realised that tackling something with teeth bigger than her fingers was not a good idea.

Trying to catch an Alsatian is not easy. Trying to catch an Alsatian while protecting a two-year-old from the trauma of watching her toy doll being savaged is next to impossible, but I did my best in shielding Rosie's eyes as I lured the dog towards us. Unfortunately the Alsatian wasn't interested in the biscuit I was offering. It wanted Bébé's blood and repeatedly tossed the doll into the air, crushing it between its jaws and paws as it landed. A row of toddlers gathered to watch the mauling. Rosie clasped both her hands around one of my legs and hid her face in my knee. Unencumbered it would have been hard enough to catch the dog, but with Rosie shackled to my leg I had to give up.

When I returned to the flat to meet Tanya and Claire I was a broken man. My clothes were covered in dirt from repeated despairing dives to try to snatch Bébé. Next to me Rosie stood in silence. Her face was still flushed red from her tirade in the playground. Only lack of energy had prevented her from crying all the way home. In one hand she held Bébé's torso, in the other its severed head. I just hoped her earliest childhood memory wouldn't be an Alsatian tearing her doll to pieces. I also hoped that she'd learn to trust me again. On the television Mary Poppins was singing, 'a spoonful of sugar helps the medicine go down,' but I couldn't help thinking that it would take a bit more than some sugar to make things right again.

I'd always been intrigued by the Tour de France. On televisions in every bar there was blanket coverage of the event. Hour upon hour was devoted to essentially the same picture – a bunch of men whizzing past on bikes. The only variety was whether they were freewheeling down sinuous bends or struggling up a hill. How could a nation be so enthralled by such a simple sport? And why did decrepit old men who could barely walk still squeeze into Lycra and pull themselves on to bikes?

I hoped to find an insight into this national obsession by watching the *peloton* stream through the suburbs of Montpellier. The 200-kilometre stretch between Carcassonne and Nîmes was an easy sprint for the riders, and the local paper had provided expected arrival times for most street corners. Unfortunately Neil and I were late. We jogged through Place de la Comédie, down a series of steps which cut through the old town and on to a long straight road that led to one of the spectator points. A helicopter flew overhead in ever decreasing circles, the heavy drone of its blades signalling the imminent arrival of the riders.

Other latecomers joined the rush along the road. A young boy pedalled furiously as his father ran alongside him, and a motorbike passed us at full throttle, enjoying the freedom of a traffic-free road. Neil and I were breathing heavily. We'd been running for half an hour, but unless we made it to the end of the road in the next couple of minutes, it would all have been for nothing. Another helicopter appeared overhead, and then a third. We were still 100 metres from the spectator point when two police bikes appeared on the brow of the hill. The riders wore helmets and wraparound sunglasses. As we joined the crowds the policemen revved their bikes and rode quickly down the side of the road, pushing everyone back on to the pavement.

We found a vantage point on a small grass bank and waited. My lungs were burning as badly as any of the Tour's cyclists. I put my hands on my knees and breathed hard. At the top of the road there were now four police motorbikes and a pace car with an enormous clock on top, but no sign of the riders. The spectators around us started nudging each other as a yellow moped appeared. 'Le moped jaune,' they whispered in awed tones.

I knew that after each stage the leader of the tour was awarded the yellow jersey, but I'd never heard of the yellow moped. Everyone clapped as it whipped down the hill, followed by the police riders and the car with the clock on top. The helicopters were now hovering directly above us, and a continuous stream of traffic was trailing down the road. There were police cars, lorries with sponsorship hoardings on the back and trucks with spare bikes mounted on their roofs. I doubted whether the President of the United States had ever travelled with such an extensive cavalcade.

Luckily I'd recovered my breath by the time the riders breasted the hill. Had I still been bent double with my hands on my knees, I'd have missed the whole Tour. The bikes flashed by leaving a blurred image of streaming colour, like a photo of city lights taken on a slow shutter speed. There was no detail, no chance to pick out individual riders, just a collective intake of breath from the crowd as the lead rider passed. And then it was over and people filtered away. For a second they'd been part of the Tour, part of the whirr of pumping legs and the faces creased with pain and part of the endeavour that would propel the *peloton* through the country. Rather than a spectator sport, the passing of the riders had been about sharing a feeling.

As Neil and I walked back to the flat I felt I finally understood the sport. Take away the doping scandals and the fact that an American called Lance Armstrong was perpetually spoiling the French party by winning the race, and you had a simple celebration of the country, a travelling festival that brought people on to the streets rejoicing in the size and diversity of France. Whether you were Parisian or Provençal, the amorphous mass of limbs, which was the Tour, united you.

I also learnt that day that sometimes wishes do come true and when I'm in trouble again I won't be afraid to whisper a small prayer to Mary Poppins. Watching the Tour had brought us to an unfamiliar part of the city, and the roadside was lined with all sorts of peculiar shops. There one selling hundreds of different sorts of beads, another specialising in bridal veils, and remarkably next door was a shop I hadn't even dared dream existed – a teddy bear and dolly repair shop.

Just possibly, Bébé's head could be reunited with her body and one little girl could go to sleep happy.

AUGUST

A minute passed and then the *gendarme* grinned. Was he celebrating catching an Englishman?

14

Gris de Gris and the Supermarket Rosé

A different type of reunion awaited us back at the flat. Sitting in the courtyard, Peter Tate puffed on his cigar, sipped on his rosé and took great delight in drip-feeding us tantalising bits of information as he declared everything around him to be 'marvellous'.

After three weeks in Saint Maximin la Sainte Baume his skin had turned a chestnut brown, and his grey hair appeared a sun-bleached snow white. His wife, Jenny, had joined him in the village, and, according to Peter, they'd blended in so well that on several occasions they'd been mistaken for locals. He'd become a regular in the central bar, eaten at every restaurant in town and visited all the local vineyards. 'There's nothing like a nine a.m. pastis to loosen tongues,' he said, as a familiar grin spread across his face.

Apparently the Etiennes' bet with a group of English tourists was common knowledge throughout the town. Like most Provençal vineyards, Château Etienne had noted a dramatic rise in UK rosé consumption and was desperate to break into the market before the opportunist Bordelais secured all the new contracts. As a result the challenge was hailed by all the locals as a smart piece of business. Nobody believed the English tourists had a chance of succeeding and so, to the envy of all the other local vignerons, the Etiennes seemed to have found themselves an importer.

And just in case we proved more successful than expected, Peter had encountered worrying rumours that the local *gendarmes* had been tipped off. A roadside breath test after a visit to a vineyard was seen as the most effective way of ending our slim chances. But despite the determination of the Etiennes to ensure we failed, Peter had rejoined us at an opportune moment. We were about to follow up one of our best leads – the *gris de gris* of the Camargue.

If you stop a Frenchman in the street and ask him to name a pale rosé, he'll probably reply Listel's *gris de gris*. If he's particularly knowledgeable he'll tell you it's a *vin de sable* or sand wine from the Camargue. And then if you're lucky, he'll warn you against visiting the vineyard. There's simply no good time of year to be in the Camargue. In the winter the mistral howls down the Rhône Valley whipping sand and ice-cold water into the air. The summer can be even worse, when the sun hammers down on the marshy swamps stirring some of France's biggest mosquitoes into a frenzy of bloodletting. The landscape is so remorseless that its only permanent inhabitants – the horse- and bull-herding *gardiens* – have build themselves windowless houses to protect themselves from the elements.

But, with a chance of finding a pale rosé, we had to investigate. We agreed to meet Claire and Neil at Listel in the afternoon and headed deep into the wilds to see if the Camargue lived up to its fearsome billing. We'd seen images of wild white horses surging through the shallow waters with their unkempt manes blowing freely in the wind. And heard how their foals were born with black or chestnut coats which took five years to change to white. The horses apparently shared the wilderness with herds of black bulls with viciously upturned horns which were bred for fighting. But driving amid the inland salt lakes, narrow canals and fields of reeds, the only white horses we encountered were tethered at endless tourist riding stables, and the only bulls we found were in fenced fields or on the lunchtime menu. At least there were the promised flocks of flamingos, searching the shallows for food.

We passed the largest town, Saintes Maries de la Mer, where gypsies flock once a year to watch the statue of the Black Saint being carried into the sea. Legend has it that after the death of Jesus Mary Magdalene fled Palestine and was washed up on the shores of the Camargue. The gypsy Black Sarah became her maid, and the local populace converted en masse. It was a romantic tale, but Saintes Maries could have been Blackpool on a blustery day. The pennants on the boats snapped in the wind, there were pleasure cruises, fortune-tellers and fripperies. And yet the sophistication of Saint Rémy was just an hour's drive away.

Our sense that the Camargue was a place apart was reinforced in the small village of Le Sambuc. We walked across a dusty square past stunted trees towards a small bar. It had a narrow terrace on which was gathered a crowd of about twenty people. The men, almost universally, had bald heads, bare chests and missing teeth, and the women wore ripped sundresses or pinnies with rags tied into their poorly dyed hair. The ashtrays were full of dead cigarettes and the tables covered in empty beer bottles. As we stepped on to the terrace a guitarist emerged from inside the bar. He took a stool and began to tap out a beat on the back of the guitar.

Everyone stood. They raised their arms skywards and curled their wrists back so the shadows on the terrace resembled a pit of snakes ready to strike. The beat quickened and another guitarist emerged from the bar, his hands moving ever quicker over the strings of the instrument. The crowd began to dance with small precise steps, keeping their backs straight and their chins arrogantly raised. They formed a circle around one of the women. Her hair was tied high into a ponytail, and there was a hint of a frill at the hem of her dress. The crowd stamped their feet as she whirled in their centre, snapping her head from side to side and fixing the men in her dark eyes. Sweat was pouring down everybody's face and just when it seemed the speed of the beat was going to prove too much, the lead guitarist cried, 'Olé,' and with one final exhausted stamp the dance was over.

More cigarettes and beers followed, accompanied by some slower music, over which the dancers chatted in scarcely recognisable French. We ordered and finished our meal before the whole terrace was called to its feet again. There was cheering and clapping as the guitarist played his final number, 'Olé Toledo'. It was a raucous, less disciplined dance. People swirled together in a mass of twirling limbs and snatched embraces as they sang with the guitarist in ever-louder voices. The energy of the dancing made me forget that the participants were all over fifty.

As we left the bar to head for our meeting with Claire and Neil, trails of cigarette smoke rose up into the air together with throaty cries of 'Venga, otra' as the crowd pleaded for another song.

We could have been in Spain.

We'd dreamed of finding France's palest rosé in a vineyard hidden in the hills, nestling amid lavender fields, forgotten by all but local custom, but our lack of success so far had brought us to Listel. On our trip we'd accosted a whole variety of people and asked about pale rosé – old men playing *pétanque* in Sainte Foy la Grande, cyclists at the water fountain in Saint Rémy, and a housewife hunting for cicadas at the bottom of her garden in Les Baux de Provence. They all had one thing in common – they'd recommended Listel to us. The vineyard was the popular choice for the source of France's palest rosé.

If the *gris de gris* was as pale as it was rumoured to be, then we were prepared to give up the moral high ground and turn up at

Madame Etienne's with a bottle. It didn't matter that in the huge courtyard outside the vineyard an open-topped double-decker bus waited to whisk hundreds of visitors around, or that Claire and Neil could take Rosie and Tristan on a more sedate ride on a tourist train. What mattered was the colour of the rosé. Or so I kept telling myself.

Listel was located on a flat sandy plain outside the town of Aigues Mortes. It was separated from the sea by two large white dunes of reclaimed salt and a shallow *étang*. Rows and rows of vines stretched to the horizon, planted at uniform widths across a uniform landscape. Sunrays bounced off the sand, and the land glowed with heat, making it hard to look into the distance. Insects buzzed around my face, and I noticed that mosquitoes had taken a couple of great lumps out of my leg.

It was early August and supposedly the *vendange* was over a month away, but the yard was full of people. Surplus wine was being stacked on to lorries, the *cuves* were being cleaned and hosed down, and parts from the presses and de-stalkers lay in huge piles waiting to be oiled. I knew that in hot years the harvest could come early, but even in the heatwave of 2003 it hadn't started until mid-August. And yet the preparations we were watching were unmistakable; the *vendange* could only be a week away, which meant that we might have as little as three weeks before being summoned to the Etiennes' harvest party.

I crossed to the vines and parted the leaves. When we began our trip, flowers rather than fruit grew from the twisted stems. By the time we reached Sancerre, the grapes had resembled tiny olives, with their skins so tight and firm I could roll them in the palm of my hand without creating any damage, but now they were dark and swollen, almost bursting at the seams. 'Mama, grape,' said Rosie, pointing at the bunches and putting her hand in her mouth to show she wanted to eat some. It wasn't a good idea – while an adult can happily eat half a dozen of the grapes used to make wine, a baby would probably be sick after just one.

Rosie, of course, didn't understand this. She promptly burst into tears as I pondered another hard-learnt lesson in parenting: never show children something they can't have.

Inside the visitor centre it was nearly impossible to hear anything. Hordes of tourists were clamouring for the free sip of the different wines included in the price of the guided tour, and over a microphone a lady wearing a Listel uniform was trying to drum up buyers. She held each bottle high in the air, reading out the price as the crowds looked at the bottom of their empty glasses. Behind me I could hear an Irish couple complaining: 'To be sure, why don't they just give us a full glass? That way we'd still have some wine left when she's asking us what it tastes like.'

'This is our new rosé for the European market,' continued the woman. 'It's designed to cater for the young drinker and introduce him or her into the world of Listel's wines. It's only nine per cent volume, so you can have a couple of glasses and still drive. If you smell the aroma, you should detect blackberries and wild strawberries.'

The Irishman ostentatiously stuck his nose deep into his empty glass, turned to his wife and with great authority said, 'Smells like potatoes to me.'

Our host, Jean-André Bonnardel, led us through to a quieter side room. He was a young man, perhaps twenty-five, with light blond hair and a hooked nose. He wore a linen suit which was a little too baggy for his thin frame, and he was only too delighted to share everything he knew about wine with us. Unfortunately Jean-André revelled in technical detail, talking about the importance of limiting the tannic reaction as if it were as simple as boiling the kettle. To make matters worse, our fluent French-speaker, Claire, was too busy flirting to translate. She twirled one of her blonde curls in her fingers and even when Rosie urgently tugged on her hand, Claire kept her big blue eyes fixed on the Frenchman. I made a mental note to tell Neil not to worry – a love of young French vignerons simply ran in the family.

Despite Claire's all-too-apparent distraction, I learnt that Listel was France's largest vineyard, stretching from Montpellier through the Camargue to Marseille, and, like the other vineyards in the area, it produced sand wines or *vin de sable*. Up until this point the French had been relatively simple, but then things got complicated. I think I understood that the Camargue vines were unique in France for having survived the phylloxera outbreak in the middle of the nineteenth century. Whereas the rest of the country's vines were subsequently crossed with American stock to protect them from future outbreaks of the disease, the Camargue vines remained 100 per cent native. They were untouched because the insect which caused phylloxera attacked the roots of the vine and, in the Camargue, these stretched through the sand to the water below, where the insect was unable to flourish.

With the technicalities over – or so I thought – Jean-André produced a bottle of *gris de gris* from the fridge. Up until now, the quest had been full of false dawns – Laurent Fournier's Marsannay rosé, which we'd briefly believed was as pale as Madame Etienne's, Nicolas Reverdy's un-sellable rosé and a fruitless trip to Bordeaux to taste the misleadingly named clairet – so I wasn't hopeful that Listel's rosé would prove as pale as promised. The average Frenchman, I'd learnt, had a tendency to want to appear knowledgeable, and to admit to ignorance about wine, even rosé, involved a real loss of face. Far better to name a wine, any wine, and hope to get away with it.

But it appeared that, as far as wine went, the man in the street knew his stuff. As they'd repeatedly told us, Listel's *gris de gris* was remarkably pale. We'd have to test it against all sorts of backgrounds and in all sorts of lights to prove it was paler than Madame Etienne's, but I felt a little surge of delight – we were back in the competition.

At least for a minute.

'Of course,' said Jean-André, 'technically speaking a *gris de gris* isn't really a rosé.' I looked despairingly at Tanya and Peter as we listened to the explanation that followed.

'The *gris de gris* gets its name from the Grenache *gris* grape. It is a grey wine from a grey grape,' Jean-André continued, 'and, as such, the appellation committee requires us to label it a *gris* rather than a rosé. It's like a sub-category.'

The quest was turning out to be a lot more complicated than we had expected. Nobody had warned us about the intricacies of appellation rules and the niceties of wine labelling. As well as finding the palest rosé in France, it appeared we now also faced the challenge of proving that whatever wine we selected as our champion was actually a rosé. All the Etiennes had to do was invoke some obscure appellation rule and disqualify our wine. In front of us we had a wonderful pale-pink wine. It looked like a rosé, it tasted like a rosé, but we were being asked to accept it wasn't a rosé. It was like clairet all over again but even more frustrating because the *gris* was a pale wine.

I was tempted to adopt Esme Johnston's attitude to appellation rules and declare that of course our *gris* was a rosé, but I didn't feel the wine was worth the fight. What would we have achieved if we turned up at the Etiennes with a bottle of France's most well-known pale rosé that we could have purchased in any off-licence in England?

'We might as well hire a team of lawyers and take them with us to the harvest party,' said Peter as we left clutching our *gris*.

On our way home we saw something rarer than a French plumber in August – the purple heron of the Camargue. Startled by the engine, it flew from its perch into the middle of a flock of flamingos. With the sun casting a corridor of light over the shallow salt-water lake, I watched as the purple crest of the heron mixed with the vibrant pink of the flamingos, and, adding to the palette of wildlife, on the horizon was a white blur moving quickly across the landscape. Perhaps our luck was changing, we'd finally seen the famous wild white horses.

★

Back at the flat Claire and Neil had organised a wine tasting with an oenologist, Michel, who arrived carrying a crate full of rosé. He was a small portly man with receding black hair from whom everything seemed to project outwards — his barrel chest, his vibrant checked green shirt and his gravelly tobacco-like voice.

Michel explained that at harvest time oenologists worked a bit like doctors on call. First they clambered up ladders and dipped various instruments into the wine, noting down their conclusions in rows of numbers and chemical formulae. They then held a consultation with the vigneron, before dispensing the necessary supplements and promising to be back in a couple of days to check on progress.

We followed Michel outside on to the terrace. Thankfully the oppressive heat of the day had vanished, leaving a gentle breeze which stirred the warm air. I was still dressed in a short-sleeved shirt and a pair of shorts, and Rosie scampered around the courtyard wearing only her nappy. Laid out on the table were plates of food to accompany the wine — tapenade spread on pieces of freshly toasted baguette, roasted peppers, anchovies, a whole *saucisson* together with a serrated knife (Neil had taught me that French men were quite particular about slicing their own pieces) and a tray of local cheeses. In the middle of all the food was our attempt at a spittoon — an enormous bucket wrapped in silver foil, which Tanya had surrounded with tea lights so that it resembled a glittering holy relic.

The wine was arranged in a line on the table, starting with the palest first, and Claire and Neil added a mystery eleventh bottle to the end of the line, which was wrapped in paper tissue. From the small private smiles I caught them swapping as they rushed to open the door to further guests, I assumed it was going to be something quite special.

After half an hour everybody had assembled. There were friends of Michel and friends of Claire and Neil, and, as is the

French way, some of the guests had even brought their parents. The introductions were made so quickly that I forgot people's names. The larger the crowd became, the happier Michel appeared, strutting in front of everybody like a barrister presenting his brief.

Two men flanked him on either shoulder, nodding their heads in accordance with his comments. The elder of the two had a neat grey beard and a gentle unassuming manner. Every now and again he asked Michel to slow down to make sure that I understood everything. The other man had dark-brown skin, a protruding jaw and enormous hands like those of a clown. Whenever Michel appeared lost for things to say, he would gently prod him on to another wine-related topic – the relative merits of Château Margaux and Domaine de la Romanée-Conti, or the American attitude to French wine. Both men appeared to think themselves deeply privileged to be in Michel's company and listened carefully to his responses. 'Although Romanée is one of the most expensive wines in the world,' opined Michel, 'my favourite is the Margaux, and, as for the Americans, they order a merlot or a syrah as if they're choosing between a Pepsi and a Coke.'

The man with the clown hands passed Michel a small briefcase, which he placed on the table and clicked open. Inside was the most incredible corkscrew I'd ever seen. It was like an electric drill with detachable parts; Michel had the option of selecting and attaching a ten-, five- or two-inch screw to the end. He had a pair of clippers to take the wrapping off the neck of the bottle and a thermometer.

The two French women present paid very little attention to Michel as he opened the bottles and checked the temperature of the wines. For them, the evening was a social event, and if the men had to discuss wine, then so be it. They were fully made-up and wore white linen trouser suits smart enough for a night at the opera house. Their hair was highlighted blonde and firmly fixed into place, and they each carried a small clutch bag loaded with mascara and mobiles. While Michel talked, they closeted themselves in a corner, where they gratefully accepted glasses of wine and talked about clothes with Tanya – yes, it was exciting that Chanel had just opened in Montpellier; ah, but for really good shopping, London was the place to go, better even than Paris.

The tasting began with the palest wine, Domaine la Colombette from near Béziers. Michel took a sip and waited for silence. 'It's quite an acidic wine, probably harvested early and designed to accompany *coquillage*.' Next came Château Puech-Haut from Saint-Drézery. 'And *voilà*, the fruits have arrived. *Frais, cassis, bonbons anglais*. It's technically a brilliant wine, but there's no *tipicité* of the ground.' And so it continued, a Tavel was described as 'explosive', a heavy rosé from near Nîmes as 'less structured but with good *tipicité*' and a Saint Chinian as a 'very masculine wine'. If nothing else, we were learning some new wine vocabulary.

By the tenth bottle we were all quite merry, particularly the two French women, who'd decided that they liked rosé so much that they wanted to know why it wasn't treated with more respect. Tossing back their hair, they cornered Michel and began interrogating him. 'Why is this your first ever rosé tasting?' quizzed one. 'Why's rosé not taken seriously by the French wine establishment?' asked the other. To begin with, Michel tried flippant responses. He pointed at a plane overhead which was well away from the usual flight path: 'Look, I think the pilot's had too much rosé.' But as the drunken questions kept coming, it became clear that he couldn't find answers.

We still had one final rosé to taste – Claire and Neil's mystery bottle. Neil removed the wrapping with the flourish of a magician and produced possibly the palest bottle of rosé any of us had ever seen. We stood and gaped as tiny tinges of pink teased across our retinas. In the fading light it appeared much paler than

Madame Etienne's. It was from Lorgues, twenty minutes down the road from Château Etienne, and made me think that the area might be an epicentre for pale rosé.

'Marvellous,' said Peter.

'Where did you find it?' I asked.

'At the local supermarket,' said Claire and Neil simultaneously as they poured glasses for everyone. 'It's only four euros.'

We raised our glasses and took our first sip of what I hoped would be the winner of our competition. It now didn't matter that the harvest might be exceptionally early this year, and the wrangling over whether Listel's *gris de gris* was or was not a rosé could be forgotten about. We could spend the next few weeks sunning ourselves in Provence, perhaps popping into the odd vineyard just to check there was nothing paler. It was also a relief not to have to worry about the bet – since Peter's return I'd become more and more concerned about how I was going to arrange to import the Etiennes' wine, and about how much a small percentage of their production amounted to. Instead, I could now look forward to a lifetime's supply of free rosé.

'*Salut*,' said Michel, beaming at us as he took his first sip, and very nearly immediately spat it back out. His face went white. He rinsed the wine around his mouth and gargled it between his teeth and gums. Finally, in a great jet, he deposited the liquid into the spittoon, quickly followed by the rest of the wine from his glass. Michel had been talking continuously all evening about wine, but now, when we most wanted to hear his opinion, he was silent. Eventually the words came haltingly to him as he recovered some of his earlier poise: 'It's very oxidised, it carries nothing, you need a wine that represents where it comes from, but this, this *n'a pas de tipicité.*'

I took a sip, convinced it couldn't be that bad. It was. The wine stripped all the moisture from the roof of my mouth and was bitterly acidic to swallow, but I was still strangely trium-phant. Our quest was based solely on the colour of the wine, and we had a possible winner. It would be churlish of the Etiennes to point out it was undrinkable, wouldn't it?

The rest of the rosé tasting has now largely faded from my memory. We finished all the bottles, apart from our winning wine, which nobody was prepared to touch, and I listened with amused interest as the two French women insisted on having a long argument with Michel about whether there was such a word as *tipicité*. But the most abiding image from the evening was Michel's friend with the clown hands and the protruding jaw unscrewing all the fearsome pieces to his corkscrew. Tanya asked him what he did for a living, and as he held the ten-inch screw up to the light, he gave a great toothless grin and answered, 'Dentistry.'

Later that night I dreamt of him prising my mouth open and holding the corkscrew above my teeth insisting that it was as effective as any dental drill.

One immediate consequence of discovering the supermarket rosé was that I was running out of excuses for not visiting Guy de Saint Victor, who lived near Béziers, just an hour from Montpellier. Previously I'd been able to persuade myself that our time was limited and that we'd be better heading for Provence rather than deeper into the Languedoc. But now, with the end of the harvest only three weeks away, and the *gris de gris* and the supermarket rosé both bubble-wrapped in the boot of the car, I felt we had to make the trip.

My telephone conversations with Guy were still rarely short of disastrous. My most recent error over a week ago had been to pronounce 'Banyuls' incorrectly. I'd mentioned the seaside town near the Spanish border because Tim Johnston had recommended a wine producer from the area and I wanted Guy's advice on the region. Instead, I got laughter and lots of it. I could almost visualise Guy shaking his head with despair as tears flowed from his eyes. 'You know, Jammie, what "*bagnole*" means in French?

It's slang for an old banger, like a car. You've just asked me whether you should look for pale rosé in an old banger.' More laughter.

And so, a week later, when I eventually picked up the phone to arrange our stay, it was with some trepidation.

15

Guy de Saint Victor

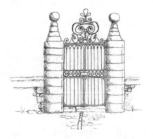

'You'll definitely get lost,' said Guy with pride when he invited us to stay at his family's country house, Rouvignac. He'd just started letting the outbuildings during the holiday season and had immediately experienced a run-in with official-dom.

'You know, Jammie, the tourist office erected a huge sign without even asking my permission. I could have sent an email complaining, but it would have been like talking Martian.' He laughed and as usual I missed the joke – if there actually was one.

'So you know what I did, Jammie? I spoke to the Mayor. Now there's no sign, just a plaque by the roadside.'

Guy was right, we did get lost. His plaque turned out to be a piece of metal not much larger than a postcard and was planted on the end of a small spike. It was dug into the ground so that a walker could easily miss it and seeing the plaque from a car was virtually impossible.

As we drove around the roads outside Béziers I became more and more nervous. I wondered if Guy was dreading our meeting as well. He couldn't, I assumed, be oblivious to our tense phone relationship, and while it would be interesting to put a name to a face, I felt we might have an uncomfortable stay. I envisaged Guy as a French version of the English country aristocrat. Instead of fox hunting, I could see him prowling the fields with a double-barrelled shotgun annihilating small birds, wild boar and the odd peasant. On the frequent occasions he'd been too busy to send the fax of his wine contacts, I imagined him to have been preoccupied with some highbrow pursuit of the French upper classes – like licking foie gras from the toes of a mistress.

When we eventually arrived, Guy was sitting on an ornate balustrade that ran the length of the outside of the house. He was a small man, with an angular nose and quick jerky movements. He wore a green polo shirt, a pair of shorts and a pair of boat shoes without socks. A smile twitched across his face as he leapt down to greet us. Somewhat strangely for someone I'd learnt to fear, he resembled a little schoolboy who'd been waiting all summer for his friends to come and stay and now they were here didn't want to reveal quite how excited he was.

Perhaps it was the size of the house behind Guy that gave this impression. Rouvignac was stunning. It was the French country mansion that every Englishman dreams of owning. Behind the balustrade the *grande face* – as Guy called it – ran the length of an Olympic swimming pool, and from every room on the ground floor a set of French windows opened out on to the garden. On the two other storeys floor-to-ceiling windows from each of the twenty or so bedrooms gave on to small cast-iron balconies with stunning views over the surrounding countryside. Completing the idyll were rows of long duck-egg-blue shutters which were hooked back to admit the perfume of the long-stemmed roses flourishing in the flower beds beneath.

'You must come and see the house and its grounds,' said Guy with evident delight. Rouvignac, we learnt, was initially a Roman settlement and, like many of the other great houses in France, its name ended in 'ac' because in Latin this meant 'near water'. Guy scampered into the luxuriously green undergrowth and beckoned us to follow. Pulling away the weeds, he uncovered a metal grill and the well beneath. 'See, the whole place is built just above the water table. We never have to water a single plant here.' Looking around the garden, I realised that the Mediterranean plants I'd become so used to were conspicuously absent. There were no pines or olive trees, but instead huge ancient oaks and drooping willows populated the garden. 'Come over here,' said Guy, a friendly smile once again spreading across his face as he stood proudly beside a man-sized terracotta pot. 'It's a Roman urn which I found in the garden. I think they used it to ferment the wine in.'

As we toured the house anecdote followed anecdote. We were shown the bishop's room, which was painted a deep red with an elaborate star emblazoned on the ceiling. Guy told us with glee that a child who went on to be a bishop was born in the bed and that 'No man or woman who's slept in this room since has ever married'. In another room a huge crucifix was mounted above a sleigh bed. 'If anything naughty happens in this bed, then the cross will fall on the lovers and pierce them through the heart.' Gradually, just gradually, I thought I was beginning to understand Guy. He was open, warm and kind but probably slightly nervous, and he used his humour to hide the nerves. The quirky nature of his house seemed to mirror his personality. There were even indications that he was a bit of an Anglophile – an old London street sign for Onslow Gardens, SW7, hung in his study, there was a picture of his great-grandfather with Prince Charles, and his drawing room was given over to a billiard table with the rules printed in English framed on the wall.

'Before I show you your bedrooms, I must warn you that we have a ghost called Jules,' he continued. According to Guy, Jules was an old family servant responsible for lighting all the candles in the house and cleaning the red tiled floors. When Jules died, the floor was dirty and as a result he was condemned to mop the tiles for eternity. 'He must get very tired,' said Peter sympathetically as he looked at a seemingly endless corridor.

Ghost or no ghost, we couldn't have been more delighted with our bedroom. It could have come straight from the set of *Les Liaisons Dangereuses* and was full of extravagant drapes and ornate furniture. The double bed was recessed into its own alcove guarded by a set of full-height curtains. There was an ancient armoire, a luxuriant armchair with curled mahogany feet and a patterned pink covering, and a huge French mirror. Two sets of windows opened out on to a balcony from which we could see a long lawn falling away into the distance, and sheltered by some trees in the far corner of the garden was a swimming pool surrounded by sunloungers.

'I don't think I ever want to leave,' said Tanya as we traipsed downstairs through the sitting room with its Directoire ceiling and the tearoom with its Louis XVI reliefs.

'Let's have a glass of pink champagne and you can tell me about your journey,' said Guy. He looked nervously into the kitchen to check his wife didn't see him disappearing into the old tack room where he stored his wine.

The champagne turned out to be named after his great-grandfather, Noel Castelnau, a famous First World War general who was awarded the Order of Bath by the Prince of Wales. Castelnau was the commander of the Second Army, which managed to halt the German attack at Nancy in 1914, and in 1915 he planned and directed the successful Champagne offensive. 'But what I don't understand, Jammie,' said Guy as he completed the family history, 'is that the Royal Family asked for the Order of Bath back after he died. Why would they do that?'

As we sat next to the pool, sipping the pink champagne, I told Guy the story of our quest to date. He nodded his head as I mentioned wine producers he approved of and wrote down some alternative suggestions for each of the areas we'd visited. Then we spoke about our plans for the next few weeks. 'Don't worry about the harvest, it's always early in the Camargue. In most of Provence it won't take place until middle to late

September. So you've still got plenty of time.' He paused, took a sip of champagne and then asked, 'The real question is, what are you going to do at the end of the quest?'

Ever since our argument in the Dordogne, Tanya and I had been avoiding this issue. I knew that staying with Claire and Neil in Montpellier had given Tanya a taste of what living in France was like, and I knew that she'd loved it. At the same time, when we'd set out on the quest, the idea had been to give ourselves a break from our London lives and some time to think about our careers. Back in April it hadn't entered my head that perhaps we wouldn't want to go back, but the longer I was in France, the more I had to agree with Tanya that it was a fantastic country that perhaps had more to offer than our lives back in Balham. Neither of us really wanted to discuss it, though, because in our hearts we knew that somehow we had to earn a living and, like it or not, that was easier for us to do in England.

'I guess we'll just enjoy the next month and then head home,' I said.

'You know, Jammie, I used to work in an office in London. Then four years ago we made a decision to come back to France. This house has been in the family for years. It was completely run-down and we had a choice – either let it fall into further disrepair or spend our lives slowly restoring it.' Guy topped up our glasses with champagne and disappeared to fetch another bottle, once again checking that his wife didn't catch him.

As he popped the cork he gave a big satisfied smile. 'I love being back.'

The next morning we took breakfast with Guy on the terrace. There was freshly squeezed orange juice, croissants and *pains au chocolat* from the local *boulangerie*. Yet again the sky was cloudless, and the heat of the sun was creeping back into the air. I could hear Guy's children already screaming with delight as they jumped in and out of the pool.

'I haven't been able to find you the palest rosé, but I've got a real treat for you this morning,' said Guy as he poured himself an enormous black coffee. Despite pressing him for information, he wouldn't say any more, but I noticed that he seemed to have dressed for a special occasion. Gone was yesterday's understated polo shirt, instead he'd chosen a bright-red shirt decorated with golden swirls. It was an extravagant piece of clothing for what turned out to be an unusual experience.

As we drove to our secret treat, Guy told us the history of Languedoc's so-called 'gold rush'. The Industrial Revolution of the late eighteenth century had led to an unprecedented demand for low-grade, low-alcohol wine to give to the workers. With the expansion of the railways, Languedoc was ideally placed to supply the whole of France with this wine. Planting took off and the wine industry experienced a mini boom. In just five years a vigneron could make enough money to build an enormous house, but because of the First World War many of the châteaux were never finished. 'The vineyard we're going to see today is typical. It has an enormous façade guarded by wrought-iron gates. It looks like your Royal Family might live in it, but the builders never finished the rear of the house and so it's actually quite small.'

Guy pulled over just before we reached our destination and led us across the road to an old warehouse. 'This was France's first ever co-operative. If you read the plaque it says, "The free vignerons of the Pays d'Enserune, each for each other." It was established in 1905 as a means of helping those disenfranchised by the gold rush.' Guy jumped up on to the step outside the door. 'And the French socialist leader Jean Jaurès stood right here and made a famous speech opposing the arms race that preceded the First World War. He said the government should spend its money on people not tanks.'

With the history lesson over, we headed towards the vineyard. Guy was still keeping quiet about what was so special about the place, but he couldn't stop himself from teasing us. 'I promise you, you'll not see a single vine.'

I'm not sure whether what followed was a tour of a garden or a comedy routine. Guy had brought us to the house of his good friend, the vigneron, François Boujol. He led us through the promised set of iron gates and round the back of an ivy-covered château. It had a square tower at one end, similar in shape to the castle on a chessboard, and a large first-floor terrace with a balustrade resembling the one at Rouvignac. As we entered the garden, white-collar doves flew up from the top of the tower, and the heavy beat of their wings alerted a dog, which barked out our presence.

'Well,' said Guy, 'this is it. We're here to see the garden.'

It didn't look like much. There was a rectangular lily-covered fish pond which stretched away from the house, a gravel path lined with large terracotta urns – which Guy later informed me were valuable Anduze pots – and a neatly mown lawn. At the bottom of the manicured part of the garden was a small wood, boasting trees with leaves which ranged in colour from the lush green of a wet English summer to the burnished red of a cold Boston fall. I'd seen houses with larger gardens in the suburbs of London, but apparently this was the unusual experience Guy had tried so hard to keep secret – a few colourful trees and a fish pond.

Alerted by the barking, the vigneron, François Boujol, emerged from his house. His short dark hair was flecked with grey, and his eyes were hidden behind a pair of sunglasses with small rectangular lenses. He wore a freshly pressed shirt, with a yellow jumper tied around his waist, boat shoes and a pair of white trousers. At his feet trotted a small brown-and-white terrier called Félicie, and, mirroring her master her fur seemed to be going grey at the tips.

Then the show began. François led us deep into the wood at

the bottom of the garden and began pointing out plants: a border filled with Vietnamese bamboo as tall as small trees; an American conker tree, the nuts on which smelled of limes; a Montpellian maple tree unique in its family because its leaves didn't turn red; and a tree bearing a fruit like green oranges which 'walked' across the earth by shedding its dead trunk and sprouting anew from a nearby spot. François gave us the Latin name for each of the plants and as he talked about them lovingly cupped their leaves in his hands.

But the real star was Guy not the plants. François pointed out a poisonous narcotic plant with hanging purple flowers which was traditionally pounded into a powder and wiped on horses' anuses to make them look sprightly before an auction. 'Try a little on your husband on Friday night,' whispered Guy to Tanya. He then plucked a citrus fruit and rubbed it under his armpits. 'Did you know people use this as a deodorant?' Soon each new plant was accompanied by a skit. A squat plant from the South American rainforests bore a fruit whose inner fibres were used to make mattresses, but, as Guy demonstrated, it had a nasty side. The small circular flowers were a trombone shape and looked innocuous enough, but the moment an insect crawled inside the flower snapped shut. Guy fell to his knees with his hands around his throat making a gurgling sound, before collapsing dead on the lawn in a graphic demonstration of what happened to the poor insect.

When we'd revived Guy, François led us into his orchid garden. He'd constructed a metal frame for the orchids to grow up and had cultivated over two hundred and fifty different varieties. The flowers were planted in narrow rows, and we walked in single file past delicate multicoloured orchids with petals as thin and brittle as sugar paper. Large insects that hovered like humming birds zigzagged between us, and François contin-ued to give us the Latin name for each plant. Hidden from the house amid rows of tropical plants, we really could have been on an expedition into the rainforest rather than in a small vineyard just outside Béziers.

Before the end of the tour there were a few final jokes from Guy. He took Peter on a detour and led him past some small round fruits randomly scattered on the earth. Little did Peter know that the fruit spread its seed by exploding into the fur of passing animals. In this case the animal was Peter, and as he trod on the ground next to the fruits one erupted, sending its green seeds flying on to his legs. He jumped in shock and of course another fruit burst and then another. Fully fifteen fruits split before Peter had calmed down enough to tiptoe out of the minefield.

Then grabbing a nearby plant with a purple flower in the shape of the horn of a gramophone, Guy used it as an improvised loudspeaker and announced that drinks would be served in the courtyard.

François's château was designed like a miniature medieval fort. The first set of wrought-iron gates brought us through into a broad sweeping yard in front of the house. Then, through a second set of gates built into the front wall, we entered a smaller courtyard, not dissimilar from a cloister at a monastery or boarding school. A large tree was planted in the middle and it rose up higher than the roof of the surrounding house, casting everything below into shade. In various small pots dotted around this courtyard were yet more intriguing plants – long thin multicoloured chillies blew this way and that in the warm wind like the tentacles of a sea anemone swaying as the water washed across them. As we pulled our chairs up to the table we crushed tiny green capers, which had fallen from a nearby plant.

François opened a bottle of his rosé, and for the next hour we sat and talked. But not about wine or our quest; instead, we chatted about the great gardens of the world, Kew in London, the Boboli in Florence and Gaudi Park in Barcelona. What was the secret to the design of a good garden? What plants flourished in different climates? How could you ensure flora and architecture successfully interacted?

We learnt that François's house dated back to the fourteenth century and, like Rouvignac, was built on land where the water table was unnaturally high, making it the perfect environment for his range of plants. And as we talked, François petted his little terrier, Félicie, whose image appeared on all his wine labels and as a pun on his bag-in-the-box wine – *Félicie mise en boîte*, literally meaning 'the dog is in the box'. His sense of humour was not so dissimilar to Guy's after all.

It was perhaps a little too early in the morning to be drinking rosé, but that morning everything seemed right. We had our first sip at 11 a.m., and it added a spice to the occasion, a sense of shared decadence. Sitting in the shade, we could sense the heat of the sun baking the thick stone walls of the house, but ours was a cool haven. We were privileged to have toured François's garden and to have seen plants that none of us knew existed. Guy was delighted to have introduced us to the experience, and François seemed to like nothing better than sharing his enjoyment of his hobby.

We'd arrived as strangers but we would leave as friends. On our quest there were always vignerons for whom we would have a special affinity – such as Nicolas Reverdy in Sancerre and Laurent Champs in Champagne – but with Guy and François we'd shared something outside the norm. At Rouvignac we'd been welcomed into Guy's family and shared the garden, the kitchen and the swimming pool with his children as they pitched tents, messily made jam sandwiches and hurled themselves screaming on to inflatable crocodiles. And it was genuinely sad when, sitting in François's courtyard, we learnt that his dog, Félicie, probably didn't have long to live and that he was considering taking her image off the labels on his wine bottles.

The vineyard Félicie Plantation might, by now, even have a different name.

So when we waved goodbye to Guy at the gates of Rouvignac, I reflected on how badly I'd misjudged him. He stood in front of the balustrade, once again dwarfed by the massive house. His face was flushed red from too much early-morning rosé, but at least it matched the vivid red of his shirt. He held both hands in the air and walked across the gravel bidding us farewell, like a member of the ground crew guiding a plane out of its station. I gave a hoot of the horn and we disappeared up the bumpy drive to continue our quest, reinforced with the knowledge that an Englishman who doesn't speak any French and a Frenchman trying to joke in English should never speak on the phone because if they do, they are liable to get quite the wrong impression.

16

De la Part de René

'Ever been to Corsica?' asked Peter, looking up from the map on his lap.

Tanya and I nodded.

'I hear it's wonderful,' continued Peter as he gazed out of the window at the passing countryside, pausing for long enough to let the idea settle into our minds. 'It's only a small detour, and you know what I always say?' There was another pause and then Peter looked over the top of his glasses, winked and said with a disarmingly delighted chuckle, 'All firm plans need a latitude.'

Dashing across the Med to Corsica was a far from sensible idea. It was mid-August and – according to Guy's estimate – we had roughly a month left to cover the rest of Provence. But Peter was adamant he wanted to make the trip, and Tanya and I had such fond memories of our last visit five years ago, that we found the idea hard to resist.

From Béziers we drove to Marseille, the edgiest town we would encounter on our travels. An internet scam meant we had to pay twice for our hotel room, and as we walked the streets, thieves tried the oldest trick in the book, repeatedly asking for the time to see if we were foolish enough to take our hands from our pockets. Driving in Marseille was even worse than in Paris.

An accident in the French capital might have resulted in a few angry gestures, but Marseille had a southern feel where tempers were quick and hitting someone's car was a personal affront – sorry would not have been nearly enough.

So it was with relief that we boarded the *Napoleon Bonaparte* and headed for Corsica. Our destination was Farinole, just a couple of kilometres from Patrimonio, the capital of the island's winemaking region. The crossing took ten hours, but thankfully French ferries turned out to be a lot more luxurious than their English counterparts. Instead of a microwave tikka massala washed down by lager, we enjoyed *steak au poivre* accompanied by a heavy Corsican red. There was a sundeck with a bar and even a small swimming pool, and, best of all, the Mediterranean reached its deepest point around Corsica, making the ferry ride perfect for dolphin and whale watching.

Dusk was falling as we stood on the prow of the boat trying to make out the silhouette of Cap Corse. Ahead of us small sailing boats tacked across the path of the ferry, heading for land before the last light drained from the day, and with a final leaping pirouette the dolphins, which had been dancing alongside for the last hour, bade us goodnight. The ferry's engine droned ever onwards, and the world dipped into shadow. Between the smooth sheen of the sea and the faded sky that still awaited the first blink of the stars, a third, blacker shape emerged. Rather than the jagged rocks I'd been expecting, the coastline of Corsica was rounded in the half-light, billowing ever larger, until, as the lights of Bastia flickered into view, the sea and the sky had almost shrunk from sight.

We arrived at our accommodation after midnight, and the bottom of the car scraped against the rutted road as we headed downhill towards the sea. The shadow of an old watchtower loomed on one corner of the bay, and behind us was a black curtain of cliffs. A candle flickered on the terrace of the house and next to it was a bottle and a note which read, 'Welcome to

Corsica. I look forward to meeting you tomorrow.' Tanya, Peter and I sat with a glass of wine listening to the gentle swish of the sea, wondering who we'd meet in the morning and what the view would be like.

We awoke to the sound of a crooning French love ballad. It went something like this:

> *'Ask me to fight the devil and the dragon,*
> *Ask me to bring down the mountain,*
> *Ask me to dive into a volcano,*
> *Anything is possible for me.*
>
> *But in front of a woman's body,*
> *I am but a paper giant.'*

The male singer had a deep luxuriant voice, and a piano played gently in the background.

> *'What can I do to caress her?*
> *What can I do to awaken her?*
> *I am just a piece of dust which she crushes beneath her feet.*
> *Despite my heart of steel,*
> *In front of her,* je suis un géant de papier.'

Rather nervously we pushed open the door to be greeted by René, the proprietor of our holiday house. He was also, we later learnt, the proud father of Manu, whose recording of 'Géant de Papier' was playing from the CD. René wore a pair of flip-flops and Bermuda shorts and whistled to himself as he meticulously completed each of his daily tasks – pruning the trees, watering the lawn, which he'd planted specially to please his English guests, and seemingly perpetually cleaning the flagstones around the swimming pool. His skin was a leathery brown and, contrasting with his otherwise dark colouring, the hairs on his chest had begun to turn snowy white. At the bottom of the immaculately kept garden a small slice of sea was visible underneath the arching branches of a palm tree. On the hilltop to our right was an old watchtower, crumbling and decrepit but with its sea-facing wall still standing, ready to repel invaders.

René's squat villa nestled beneath the hilltop hamlet of Farinole. From our distant perspective, Farinole's rows of small rectangular buildings with their symmetrical dark, square windows looked like toy houses perched precariously on the cliff. They were periodically covered in swathes of cloud as the *nebbio*, or mist, swirled lower into the valley. Interspersed across the hillside were fields of vines. In France, we'd become accustomed to seeing whole landscapes filled with vineyards, but, in Corsica, viticulture appeared a much more piecemeal affair. Farmable land had to be reclaimed from the *maquis*, a dense hillside bramble. Although it smelt of a heavenly concoction of herbs – thyme, marjoram, basil, fennel and rosemary – it was also full of thorns, spikes and prickly fruits, the perfect habitat for the thick-skinned wild boar.

Before we left to visit our first vineyard, René clasped me by the hand. 'Remember, say that you are friends of René,' he urged, 'then you'll be treated properly.' And so everywhere we went our watchwords became 'de la part de René de Farinole'. People began to hoot their horns as they passed us in the street, and after just a few days we felt part of the small community. Meeting Mark Giovannetti at Domaine Pastricciola was typical of the reception we received. Mark was a small man, barely five feet three inches, with a round cherubic face covered in wrinkles and laughter lines. The moment he greeted us he gave the broadest smile, which became even wider when we told him we knew René.

'René and I used to go to school together. I still don't quite know how he managed to marry Louisa. Such a pretty girl. I've told her that when René dies, we'll marry.' He poured us some of the local Muscat. 'It'll be an expensive business, though – have you seen her jewellery?' He reminded me of an old comedian who'd been on the circuit for years and was confident in his charm. His humour was gentle, instinctive and self-deprecating.

Tanya tasted the Muscat. 'Apples and maybe aniseed,' she said. 'Am I right?'

'Nearly,' replied Mark, 'you missed the sunrays, we added them at the last minute.'

Just a couple of hours later we were wandering through the streets of Saint Florent when we came across Mark again, sitting on a stool outside the hairdresser's. 'It's my harvest haircut,' he shouted across the road. Mark was nearly bald, and he must have seen our somewhat bemused faces. 'You'd be amazed – just snipping a few hairs off makes you sweat a lot less.' We bought an ice cream from the *gelateria* – Corsica is closer to Italy than France and many of the businesses have adopted Italian names – and talked with Mark as he waited.

Rather than wine, he wanted to discuss women. He knew a pretty girl in each of the wine-growing areas we'd visited. 'None of them want to marry me, though,' he sighed dramatically. 'Still, there's always Louisa.' As Mark was called into the barber's chair, he turned to Tanya. 'Give me a day and the phone numbers of a couple of your girlfriends and I'll arrange a tasting with the President of the appellation. He knows all the rosés on the island.'

Although Tanya was more than willing to sacrifice the requisite phone numbers, for a while we didn't see any more of Mark. Reassured from our time in Montpellier that we had at least one rosé which could compete with Madame Etienne's, we spent most of our first week simply enjoying the island.

Corsica was more beautiful than I remembered. I'd visualised sandy beaches framed by hills, but, even close to the coast, the hills were jagged mountains as high as the Alps and the beaches too varied for the memory. Wide half-moon bays of white sand fringed by pines, deserted turquoise coves guarded by old watchtowers and hidden lagoons accessible only by René's boat, and whereas the south of France overflowed with people, Corsica remained calm. In restaurants we listened as guitarists practised ballads in their native tongue, not to earn money from tourists but to prevent the language fading from memory.

And each day we swam, seemingly in slow motion, buoyed by the salt-rich sea. Behind one beach, Plage du Loto, René showed us the land that his father used to plough with oxen. When the food ran out, René's father would light a fire to signal to René's mother on the other side of the bay. The crossing took her all day on a canoe, but it was the only farmable land available. 'Now the beach is one of the most famous in Corsica,' commented René, 'but it wasn't always that way. You must remember how poor this island was.'

It was difficult to forget. Everywhere we went there were reminders of Corsica's turbulent history. The Corsican flag – a black silhouette of a proud face wearing the bandanna of a freedom fighter – fluttered from all the coastal watchtowers. Over the years the island had been occupied by the Genoese, the English and for the last 200 years the French. The late 1960s saw an upsurge in Corsican nationalism, when the only work people such as René's father could find was in the asbestos mines of Nonsa. At the same time, to the anger of the islanders, French immigrants from the collapsing Algerian empire were granted land on the east coast and loans to fund development.

But recent prosperity and a more sympathetic French government had quelled much of the nationalist anger. As one shop owner told us, 'Most Corsicans can't even be bothered to find out what's happening on the other side of the road, let alone join the nationalist party.' With the influx of French money as few as two per cent of Corsicans still wanted independence. And the graffiti painted on the road surface overnight denounced drug gangs, which used the island as a staging point for trafficking to the mainland, rather than the French.

Back on the mainland we'd found it interesting that people still described the island as savage. Why would they choose to emphasise the turbulent past rather than the obvious beauty of Corsica? But after a little time on the island we realised the landscape and the people were intrinsically linked. Nature still ruled much of inland Corsica. Mountain roads were swept into crevices by flash floods, uninhabited deserts blocked the access to some of Europe's most picturesque beaches, and inland the old capital of Corte, ringed by a high mountain range, crumbled away, completely forgotten by most visitors.

Except, that is, Peter, for whom the area around Corte seemed to exert a strange pull. For a couple of days Peter abandoned all thoughts of pale rosé and persuaded us to travel inland. By now I was accustomed to his habit of exploring each village he came across, but as we drove through the hills of Corsica, Peter began to insist on stopping at every ramshackle collection of houses. It would be grandiose to describe these places as hamlets. The buildings were constructed from irregular-shaped stones, and dogs and cats were content to put aside animosity and lie side by side in the shade of their crumbling walls. There were stray pigs, the odd noisy cockerel and cars with bricks for tyres. All that was needed to complete the picture of desolation was some balls of tumbleweed chasing down the road.

But Peter wasn't to be deterred. While Tanya and I looked on, he meandered among the ruins, occasionally knocking on the door of a dilapidated building. On average one in ten was answered, and the occupant sheltered in Peter's shadow for a couple of minutes before shaking his or her head.

Then, just as I was on the point of demanding an explanation for his strange behaviour, Peter returned from one of his solo house visits with a triumphant smile on his face. Clasped in his hand was a small pot. Around the lid was an orange plastic seal, and inside I could make out a thin layer of yellow, presumably fat, and then a dark coarse material underneath.

'What is that?' Tanya and I asked in unison.

'You don't want to know,' said Peter, still unable to take the massive grin from his face.

'Oh, we do,' I said, removing the keys from the ignition and turning towards him.

'Well,' said Peter, quickly settling into his story, 'years ago a friend returned from holiday in Lapland with a small present for me – some reindeer pâté. Ever since we've been exchanging exotic terrines – wild boar, pigeon, squirrel, pheasant, quail, bear. It's like Top Trumps – guinea pig beats goat – you get the idea. And now,' said Peter, putting the pot in the glove compartment and still beaming like a schoolboy who'd made a clean sweep at sports day, 'I've found the ultimate – blackbird. Isn't it marvellous?'

There was still no news from Mark Giovannetti about our prospective meeting with the President of the appellation, and so, ensuring that Peter kept the blackbird pâté stored deep in the boot, we indulged our curiosity about the island's history.

Just up the road from the villa was another vigneron recommended by René – Jean Marie Paoli. As well as hunting for rosé, we were curious about the vigneron's surname. In the eighteenth century Pascal Paoli was a kind of Corsican super-hero. His nickname was 'the General' and he was credited with ridding Corsica of its damaging vendettas, establishing an enlightened system of government and, just for good measure, inflicting one of Napoleon's rare military defeats.

So we headed up a bumpy dirt track, hoping to meet one of Pascal Paoli's descendants. In the middle of a field full of vines was a small log cabin with a raised terrace and sliding glass doors. Resting on a chair facing out to sea was an old man with a baseball cap pulled down over his eyes. His white hair sprouted out from the cap around the ears, and he wore an unbuttoned faded checked shirt over a white vest. Inside the cabin a large upturned oak barrel had been converted into a table, and a set of iron stairs wound towards a mezzanine level just below the ceiling.

Rocking gently in his chair and with the sea breeze playing in his hair, Jean Marie Paoli looked almost too comfortable to disturb, but when we asked about the provenance of his name, one eye blinked open. Pulling himself slowly from his seat, he ducked inside and returned with a dusty book on Corsican history. Seconds later his wife shuffled out carrying a bottle of golden Muscat. The wine was delicious, coating the back of our throats with a wonderful rich sweetness as we flicked through the history book and listened to the story of Pascal Paoli.

In the mid-eighteenth century Corsica was a battleground. The Genoese had exploited the island for over four centuries and encouraged blood-soaked vendettas between the various clans. But then, at the age of twenty-nine, Pascal Paoli was elected by the Corsican nationalists to be their leader. Within years he had managed to drive the Genoese occupiers to the coastal towns and had developed the interior of the island.

'Do you know,' asked Jean Marie proudly, 'that the constitution Paoli established was used as a model by the Americans?'

We shook our heads and let Jean Marie continue.

'By seventeen sixty-eight the Genoese were so annoyed with Paoli and his burgeoning Corsican state that they sold the island. Unfortunately the French buyers proved rather more determined than their Italian predecessors and drove Paoli into exile.'

As Jean Marie talked, I saw that Tanya had her fingers crossed. She was hoping that we'd found one of Pascal's descendants. I hated to tell her, but, to me, an old man wearing a Kangol baseball cap who rocked his days away asleep on a terrace by the sea was hardly likely to be related to a ruler who, in his wilder moments, was reputed to have signed his cousin's death warrant. Only Corsicans could see this as a good way of putting a stop to a vendetta. Jean Marie's story continued, and Tanya shuffled forwards, anxious to ask about the family connection.

In the 1790s, presumably at the same time that Tim Johnston's relative David was stealing a part from the guillotine in Bordeaux, Paoli returned to Corsica. But, having spent his youth training in the French army, Napoleon was also back on the island of his birth, and the two men quickly became enemies. So when Napoleon attempted to seize control of the citadel in Ajaccio, he was chased from the island by the Paolists.

At this point, with France in the grip of revolution, Pascal Paoli must have thought his chance had come to finally establish Corsican independence, but things didn't end happily. Unable to halt the endemic violence and create the Corsican state he dreamt of, he called on the English for support. But rather than appoint Paoli Corsica's viceroy, in 1794 George III was declared King of Corsica, and twelve years later Paoli died in exile in England.

'We've done some research into our family. When Paoli returned to face Napoleon, relatives of mine lived in the same village as him,' said Jean Marie, as he closed the book. Tanya smiled, relieved. At last we were getting on to the part that really interested her. Could Jean Marie be Paoli's great-great-grandson?

'Unfortunately the church records were destroyed in a fire. There could easily have been two or three families of Paolis living in the same village at the same time. It's nice to think we're related, but there's no evidence.' Seeing our Muscat was finished, he poured us some heavy oak-aged red, which he insisted was good for our heart. As we drank he grew concerned that we'd understood him properly. He grasped me by the arm and looked at me with his clear blue eyes. 'I don't want you to leave thinking I might be related to Paoli. Remember I'm not. There's no evidence.'

Tanya sighed with disappointment as we left, and it took us a few minutes to realise we'd forgotten to ask about his rosé. Fortunately we didn't have to wait long for another encounter with the island's past.

We drove back along the road from Farinole towards Saint Florent intending to stop in on Mark. Instead, we noticed Domaine Gentile. Our guidebooks told us that from the thirteenth century two local families had dominated Cap Corse – the da Gentile family in the south near Saint Florent and the da Mare family in the north. In the 1450s the da Gentile family was split by a family feud when the wife of the head of the family began an affair with her husband's cousin. Castles were built and then razed to the ground, towns pillaged, and for 200 years nobody would say sorry.

So as we arrived at the vineyard, Tanya, Peter and I formulated our list of questions: could we taste their rosé? Could they tell us how it was made? What factors determined the final colour of the wine? And, by the way, are you related in any way to the da Gentile family which wreaked havoc across Cap Corse for two centuries?

The rosé was disappointingly dark, but the historic link more than lived up to our expectations. Above the fireplace was a series of black-and-white photos of recent heads of the family. They were shot in portrait style and could easily have been used as promotional material for *The Godfather* – men reclining in chairs smoking pencil-thin cigarettes, with hair greased so tightly to their scalps bullets would skid off the top.

We met Vivienne Gentile and her son, Jean-Paul. To me, they appeared perfectly nice ordinary people, like any number we'd bumped into in the streets of Saint Florent. Vivienne was barely as high as the counter from which she served the rosé. She was chatty and anxious to explain about the latest winemaking techniques. Her son, Jean-Paul, had dark hair, dark eyes and a slightly heavy, lumbering manner. To look at, he wasn't dissimilar to his ancestors, although he probably needed to add a little more grease to his hair for the full bullet-proofing effect. He shifted boxes of wine, took a passing interest in our quest and gave a friendly nod when we mentioned René's name. Although acknowledging the family link with the da Gentiles, both Vivienne and Jean-Paul were unwilling to talk too much about the history of the feuds. So we left with our box of wine.

Only then did I learn that Tanya had apparently been at a completely different wine tasting. 'When Jean-Paul punched out the wine box, it was like he was pummelling somebody's face,' she whispered as we got into the car. 'And look at him now, he's staring at us through the door. Don't you feel that his eyes are looking right through you?' As Tanya crouched down in the seat, trying to avoid eye contact, I resolved not to visit any more vineyards with even the remotest connection to Corsican history. The tales of the past were clearly going to Tanya's head.

'Quick, let's get out of here before he writes down the number plate,' she urged, conveniently forgetting that the Gentiles knew we were staying with René.

17

Tipicité fatigue

News from Mark Giovannetti, not a crack squad of Gentile-family heavies, awaited us back at the villa. He'd arranged the promised tasting with the President of the appellation of Patrimonio, Jean-Laurent Bernardi. We should all have been really excited, particularly because we'd probably be offered a full tour of the vineyard, but we were showing signs of *tipicité* fatigue.

We'd spent nearly our entire time in the last months chatting about the difference between *macération* and *saignée*, debating the relative merits of machine versus hand harvesting and discussing the effects of soil type and grape variety on a wine's colour. It had taken us over one hundred visits to vineyards to piece together in our heads exactly how a rosé was made, but we'd done it, and inadvertently we'd created a problem.

Every vigneron we visited still insisted on explaining the whole process to us. When they talked about planting Grenache in a sandy soil and harvesting late to allow more time for the flavours of the soil to develop in the grape, the symptoms of *tipicité* fatigue began to manifest. Our eyes glazed over, our heads nodded in unison and, to be polite, we asked a series of questions we already knew the answers to. So, where possible, rather than spend hours discussing technicalities, we'd learnt to dash in and quickly ascertain the colour of a rosé. Short visits, preferably with a historical connection, were what we enjoyed most, and measured against these criteria the impending tasting didn't appear promising.

But one of the joys of our quest was that *tipicité* fatigue never lasted long. Whenever we were complacent enough to think we knew everything worth knowing about rosé, we were quickly proved wrong.

In our first week on the island we'd got to know Patrimonio well. It was about five kilometres from the coast, and there were no hotels or guesthouses. The liveliest it became was at four o'clock every morning when teenagers used the pavements as impromptu chicanes when snaking their way home from Bastia's discos. The story of a roadside fence in the hills above the village seemed typical of the place.

Years ago a shepherd complained that a landowner, in contravention of local law, had built his fence too close to the road. After a suitably Corsican amount of time had elapsed – say two or three years – an official from Ajaccio was dispatched to examine the offending fence. There was some head scratching and pacing out of distances (the official left his tape measure in Ajaccio) before it was confirmed that the fence was indeed too close to the road.

But then, after thanking the landowner for a glass of Muscat, the official took another look and noted that the bend in the road was so severe that a brick wall was required. While the road traffic department raised the necessary funds the official declared that the illegal fence could remain. The money was never raised, and the fence still stands.

Like the fence, little else in Patrimonio seemed to have changed for years. Architecturally the village was dominated by the fifteenth-century church of Saint Martin, which stood isolated on a rocky outcrop. A single dirt track wound towards it, past outlying houses and then through trees and rocks towards the bell tower. The binding between the bricks had eroded away, and the nave was supported by a set of flying buttresses that looked like they might collapse inwards. But standing on the steps of the church and risking being hit by crumbling masonry was the best way to appreciate Patrimonio's unique positioning. The village was raised on a natural pedestal in the middle of a crater formed by the slopes of a circle of mountains. Vines fell steeply away on all sides before rising towards the mountains at the far side of the valley. Through a narrow gap in the cliffs, towards the port of Saint Florent, a crescent of sea was visible.

And halfway up the narrow road that rose through Patrimonio, past the eleventh-century chapel at the base of the village but not quite as high as the church of Saint Martin, was the home of the President of the appellation, Jean-Laurent Bernardi. The house was opposite a small supermarket that had bins full of French bread arranged in the street outside. Slightly further up the hill was the town's bar, where earlier in the week we'd enjoyed a *maquis* liqueur.

Underneath an old plane tree, facing the entrance to the President's cave, was a thin gaunt man sitting on a low wall with his face hidden in the shade. I could make out an uneven stubble flecked with grey hair and a pair of dark sunken eyes. The man wore loose-fitting work overalls that were stained with mud, and a ragged shirt.

We parked the car and crossed to the cave. Although the door was open, the room was empty. A row of wine bottles was arranged in a line on top of a wooden counter, next to a couple of fluted wine glasses. Cases of wine were stacked to the ceiling in the far corner, and it was just possible that they concealed our missing vigneron. 'We're looking for Jean-Laurent,' I announced in a loud voice. 'We're friends of Mark and René.'

'Well, if you'll come back outside, we can talk in the shade of the tree,' said a voice. The head of the appellation of Patrimonio waved from the low wall behind us. 'He doesn't look much like the President,' I whispered to Tanya as we sat on a couple of upturned logs opposite Jean-Laurent.

The house was built on a small plateau about ten feet above the road and from where the President sat he could see every car that passed, wave at people in the queue for their lunchtime baguette and spot men idling away their afternoon in the village bar.

Jean-Laurent gave us a brief history of the wine-growing area. It was thought that the Phoenicians were the first to bring viticulture to Corsica. They named the island Korai, meaning covered in forests. The Romans followed and encouraged the development of the industry, and since the eleventh century there'd been a Christian community in the town. 'Where there are priests, you'll always need wine,' said Jean-Laurent in a voice so quiet we had to strain to hear.

It was lunchtime and, below us in the street, people were making their way home. Every other car seemed to hoot at Jean-Laurent and he waved a familiar hello as he continued his explanation. 'Today, we try and stay faithful to the traditional Corsican methods of producing wine; we use only the strains of grapes which have been native to the island for centuries – Sciaccarello, Niellucio and Vermentino. If a vigneron came to me and asked permission to plant Cabernet Sauvignon, I'd refuse.'

Fierce lines of light pierced the shade of the foliage above, reminding us of the beating heat of the day. A warm wind stirred the branches of the tree, and the noise of the passing traffic seemed to swallow Jean-Laurent's words. He continued talking in his gentle voice, explaining how the upsurge in Corsican nationalism in the latter half of the twentieth century had been intrinsically linked with the wine industry. Algerian independence had deprived France of a major source of cheap wine to mix with its own production to make *vin de table*. Many of the French Algerians had been involved in the wine industry, and the east coast of Corsica was seen as the ideal place to resettle. Massive vineyards were planted and to this day the area produces much of Corsica's cheaper wine. But the immigration and the grant of the land had sparked resentment.

Although Jean-Laurent's manner was unassuming, I could imagine him sitting under the tree, dispensing advice that people feared to gainsay. The leaves would turn golden brown and fall to the ground and each of the region's thirty-two producers would visit and talk through their problems. Then when the snow lay heavy on the high mountain passes, they'd move inside to his warm cave. As spring came and Jean-Laurent resumed his station on the wall, he'd call the vignerons from Farinole, Oletta and Poggio de Oletta and remind them to stay true to the values of the appellation.

After we'd talked for an hour, Mark arrived. He sat next to Jean-Laurent on the wall, with his little legs dangling above the ground. 'I always like to have a beer with the President.' His facial expression remained neutral, but his round cherubic face and shining eyes made us want to smile. 'That way, I can do what I want, when I want.' He paused. 'And if the President doesn't approve, my partner's the Mayor.'

He produced a booklet on Corsican wine that he'd promised us and put his arm around Tanya. 'Have you remembered the phone numbers of your girlfriends?'

So far we'd been spared another discussion about the technicalities of winemaking, but if we handed over the phone numbers, I sensed we'd be rewarded with one. My eyes began to glaze as I waited for someone to mention *macération* or *saignée*.

But, instead, Jean-Laurent began to talk in his gentle voice not about pneumatic presses, de-stalkers or, God forbid, *tipicité* but about the history of a unique rosé festival – the Fête de Saint

Martin. Every year the vignerons strapped a huge barrel of wine between two long poles and hoisted the contraption on to their shoulders. They wound their way through the streets, and the whole town formed a column behind them. When the weight of the barrel became too much for one man another took over. The procession ended at the church of Saint Martin, where a priest swinging incense on the end of a long metal chain led the struggling vignerons and their cask of wine to the altar. After prayers and a reading, the priest reached for his sceptre and pierced the barrel, allowing rosé to gush forth. Each of the town's vignerons contributed a small amount of their newly made rosé to the contents of a barrel, which was used in the Mass to celebrate the harvest. Afterwards the remaining wine was taken to the central square and given away for free, in honour of the generosity of Saint Martin. The Mayor donated a spit-roast calf to the party, and the townspeople contributed home-baked cakes.

Tanya, Peter and I looked at each other. A church service based around rosé and the streets of the village filled with a massive fiesta. It was the first festival to celebrate rosé we'd come across in our time in France. Despite travelling throughout the mainland and asking thousands of questions about wine, nobody had mentioned it to us. Instead, we'd just stumbled upon it. And it was held in the shadow of the mountains, with a view of the vines escaping through the valley to the sea. What was more, we'd been personally invited by the appellation's President, Mark would be there, and René. The only question was, when did it start?

'Not till the eleventh of November,' replied Jean-Laurent.

Mark coughed. 'Now, about those numbers.'

The next day Peter received a call from the mainland. It was the proprietor of Café du Marché in Saint Maximin, whom Peter had befriended during his time in the town. In return for a bottle of rare Scottish whisky he'd agreed to give Peter early warning of the date of the harvest.

According to our source, or Gitanes, as Peter affectionately called him – due to his remarkable propensity to smoke a packet an hour – it was so hot in Saint Maximin that the town's dogs were still panting at midnight. The sugar level in the grapes was rising fast, and if the heatwave continued, picking could start within two weeks.

A return to Provence was overdue, but first we had one more lead to follow up. Our visit to the island had reawakened memories of the time Tanya and I had spent on holiday in Corsica five years ago. Then, near the port of Calvi, we'd enjoyed a week in a hotel overlooking a wide sandy bay. In the corner of the bay, no more than five metres from the sea, was a wind-blasted house that sold one of the best rosés we'd ever tasted. The house was so dilapidated it might have fallen into the sea by now, but we had to return, just in case.

We thought – wrongly, as it turned out – that nothing could be as eventful as when we first made the journey to this bay five years ago. Then, we were strangers to the island and we'd arrived in the middle of a savage storm. People had told us that Corsica was full of bandits and that rather than welcome tourists, the locals periodically blew up their houses. Kidnapping was, apparently, not uncommon. Drenched, lost and nervous, we'd entered a local bar to get directions. Instead of the expected unfriendly welcome, we were invited to supper with the regulars.

After our meal we were offered a lift to our hotel. As we sat in the back of the car, with the wipers thudding heavily against the windscreen, our driver began telling us a story. It concerned the French governor at the time, Prefect Bonnet. Like many Corsican stories, it began with a murder, in this case the assassination of Bonnet's predecessor by terrorists. We drove into the middle of the mountains, miles from the nearest town, and I recall Tanya and I looking nervously at each other – had our local host been just a little too friendly in the bar?

While we fretted about his terrorist connections, our driver continued talking. And since he was going far too quickly for us to consider leaping from the car, we listened. Following the death of the previous Prefect, Bonnet was given the mandate to implement a zero-tolerance campaign on crime and become a kind of Corsican Mayor Giuliani. He started with an assault on illegal beach bars, commandeering a squad of army engineers from the mainland to bulldoze them. 'Or so he wished,' said our driver, winking at us.

Unfortunately for Bonnet, the owner of the first bar to be targeted handcuffed himself together with his wife and children to the nearest wall. The engines of the French army diggers chugged over, waiting for the order to go in. Was Bonnet strong enough to implement the zero-tolerance policy and perhaps kill those inside?

Our local storyteller paused, turned the car engine off and flicked out the headlights. I remember thinking that either we'd arrived at the hotel or we were about to be kidnapped. 'Of course, Bonnet backed down, but that was when things got worse for him.' Raindrops ricocheted off the stationary car, and, try as I might, I couldn't see the lights of the hotel. The story then became even more bizarre.

Our driver told us that two days ago Bonnet had been arrested in connection with an arson attack on another illegal beach bar. It was alleged that he'd ordered the police secret service to burn the place to the ground. While Bonnet admitted that the fire seemed suspicious, he claimed that he'd been set up by nationalists. 'After all, the secret service wouldn't have been clumsy enough to leave police equipment scattered all over the burnt shell of the bar, would they?' said our driver as he made us jump by turning the ignition on on the car. 'If you want, I can drive you to the beach bar later in the week so you can see for yourselves.'

The next morning when we woke, thankfully in our hotel room, the previous night's experience seemed like a strange dream. We opened the bedroom windows to a clear blue sky and hidden among the trees in the corner of the bay was the wind-blasted house we would become so familiar with.

Five years later as we were packing our suitcases, readying ourselves to make the same trip, René came in to warn us. We'd planned to leave at 5 a.m. to allow enough time to get to Calvi, find the rosé and catch an early-evening ferry back to the mainland, but René wanted us to delay our departure.

Rather than terrorists hiding in the hills, the problem was teenage Corsicans fresh from the discos of Bastia and Calvi. The island had some of the worst roads and worst drivers in the world. Even on a sleepy Sunday afternoon, a typical Corsican would prefer to lay down his life than suffer the ignominy of using his brakes. And at night things got much much worse. 'Remember, road safety,' counselled René, 'is not at the forefront of a young partygoer's mind. If I were you I'd take the back roads.'

18

Extremely Pale Rosé

Corsican B-roads are narrow, potholed and littered with skid marks. Cars slingshot out of tight bends, and kissing wing mirrors with passing drivers is so common it's considered a form of friendly greeting. Falling off a precipice on one of these mountain tracks didn't seem a good way to go and so we ignored René and headed for Calvi on the main road. And as we set out on the same route Tanya and I had taken five years ago, in the dark again – the sun wouldn't rise until nearly 7 a.m. – we reminisced about our late-night adventure. This time, Peter argued, we should worry about nocturnal teenage Corsicans, rather than invent fantasies about bandits, but these two groups proved to be the least of our problems.

Just ten minutes from our villa, outside the town of Saint Florent, we encountered a roadblock. To begin with, I thought there'd been an accident. I could see four or five blue sirens revolving in the darkness ahead of us. There were also some smaller white lights, probably torches, that winked on and off. I slowed the car, and we crawled towards the roundabout, crossing an iron bridge and passing the dark shadows of boats in the marina to our right. It was only when the car ahead of us did a quick U-turn, flicked off its lights and sped back into the darkness that I realised we were arriving at a checkpoint.

Our headlights caught the reflective strip sewn into the uniform of one of the police officers and a beam of torchlight swung towards us. I noticed that a long line of cars had been pulled to the kerbside. The drivers were all young men with gelled spiky hair and shirts stained with sweat. In the back seats teenage girls sat nervously talking to each other as they watched their driver blow into a little white bag.

I hoped that the *gendarmes* would be too busy with the disco-going kids to worry about us, but there were police everywhere, and it seemed inevitable that I'd be pulled aside for a breath test. I knew I shouldn't have a problem – my last drink had been at 11 p.m. the previous evening. But, according to French law, even a tiny amount of alcohol in my bloodstream would lead to my licence being ripped up. I could even go to gaol. As the engine of the car idled over and we drove through the line of police at the stately pace of about 2 m.p.h., I couldn't have felt more stupid. Why hadn't we waited another hour before leaving? I knew we had a long day ahead and that we might be pushed for time to catch our ferry back to the mainland, but if I was stopped now, there was a possibility we'd be stranded in Corsica.

Luckily rather than guide us to the kerb, the police torches lit a path to the open road. It appeared that it was too much hassle to stop a car with a foreign number plate. We continued driving into the Désert des Agriates – a vast area of uninhabited land that was protected from development by the government. We'd read that it was home to the island's purest species of wild boar – many of Corsica's boars had inbred with domestic pigs – and that rare birds, such as bee-eaters, shrikes and warblers, nested in the *maquis*.

It should therefore have been the last place to encounter another police roadblock, but after ten minutes passing cars began to repeatedly flash their headlights. At first I presumed our English lights hadn't been dipped properly, but then I noticed several cars full of the now-familiar teenage Corsicans waiting by the side of the road. The occupants were all talking into their mobile phones. Eventually, the lead car pulled off and headed down a dirt track.

Instead of following, we kept going, presuming that once again the police wouldn't be interested in a foreign car. We were wrong. Around the next bend waited the same combination of revolving blue lights and torches dancing in the dark, however, this time the corridor of lights led not to the open road but to a lay-by.

I heard the crunch of the policeman's boots as he approached the car. I wound down my window and waited for the breathalyser. Instead, there was a knock on Tanya's door. She opened the window and was handed a bag to blow into. Right-hand drive cars obviously didn't make it to Corsica that often.

Rather than risk the possibility of Tanya being arrested for drink-driving a car she hadn't been driving, I got out and walked round to the passenger's side. Although I knew I should be fine, my legs were light, as if all the muscles in them had relaxed at the same moment. I rested my hand on the roof and looked at the police officer. The torch was clasped to his chest so that a wide beam of light illuminated both our faces. His hair must have been cropped short because not a lock protruded from underneath his cap. He had a large hooked nose and the seemingly ubiquitous dark Corsican eyes. I searched for an expression on his face as he handed me the bag. There wasn't even a hint of a smile.

As I prepared to blow, conspiracy theories came flooding into my head. Why had we been stopped at this roadblock and not the other one? If the nationalists had sympathisers within the police, who'd allegedly framed Prefect Bonnet, presumably they might also have bribed a few of the *gendarmes* to arrest tourists.

I was hyperventilating as I blew for the first time and so the bag only half-filled with air. The *gendarme* handed it back to me, and I noticed that a small smile twitched across his face. He was enjoying my discomfort. 'You must blow harder for us to get a result.'

I inflated the bag, and we both waited, with the torchlight illuminating our very different faces. My eyes flitted everywhere – to Tanya drumming her fingers on the dashboard, to Peter flicking quickly through the pages of the map, to the impassive *gendarme* and to the first rays of morning light creeping over the desert hills.

A minute passed and then the French policeman grinned. Was he celebrating catching an Englishman?

'*C'est parfait,*' he said as he waved the torch and ushered us back on to the road. I was clean.

We thought the rest of the trip would be easy. We were wrong. We took a left rather than a right and ended up on a mountain pass. By now I was a little fraught and driving too quickly, unaware that where the dirt track ended a 500-feet drop began. On the inside of each bend metal wiring was mounted on the cliff to prevent landslides, and on the outside the only thing protecting us from plunging into the valley below was a low crumbling wall. To make matters worse, as we approached each turn the road concertinaed into a single lane.

But with each passing minute more light entered the morning sky, and I began to feel a mixture of relief and exhilaration from my close call with the *gendarme*. Thankfully I would never see the inside of a Corsican gaol. The roads were empty, and I enjoyed the feeling of letting the car drift wide on to the apex of the bend before accelerating and cutting across the inside of the turn, sending the loose gravel flying into the air behind us.

I'd got into a nice rhythm until rounding yet another bend, I fought to keep the car straight. Tanya grabbed my arm, jabbing her nails into my flesh, and shouted, 'Cow!' I thought this was just a polite expletive and that yet another staggeringly dangerous turn awaited us. Wincing from the pain, I momentarily closed my eyes. When I blinked them open, I had to make an immediate choice between ditching the car off the cliff or ploughing into the two mountain cows walking casually down the middle of the road.

In the end I nearly managed both, clipping the swaying stomach of a cow with my wing mirror and dangling half the car over the edge of the mountain. When I'd extricated my head from the steering wheel and ascertained that we were all still alive, I opened the driver's door. There was nothing but air beneath my feet. Tanya was too scared to say anything, and I sat frozen, worried that any sudden movement might tip us over the edge. Then the cows came to investigate.

'This is far from marvellous,' said Peter.

When the wheels of your car are straddling a canyon, the last thing you want is some friendly animals poking their muzzles against the window. The car began to rock as the cows butted their heads against it, no doubt looking for food. Tanya still hadn't spoken. Rather than bandits, terrorists or the Gentiles, it appeared that something as prosaic as a farmyard animal was going to bring our quest to an end.

I took the only option available, put the car into reverse, pressed on the accelerator and hoped that the majority of the heavy luggage was on Tanya's side of the car.

All that remains of our adventure now is a set of black skid marks on the road. They get darker and darker as they head towards the cliff edge, and right where they end there are some scattered hoof marks.

Half a mile later – fortunately on what appeared to be the only straight stretch of road in the mountains – we met the rest of the herd and the shepherd. He was a young boy, maybe fourteen or fifteen. Little tufts of hair sprouted from either cheek, and a soft moustache was growing on his upper lip. He wore jeans and a thick woollen jumper covered with holes. Behind him were maybe twenty cows blocking the road. We wound down the window and asked him for directions to Calvi, but he shook his head.

'You are truly lost.'

'So are some of your herd,' called Peter, pointing back down the road to where two cows were ambling into view.

The house on the beach just outside Calvi was exactly as I'd remembered it. Four small yachts sat at anchor in a wide bay, their masts clinking gently in the wind. Umbrella pines and eucalyptus trees grew on the fringes of the sea, and in their midst we could make out our wind-blasted house. It was surrounded by a few large boulders, a discarded surfboard and tufts of thigh-high grass. Hanging over the side of the terrace were four terracotta pots holding rows of thirsty-looking geraniums. A white parasol stood redundant and faded in the sun, and the house rose three floors above it, with three sets of red shutters on each floor. The whole building was made of crumbling concrete, sand-smattered and streaked orange and red, collapsing inwards around each window. If a Surrey housewife had the misfortune to rent such a house, it would probably give her apoplexy, but it was so ugly and so run-down that I couldn't help but love it.

Rather than head to the cave underneath the house, we had lunch in a little restaurant overlooking the bay. It remains my favourite place to eat in the world – surrounded by palm trees, with the yachts bobbing gently in the sea and with the faded glory of the wind-blasted house nestling in the corner of the bay. In the distance, on the tip of the headland, the huge medieval citadel of Calvi stood sentinel with a tricolore just visible fluttering from the highest turret.

Every evening five years ago Tanya and I had sat in this bar watching as the sun turned a gentle orange and then a fierce red. Then we'd been planning our wedding and I remembered the final remnants of light clinging to the slim silhouettes of the yacht masts and in the last seconds the red of the sun becoming so intense that the waves could have been breaking on to a Martian beach.

After a long lazy lunch we stumbled along the beach towards the house. The paint was flaking from the upper storeys of the building, and the single faded white parasol was still tied back, with the cloth flapping noisily in the sea breeze. The pillars which raised the structure up from the beach looked on the point of collapse, but we ducked our heads and followed the arrow leading to the hollowed-out cavern underneath.

We were keen to get inside and taste the rosé. Tanya clutched my hand, and we pushed the door. It was locked tight. We knocked and waited, with only the sound of our quick anxious breathing for company. Still nothing. We retreated back into the sunlight and looked up at the empty terrace. Only then did I notice a small sign hanging from a piece of wire above the entrance to the cave: 'Closed until 4.30.'

Waiting an extra hour for the cave to open wasn't really much of an inconvenience. Our ferry didn't leave till eight and so we had time. The beach was deserted apart from an old woman doing yoga on a rocky island some fifteen metres out to sea. There was even a small rock pool about the size of a home Jacuzzi into which the sea water rushed and retreated with a soothing regularity. We spread out our towels on the empty beach and dozed in the hot afternoon sun.

But over an hour later the door was still shut and I began to get worried – the day before, the port of Calvi had been hit by strikes, and if we missed our crossing, getting another booking would be difficult. We could end up stuck in Corsica for weeks, with the harvest getting ever closer, and the whole of Provence still to search.

At 6 p.m. there were signs of movement. A small girl and a boy emerged from the house and began kicking a ball around. Tanya approached and asked if they could open up.

'You'll have to wait for our parents,' said the boy.

'And where are they?'

'Asleep,' the girl replied and returned to kicking the ball.

By 7 p.m. their parents had still not appeared. We both knew that to catch our ferry we had to leave immediately, but we'd braved bandits, police roadblocks and stray cows to taste this wine. Surely the children could be persuaded to let us buy a bottle. I hoped the universal language of football might help and spent the next ten minutes kicking the ball around. Despite outnumbering them and managing to lose 1–0, we were told we still had to wait for the sleepy parents. It was 7.15 and we had to make a decision.

In the distance out at sea, almost camouflaged by the backdrop of high mountains, I could see our ferry turning towards land. Thankfully it was late, and it looked like we'd have time to make it through the congested streets to the dock.

'Wait here, and see if you can get them to open up. I'll go and fetch the car,' I said, as I turned to run back towards the restaurant.

I collected the car and turned down the track which led from the road to the house. It was rough and potholed and completely unsuitable for anything other than a 4×4. Halfway down the drive I winced at a loud bang as the rear tyre crunched into a particularly enormous rut and then jarred out of the hole. It sounded like it could only be one thing – a flat. Across the bay our ferry had now docked, and cars were rolling off the ramp. I examined the first three tyres. They were fine, but although the fourth looked okay, a pool of liquid was quickly forming around it. Had I ruptured the petrol tank? I flipped the boot to get the owner's manual and found broken glass everywhere. Our final bottle of champagne had just exploded, but at least we still had a chance of making the ferry.

Glancing up, I saw Tanya and Peter running towards me. Tanya had a bottle of wine clutched to her chest.

'Look at this, just look at this. It's even paler than we remembered.'

She jumped into my arms and clasped me in a bear hug so tight it imprinted a mould of the bottle into my back. When she'd calmed down enough to stand still, I took the wine from her and held it up to the last of the day's light. She was right. It was far paler than anything we'd encountered on the mainland and could easily have been confused with a white. Looking through the liquid, the whole landscape assumed a gentle yellow tint – the palm trees, the swollen grapes on the vines and the cars now rolling on to our ferry.

'Come on, let's see if we can make it,' I said.

Peter, however, was oblivious to the impending departure of our ferry. He was doing a little jig of delight on the beach, leaping in the air and kicking his heels together in a manner that entirely belied his age.

I started the engine to encourage him to get into the car, but the jig of delight continued so I moved off slowly. Trying to plot an explosion-free path through the potholes while looking in my rear-view mirror to see if Peter was following wasn't easy, but as it turned out, it was the least of my problems.

Before I'd gone five metres a police car turned on to the bottom of the drive. It drove slowly towards us, stirring dust into the air. We sat, stared and waited. When the car was twenty metres away, I recognised him. The same *gendarme*, with the same hooked nose, who'd given me the breath test in the middle of the Agriates Desert. I couldn't believe they were still patrolling. Didn't Corsican policemen ever rest?

The car pulled up beside us, and I could see piles of breathalyser bags and fresh plastic tubes to blow into on the back seat. It was over four hours since our long lunch when, in the excitement of returning to one of our favourite places, I'd had a little more to drink than usual. If the French drink-driving limit was as draconian as I understood, then I was in real trouble. The officer got out of the car and gave the same twitchy smile that had terrified me in the early hours of the morning. He looked delighted to have finally caught his prey.

SEPTEMBER

'Remember, English, don't jump in the swimming pool or you'll turn it pink,' cried Dominic from the back of the tractor.

19

Beckham's Rosé

It was the beginning of September and Provence had gone mad. A wild boar was discovered lost on the beach near Nice. It trotted through the surf, charged aggressively at a couple of holidaymakers and then disappeared into the hills. The next day a mini tornado struck the coast, ripping roofs from houses and capsizing boats.

Peter also appeared to have gone slightly mad. Left alone for an hour in Marseille, we discovered him in a port-side bar wearing an enormous pair of new sunglasses and a panama hat. Fine for watching a cricket match in England on a lazy Sunday afternoon, but a bit out of place in the south of France. 'They are very this season,' he said proudly, before continuing his conversation with an English tourist he'd accosted.

'So, after spending a night busting people for drink-driving, what does the typical Corsican *gendarme* do?' continued Peter, obviously enjoying describing our narrow escape. 'Well, he goes on a tour of the local vineyards.' He paused, only too conscious that the audience for his story was gradually growing. 'For a second it looked like the end of our quest. The raised boot of the car obscured the *gendarme*'s face, and we stood and waited, expecting another breath test, and then the most extraordinary thing happened, the *gendarme* handed us a bottle of wine. He'd just been to a tasting and had bought twelve bottles. Perhaps it was his way of apologising for stopping us in the early hours of that morning. In any event . . .'

But there the story tailed off. Peter stood motionless staring across the square at the car park. Finally he blurted out one word, 'Betty.'

As I scanned the rows of vehicles looking for his car, I couldn't think what all the fuss was about. Apart from nearly driving off a Corsican cliff and plunging into the odd pothole, we'd looked after Peter's car really well. We'd even recently put it through a car wash so it was all shiny for the upcoming harvest. It was parked legally, in the far corner of the car park next to some newly erected scaffolding.

As Peter left his drink and broke into a run, I realised what the problem was. A truck with a small crane on the back was trying to deliver a skip to the building site next to where we'd parked. It couldn't squeeze through the narrow lanes, so instead the driver was trying to winch his cargo into position. The skip was now swaying from two metal chains above Betty's roof. A crowd of over a dozen labourers had gathered around to watch the operation, which seemed to have come to a halt because the arm of the crane wasn't long enough.

The distance between the sprinting Peter and his car narrowed, but then the labourers hit upon another idea. They would pick Betty up and move her. So they formed a circle around the car and squatted down on their haunches. For a moment they resembled a troupe of Russian dancers, rather than Provençal workmen. And, as if we hadn't had enough trouble with the police, as I got closer I noticed that their every move was being supervised by the local *gendarmerie*. As the officer in charge raised his hand, they all gripped the undercarriage and began to lift.

The car inched gradually off the ground. Then, to the relief of the labourers, Peter arrived. There was no fuss, no cursing of the

English, not even a reprimand from the police officer. Cigarettes were lit, and the workmen splintered away into smaller chattering groups. The *gendarme* even had the courtesy to admit that the car was parked legally. 'We just needed to move it to deliver the skip,' he said as if it was the most natural thing in the world.

Peter drove away shaking his head. 'Maybe there was something in that rumour about the Etiennes and the local police.'

That afternoon we tried to book a hotel in picturesque Cassis and Peter insisted on using his sorbet test. According to Peter, if you want a hotel that serves decent food, then you should always ask whether the chef makes his own sorbet. 'Sorbet,' continued Peter, 'is easy to buy in, but a good chef will always make his own.' In principle this was fine, but the south of France in August was hardly a place to be picky.

There wasn't a hotel in Cassis with two rooms and a sorbet-making chef. In fact, there weren't any hotels with rooms. Finally we found a small local guesthouse in Les Lecques, a couple of kilometres from the vineyards of Bandol. 'The owner's the chef and he serves the most fantastic bouillabaisse,' said Peter. And as we unloaded our bags, I prayed that Tanya would have the sense not to mention sorbet.

It was the first time we'd stayed on the Provençal coast at this time of year. An hour east of Marseille, Les Lecques was supposed to be a small, unpretentious seaside resort, free from the overstated glamour of the Côte d'Azur. It was built on one of the few naturally sandy beaches in Provence. Pine- and villa-filled hills overlooked the bay, and in the far corner was a small port, where fortunately there wasn't a gin palace in sight.

But, like the rest of the French coast, it was absolutely packed. The narrow high street was clogged with traffic, and on the beach you needed a degree in spatial dynamics to find somewhere to put your towel. The sea was little better than the land – the shallows were filled with people playing bat and ball and teenagers flinging themselves at footballs practising scissor kicks. If we wanted to swim we had to zigzag through canoodling couples demonstrating an array of Kama Sutra positions in the buoyant sea water.

It made me worry about what awaited us on the more popular stretch of coast to the east. Letting Tanya loose in Les Lecques, let alone Saint Tropez, was potentially ruinous. The high street was lined with boutiques, and long-limbed female shop assistants lounged on the pavement. Just walking past them could generate more insecurities than a lifetime of reading *Marie Claire*. By the end of the week Tanya was on first-name terms with most of them, and barely a day passed without her being lured inside.

But whereas Tanya was mostly too sensible to purchase, the French holidaymakers showed no such discretion. My favourite shopaholic was the middle-aged woman with two pet poodles who walked past our hotel every morning treating us to her latest fashion faux pas. The wide-rimmed sunglasses and designer blouses were garish, yet acceptable, particularly in the south of France, but a pair of red leather trousers with 'Glamour' printed in bold gold lettering over her copious bottom was enough to make me choke on my croissant. 'Wait till we get further up the coast,' said Tanya with a delighted smile.

Peter was in his element. We'd lose him for hours on end as he wandered off to check out the restaurants and bars. Inevitably he ended up in the Epicerie du Port, a small delicatessen and off-licence which was the centre of all the local gossip. Dried bushels of bay leaves and bunches of lavender hung from the ceiling, and behind the deli counter Michelle Stenta served rice wrapped in vine leaves, goat cheeses on the verge of combustion, marinated peppers and cuts of cured ham. A daily delivery of fresh peaches, pears, apples, strawberries and raspberries arrived in wooden boxes, which were stacked outside. There were trays of *girolles*, baskets of croissants, sacks full of bread and queues full of locals for Peter to accost and talk to about pale rosé. And whereas most shops in France only sell local wine, the *épicerie* had a selection from across France – Pouilly Fumé and Fuissé, Banyuls, Beaune and of course Bandol.

Early on our first evening in Les Lecques Tanya and I were worried we'd lost Peter. He'd disappeared after lunch, ostensibly to find a locksmith to open his new suitcase for which he'd mislaid the key. We expected him to have a few cheeky pastis to help him on his way, but three hours later when he still hadn't returned we became concerned. Thankfully the town emptied and most of the boutiques had shut, so after asking unsuccessfully after Peter in the *épicerie*, we wandered along the seafront looking for him, as small waves broke lazily on to the sand.

We found him at the far end of the bay giving a long-jump lesson to a couple of five-year-old boys. He was trying to explain, through a mixture of halting French and graphic gestures, that their run-ups were too long. Oblivious to the instructions of the strange Englishman, the boys were tearing across the sand and exhausting themselves before they reached the point from which they had to jump.

'Tanya, can you tell them,' said Peter as we tried to drag him away to supper, 'that they'd be much better using a shorter run? That way, they'd hit the mark at full pace.'

'Why not demonstrate?' I asked.

Peter ignored me and turned back to the children. He sat on the beach and drew a miniature long-jump pit in the sand, simulating a running motion with his fingers. In his youth he was a very able sportsman, playing rugby and cricket for his county. Years ago when his daughter was ten, he ran all the way around the inside of the school athletics track, acting as a pacemaker for her attempt on the junior 400-metres record. And in situations like this his urge to pass on advice even outstripped his desire to sit down to supper.

But oblivious to his promptings, the two French boys once more careered off across the sand. How were they to know that they were being coached by the joint holder of the Kent girls' 400-metres record?

'Just visualise twelve Provençal workmen trying to pick up your car on the far side of the long-jump pit,' I added unhelpfully, 'then you can show them how it's supposed to be done.'

We'd noticed that experts tended to turn their noses up at Provençal wine, but if there was one appellation they were serious about, it was Bandol, just inland from Les Lecques. Clive Coates, author of *An Encyclopedia of the Wines and Domaines of France*, had recently visited one of its most prominent vineyards, Domaine Tempier, and when Catherine Peyraud, of the Tempier family, told us that Coates had tasted over fifty vintages from 1950 to 2001, we felt a lot better about ourselves. In this context our summer of decadent drinking appeared like little more than the odd lunchtime spritzer. We felt even better when Catherine insisted that drinking was 'like reading different books, if you do it a lot, it expands your mind'.

On our trip we'd discovered that every French appellation had to have a bizarre rule – insisting that all grapes were hand-picked, limiting the yield of the vines to an arbitrary number of hectolitres or only pruning in a certain way. Bandol had excelled itself with so many regulations it was rumoured that even the mighty Bordeaux was considering copying it. My favourite was that only vines growing over seven metres above the River Sale, which ran through the middle of the valley, could be classified as Appellation Bandol Contrôlée. Everything else was mere *vin de pays* and retailed for €3 or €4 less a bottle, but, as a barman in Les Lecques told us, 'It's all exactly the same stuff.'

We'd come to Bandol for its rosé – the area produced some of France's finest, made from a mixture of Mourvèdre, Grenache and Cinsault. It was universally exceptionally pale, and the colour was considered so important that one female vigneron, mistaking us for experts, even asked our opinion. She leant dramatically across the table and gripped my hand. 'Do you think it would help sales if I made it paler?' she asked earnestly.

Each vineyard was racing against the weather to be ready for the harvest. Day after day dawned with a clear blue sky, and by noon the sand on the beach was too hot to walk on. Not that the vignerons cared – typical of their new industriousness was Domaine les Luquettes, where we were greeted by a stainless-steel *cuve* that appeared to be singing. The words '*Je ne voudrais plus travailler*' rang out metallically round the small courtyard, but there was no vigneron in sight. On closer inspection we found a pair of wellington boots and Elisabeth Lafourcade's upended bottom poking from the end of the barrel. She was scrubbing the *cuves* in preparation for this year's wine, and she just about had time to slosh some rosé into glasses for us before dashing away to pick the children up from school.

Finally, one morning, as we rounded the bend out of Les Lecques and headed for the vineyards, Tanya cried out, 'Look, it's begun.' Cars were parked on the verges of all the fields, and people in their scruffiest clothing were making their way through rows of vines. Some had little stools, others just knelt, shifting from one knee to the other. They all carried secateurs and buckets and kept close to the small tractors of the vignerons, which were piled high with freshly harvested grapes.

Throughout our trip we'd idled along behind these chugging blue machines, but come the harvest, they discovered a new gear. The flashing orange lights at the back were illuminated, and old men hunched over the wheels and wrenched at the gearstick. At best they managed to coax an extra couple of kilometres an hour out of the engines, but to us, accustomed to the crawling pace of the rest of the year, the vignerons appeared to whip through the narrow lanes carrying their precious cargo of grapes back to the cave for pressing.

Inevitably there were accidents. Outside the town of Le Castellet, just inland from the port of Bandol, we passed a vigneron sitting by the kerbside with his head in his hands. The rear wheel of his trailer had caught the edge of a ditch, pitching on to its side. All the vigneron could do was wait for the inevitable, as the pressure of the grapes piling on top of each other forced the juice out. Soon there was a purple-red stream running down the side of the road. A year's work had just disappeared in a moment, and making matters worse the co-operative was only a couple of hundred metres up the road.

With the harvest underway, we spent most of the rest of the day anxiously glancing at our mobile phone. Had the *vendange* started at Château Etienne? How much longer did we have? Peter's source, Gitanes, was mysteriously absent from the Bar du Marché and so, with no news, or credible intelligence – as Peter liked to call it – we continued with the hunt.

'If you wait in the courtyard, then Régine will be with you in a minute.'

The courtyard we were shown into would have been a perfect setting for a Bacchanalian orgy. Grapes dripped from the overhead wooden trellis, a fountain bubbled into a pond full of lily pads, and through the open door of the cave we could see barrels and barrels of wine. All we needed was a toga each, some sunloungers to recline on and perhaps the odd whole roasted wild boar.

We were at Domaine Ott, the vineyard credited with reviving the fortunes of Provençal wine. Throughout France people had reverentially whispered its name to us. If there was a tourist itinerary for rosé wine, then Domaine Ott was apparently the Eiffel Tower of the whole trip. For months I'd just nodded along when people had mentioned the vineyard's name. It had seemed too much of an expression of ignorance to ask them to write it down or to ask for directions. So, on our arrival in Provence, I'd scoured my wine books looking for a Domaine Haute or a Domaine Hote. Nothing. Then one day, driving through the vines outside Le Castellet, I'd seen a roadside sign and looked up at an imposing red-brick villa. At that moment the pronunciation and spelling had clicked in my head – Domaine Ott.

It's difficult to find any top chef to rave about rosé, but not apparently Domaine Ott's Coeur de Grain. In the marketing literature we were handed to read while we waited, the restaurateurs of France formed an almost embarrassing queue to be nice about the wine. 'I've always had a fondness for Domaine Ott wines, particularly the rosés, which rank among the most distinguished rosés in the world,' says Jean-Pierre Legoff of Lasserre restaurant in Paris. 'The distinguished rosé Coeur de Grain Bandol ranks among the great Bandol wines,' adds Pierre Laroche of Le Divellec in Paris, and André Toscano of La Palme d'Or in Cannes gushed that the 'Ott family are and will remain the prime movers who've restored Provence to its former greatness'.

Either the vineyard had one of the most impressive publicity machines in the industry or the rosé they produced was quite special. Régine, who I think produced the marketing brochure, turned out to glow almost as much as the reviews. She had a neat bob haircut, a cute button nose and wore a classic summer dress over her tanned trim neat body. She'd have turned heads on the Champ-Elysées. Instead, she had to conduct our tasting. To revive her effortless chichiness, she periodically disappeared into a side room to giggle on her mobile with her fashionable friends.

Peter had stayed in Les Lecques to choose the restaurant for the evening, so, left alone by Régine, Tanya and I tasted the fabled rosé. To look at, it was pale but nowhere near as pale as our Corsican *gris*. After her first sip Tanya, happy to go against the arrayed wisdom of a phalanx of Parisian restaurateurs, declared it to be nothing special. But for once on the trip I think my taste buds, if not my wine vocabulary, trumped my wife's. The flavour of the Coeur de Grain did seem to stay in the mouth far longer than other rosés. I thought back to Jean Gazaniol's at Château de Parenchère in the Dordogne. He'd said that 'if the taste of a wine stays in the mouth for ten seconds, it is interesting. If it remains for fifteen seconds, it is a fantastic wine.' On this scale I could safely declare that Domaine Ott's rosé was interesting, but for some reason I didn't, instead, just as Régine wafted back into the room, I commented that it had 'an undercurrent of sweetness like a good vindaloo'.

Suitably unimpressed, Régine handed us some Domaine Ott press cuttings. There were plenty of French celebrities pictured embracing their favourite Provençal wine and a picture of our own Kate Moss sitting on a beach in Saint Tropez with a bottle of Domaine Ott bobbing in an ice bucket. Then we flicked to an article about David Beckham. I knew that Victoria liked her designer labels, but I hadn't quite appreciated just how famous a brand Domaine Ott was. Did it really rank alongside the Versaces and Chanels of this world? Was no celebrity dinner party complete without a bottle of Coeur de Grain rosé?

The answer was contained in tiny italic writing at the end of the article: '*This imaginary interview with David Beckham was written after the author had sat in the sun for too long drinking Domaine Ott.*' So while Kate liked the rosé and journalists considered it enough of a French cultural icon to include in spoof articles, disappointingly we'd never know whether David and Victoria were partial to a glass.

Peter had chosen a restaurant on the far corner of the crescent-shaped sandy bay of Les Lecques. Throughout the day firefighting planes had made low lumbering passes over the resort. As their great bellies slapped down on to the water, their nose cones opened like the yawning mouth of a hungry whale, gulping water into the cargo hold. Then slowly they clawed their way back into the sky, trailing water as they headed into the hills. As we sat down to eat we heard their throaty engines and looked out to sea just as five of them splashed into the still, evening water and then climbed agonisingly into the sky, shrouding the restaurant in shadow as they pulled away for their last run of the day.

We ate by the harbour-side, amid the clinking masts of a flotilla of small yachts. On the foredeck of one of them a young child lay flat on her belly. She wore a pretty pink sundress, and her hair was tied back in a ponytail. This swished in front of her face as she tried to scoop fish into a net fastened on the end of a long wooden pole. The light on the mast above her blinked into existence as darkness fell, but still she fished, as we ate fried calamari and grilled sea bass. And an hour later as we were sipping our espresso, the girl still remained flat on her belly, lazily dragging her net through the water.

Across from us we could see the lights from villas winking out from the dark shadows of the pine-covered hills of La Madrague. Out at sea a cruise liner floated past, lit up like a high street at Christmas time. All along the promenade couples walked hand in hand, sharing ice creams, stopping for a nightcap on one of the seaside terraces and then slipping away to bed.

Less romantically, on our table was a pile of post, which Peter's wife Jenny had brought for us. Peter had forgotten about it for a couple of weeks and then locked it in his suitcase, before finally retrieving it. There were letters from the bank, flyers for home-improvement companies, invitations to weddings and notices of new births. We'd apparently missed five opportunities to participate in the investment opportunity of a lifetime, and rather incongruously our local supermarket had kindly offered to supply our gas and electricity. And if we signed up to cheaper phone calls and broadband internet, then our names would be entered into a raffle to win a brand-new Thames-side flat. We knew the development and they hadn't mentioned the wonderful views of the local refuse tip.

Unbidden, a couple of recruitment agents had sent us letters telling us not to despair, we were valuable commodities in the London job market. All we had to do was give them a call. But at least the last item was nice – a birthday card from my nan, with some crisp £10 notes inside, inviting us to have a celebration meal on her.

'Do you know,' said Tanya sifting through the pile, 'I don't miss home at all.'

20

The Rosé Laboratory

The next day Madame Etienne, or Miriam as she called herself on the phone, finally contacted us. We hadn't spoken with her since our fateful lunch the previous summer, so it was something of a shock to finally hear her voice. Tanya took the call and reported that she sounded much nicer than the fearsome woman who'd nearly garrotted Rosie's teddy. Apparently the harvest at Château Etienne had begun, and Miriam estimated, depending on the weather, that the *fête de vendange* would be in two weeks' time, on 15 September.

This gave us nearly a week longer than we'd thought, and immediately after the phone call we adjourned to a seafront café in Les Lecques to discuss our plans. It was early in the morning and a strong overnight wind had deposited strands of seaweed across the beach. The storm-churned water didn't deter the resort's pensioners. 10 a.m. was aqua-aerobics time. They stood together in the shallows in a circle of bathing hats, chatting happily away as they completed a minimal exercise routine. Back on the shore their pet dogs sat obediently in a row, waiting for the end of this daily ritual.

After twenty minutes they emerged from the water coated in seaweed, wrapped towels around their midriffs, collected their dogs and came to sit in our café. Dripping wet, with their bathing hats still on their heads, they then started a conversation about how inappropriate it was for us to have a bottle of rosé on our table at this time in the morning. We were only marvelling at its colour not drinking it, but we'd become accustomed to being criticised in this manner in restaurants. The moment the French heard us speaking English they assumed we couldn't understand their language and took this as a licence to say whatever they wanted.

We added sugar and water to our orange pressé and shifted our Corsican *gris* to a more prominent position amid the croissants and the *pains au chocolat*. We'd been in such a rush to catch the ferry in Calvi, that Tanya hadn't even paused to taste the wine. She'd bought a single bottle and run back to the car. Thinking about it now, this appeared a blessing – none of us really wanted to rely on Claire and Neil's supermarket rosé because we knew that in a blind tasting it could easily be mistaken for paint stripper, but with the Corsican wine we could arrive at the Etiennes' with clean consciences. We had no way of knowing whether it was any good until after the colour comparison with Bernard's wine. And by then it would not matter. Colour really was everything and just looking at our wonderfully pale bottle gave me a victorious glow. But I did still have one nagging doubt.

The Corsican wine was a *gris*, and we'd heard at Listel that some people considered a *gris* a separate category of wine. We had the two remaining weeks to establish whether they were right and, if they were, to scour Provence for another contender. We also had another good reason to keep searching. Wincing at the tartness of his orange juice and pulling his glasses down so that they almost rested on his nostrils, Peter gave us both an intense gaze.

'You don't really think the Etiennes would have made this bet unless they knew they were going to win, do you?'

Tanya and I both looked nonplussed.

'It's obvious,' continued Peter, 'they must have a plan.'

'So what is it?'

'Ah, if we knew that, it wouldn't be nearly so much fun.'

Over the next few days we scoured the Var region, visiting Lorgues, Pourrières, Cotignac and Trets. Lazy Provençal villages where it felt like a crime to be in a hurry, but each morning we crammed our cases into the car and headed for a new destination. The time pressure was so acute that it even curbed Peter and Tanya's usual wanderlust.

In the town of Barjols we discovered the largest plane tree in Provence. It had a trunk twelve metres in circumference and a pretty café underneath its heavy green canopy. Usually Tanya would have wrapped herself in its shady embrace and happily spent an hour people-watching, but instead she restricted herself to a longing glance. And, in the villa-laden hills above Nice, Peter refused to be tempted by a meal at the La Colombe d'Or, the restaurant where Picasso and Matisse painted for their supper. The halls of the attached hotel were draped with work from these and other artists, and Tanya and I confidently expected to lose him for an afternoon as he pottered from painting to painting, but Peter resisted and instead settled for a quick *croque-monsieur* outside the wine-producing town of Bellet.

We traipsed down roads so rough they would have torn the undercarriage from Peter's car to vineyards clinging to the corner of mountains, forgotten by the locals and the French road system. We were attacked by dogs, cockerels, cats and even a domesticated pig–wild boar cross. At one domaine, rather than rush to our aid, the owner salivated as we were surrounded by a prowling ring of Rottweilers, Jack Russells and bull terriers.

'I have no name, only a number,' he cried wildly. 'Address me as E147 or they'll find out.'

Against this sort of arrayed pet firepower and obvious madness, a polite question about the paleness of his rosé didn't seem worth the risk. We later found out that each vigneron in a co-operative was usually given a number, and E147 was presumably his. But this still didn't explain why he'd pranced around us like a cannibal doing a war dance. 'Probably out of dog food,' was Peter's sanguine conclusion.

Thankfully, after a week spent careering haphazardly from vineyard to vineyard, we were able to give our traumatised noses a rest. In the town of Les Arcs in the central Var we made a belated discovery – the Conseil Interprofessionel des Vins de Provence. It had smart modern offices and a marketing department that was launching a new initiative to wean the British consumer off Mateus. They'd even invented a swish catchphrase to launch the campaign: 'Dry rosé de Provence – why should the French have it all?'

'Do you think I could be their mascot?' said Peter, as we were shown into the Conseil's Maison des Vins, a shop that held a bottle of rosé from each major producer in the Var.

'Instead of running around like lunatics for five months, we should have come straight here,' I said ruefully.

'Nowhere near as much fun,' replied Peter, as he helped himself to a free *dégustation*.

There were over one hundred rosés and, with the kind help of our guide, Maximillian, we spent an hour measuring them against our Corsican *gris* and the Etiennes' wine. Nothing came close in terms of paleness, and as we discarded the final Provençal contender, we shook hands, hugged and drank some of the Maison's free wine. The quest, it seemed, was all but won.

But then Maximillian looked closely at the label of our Corsican wine and shattered our celebrations: '*Ce n'est pas un rosé, c'est un gris.*'

With seven days to go until the harvest party I was sitting in a café in the centre of Vidauban. It was pouring with rain, not the stencilled slices of an English thunderstorm but thick heavy globules that smacked repetitively on the awning over my head. Peter and Tanya were in the local co-operative investigating a pale rosé lead, and I was left stirring a coffee, and keeping an eye on our illegally parked car.

Vidauban was probably the least attractive Provençal town I'd ever come across. Its centre was split by a *route nationale*, and it was just off a motorway. The town square was a natural crossroads and rammed with cars, lorries and even army trucks. There were signs to Draguignan, Lorgues, Brignoles and Saint Tropez, and soldiers and tourists fought for right of way. One enormous café struggled to serve travelling salesmen, shop assistants, holidaymakers and me.

For the first time in weeks I'd treated myself to a British paper. I looked ruefully at the front cover – pictures of a September seaside rush as temperatures stayed in the eighties for the second week running. Unlike Tanya, I'd not fallen in love with France from an early age. As a reluctant student at school, I'd dreaded exchange trips to Paris. Even as I grew older and learnt to appreciate the food and the culture, I always felt alienated in France. It was as if the whole nation was laughing at my inability to speak the language. But I hadn't realised how much the trip had changed my attitude to the country until that hour alone in Vidauban.

I thought I still believed in my mother's mantra that there was no place like England on a sunny summer's day. I visualised myself sitting outside a country pub in a Devonshire village. A row of thatched cottages stretched away from me, each with a window box full of geraniums and a neatly trimmed garden hedge punctuated by a freshly painted wooden fence. At the end of the road there was a small stream, which bent away down a gentle hill, trickling past the village school. I was wearing jeans and a T-shirt, and the temperature was in the comfortable seventies. Through a gap in the trees down the lane, I caught the white flash of a fast bowler's run-up. Swallows circled overhead, and as I drained my pint, I heard the excited chatter of the children as school ended for the day.

What could be better?

Strangely, at that moment I felt that sitting alone in Vidauban in the pouring rain was preferable. There was something comfortingly familiar about these unfamiliar Provençal towns and villages. My favourite time was late afternoon when I could wander through them and not see a soul. The doors of houses fed right on to the street, but not a net curtain would twitch. Even the central square could be a lonely place, with the iron grills pulled down over the shopfronts, and tables and chairs from bars stacked and chained to lamp-posts. But when they were dozing in the fading sun, they held a promise which I'd been struggling to decipher.

If I lived in a flat overlooking one of the ubiquitous intertwined narrow lanes, I knew I wouldn't become any kinder or any less quick to anger, and I wouldn't laugh more or less than I had always laughed. But I would be a subtly different person. I would have changed the boundaries of my life, invented a new set of rules.

Work hard and everything will be yours was the motto, laid down by my parents at my birth. Whether the world had changed, or I was just an ill-gotten son, I'd ceased to believe in it. Following their mantra meant accepting my life would be swallowed by work. I had to believe there was something more, which is why, when the opportunity came, I was happy to search for pale rosé. And eerily, just as the psychoanalyst in Burgundy had predicted, I now understood that 'People on a quest only think they know what they're searching for'.

What France had delivered over the last few months was the chance to live freely. To never have to judge myself against my contemporaries. To forget the savage world run by bonuses, pay packets and promotions and just be. Of course, now it was coming to an end. The savage world had to intrude again. There wasn't really life for us in France, was there?

At the beginning of our journey I would have answered a definitive no. But now I wasn't so certain. Thanks to our experiences, Tanya and I had grown even closer. I'd finally appreciated Tanya's view that the beauty of our surroundings was just as important as our jobs. If we spent so much time, and effort, worrying about one, why not the other? Waking up to the smell of wild herbs carried on warm air through open windows, walking hand in hand through cobbled lanes and stopping to have a drink as the theatre of street life continued around us. It was life in a painting, festooned with sights and full of rich swathes of colour.

And ever so slowly, as the grapes ripened, I'd relinquished my belief that I would be a London lawyer for the rest of my life. I'd learnt to be a little more like Peter Tate – to enjoy every second of every day and to be positive rather than negative. But, above all, I was in love with Tanya and through her I'd fallen in love with France.

So, I sat in the café in Vidauban and tried to figure out the answer. Tried to invent a new set of rules that wouldn't lead to disaster. And as I'd been doing since I was a child, tried to prove everyone wrong.

When they returned Peter and Tanya were really excited. Apparently Vidauban hid a secret, a secret too important to allow me to finish my coffee. As we walked to the outskirts of the town they could barely keep the grins from their faces. They stopped in front of a pair of small wrought-iron gates. There was no plaque, just a house number and a long tree-lined gravel drive, at the end of which sat a modern, unremarkable building fronted by a small courtyard. It was 2 p.m. and the glass door to the house was locked. And so we waited, and listened as the sound of the lunch-hour traffic faded, the clouds parted, and the beat of the crickets grew with the afternoon heat.

Peter peered through each of the ground-floor windows, and Tanya rattled the door for the fourth time. A little annoyed that nobody would tell me what was going on, I began to walk back up the drive, scuffing clouds of dust into the air. When I was halfway back to the gate, a young man wearing jeans and a T-shirt came ambling out from behind the house. He looked curiously at us. All too apparently the place did not usually have visitors. But when Tanya explained our purpose, he suddenly became excited. Then he disappeared.

'Do you think,' said Peter, 'that if you drink too much rosé you turn pink?'

'What?' I replied a little too sharply.

'Kids turn yellow drinking Sunny Delight so it follows that a rosé overdose should turn us pink.'

'And?'

'I just thought they might know the answer, that's all.'

'Who are "they"?'

Peter just tapped his nose and winked at me, only too aware that I was now quite irritated.

Minutes later all was revealed. Gilles Masson opened the doors and admitted us to the Centre de Recherche et d'Expérimentation sur le Vin Rosé. The world's first and only rosé laboratory. Gilles was a scientist who'd devoted his whole life to rosé. He was one of the judges at the Concours Mondial du Vin Rosé in Cannes – a competition to find the best rosés in the world – and his job at the centre was to protect Provence's position as the leading producer of rosé. He was a serious, intent man who appraised people with his clear blue eyes as he spoke. To begin with, quite understandably, he couldn't believe that we'd spent our summer trying to find France's palest rosé. Didn't we have something more sensible to do? And so for the first twenty minutes we struggled to convince him that we weren't pranksters.

We wanted the definitive answers to the problems we'd encountered over the last few months: was pale rosé inferior to darker rosé? Why was the French wine establishment so dismissive towards rosé? And why was rosé enjoying such a resurgence? Most importantly of all, Gilles could tell us with authority whether our Corsican *gris* was actually a rosé. It was imperative that he liked us, and thankfully as we asked question after question he began to soften.

First he showed us his colour chart, a tube-shaped piece of Perspex containing over fifteen miniature glasses of rosé, each a slightly different shade of pink. Underneath each glass the colour was labelled – *Framboise, Bois de Rose, Clair, Marbre de Rose, Saumon, Peillure d'Oignon, Brique, Corail,* etc. Opening a door, he took us down into the cellar, where he stored a bottle of each of the 500 rosés from the Concours Mondial. He explained that he was conducting an experiment to analyse the effect of soil type, weather and age on the colour and taste of each wine. All the information gathered from his research would then be passed back to the vignerons who were funding the centre.

Next he led us up some stairs to the laboratory. It felt like being on the set of a James Bond film. There were men and women in long white coats carrying what could have been hazardous material in tiny phials. The phials were arranged in row upon row, and little droplets were placed in petri dishes and analysed by microscope. The results flashed up on a computer screen showing the exact chemical composition of the liquid at any one time. Outside we were just moments away from a landscape full of wild copses of olive trees, flowering bougainvillea and mimosa-draped buildings, but in the laboratory all that was needed to complete the surreal feel was an evil genius, a hacking laugh and a thin story line about a plot to take over the world.

Instead, the scientists were analysing the differing composi-tions of the rosés they made in their cave. As we toured the laboratory we talked about the reasons for the growing popularity of rosé. Gilles thought it was primarily down to the increasing quality of the wine produced. New technology, such as better pneumatic presses, and the changing attitude of the vignerons – who saw a growing market for their product – meant that French rosés were being transformed. There was now a rosé to accompany most meals, and with people increasingly worried about drink-driving, rather than order and not finish a separate bottle of red and white, people compromised with rosé.

Gilles also argued that French consumers were fed up with the heavy tannic reds that had dominated the market for the last ten years. They wanted something lighter, and rosé was ideally placed to capitalise on this trend. Additionally rosé was an attractive drink for the youth market. Rather than sit around the dinner table and discuss the qualities of red or white wines for hours on end, young adults wanted a drink that wasn't too intellectually demanding, one that could be slugged back, rather than debated.

Finally Gilles somewhat questionably argued that rosé was the colour of love and passion, which is why women adored it, and that sales were increasing because women were buying more wine.

So the French nation was divided. You had the traditionalists, such as the Parisian wine collector we met, François Gilbert, who couldn't see any point in rosé and who would be deeply offended if it were served to accompany a meal of any substance. And you had people prepared to be more open-minded and who recognised that there were now some great rosés.

Next Gilles moved on to the subject of colour. It was far too simplistic to say that a dark rosé was necessarily a better wine. Rosé was the most complex wine for a vigneron to make; each of the different methods of making rosé required a delicate touch and real skill. 'Every vigneron seeks the elusive equilibrium between colour and taste, although the two are not directly related,' said Gilles. 'The trend at the moment is for paler and paler rosés.'

We'd seen and heard more than enough to convince us that even if we searched France for the next decade, we'd be unlikely to find anyone more knowledgeable about rosé than Gilles. Having spent the whole summer immersed in the technicalities of winemaking, it seemed only right that the quest should end in a place like this. Completely by accident we'd stumbled upon a rosé Mecca. Any vigneron who had a question about rosé could make a pilgrimage here and expect to find the answer. And the time had come for what we hoped would be the final question of our trip. We removed our Corsican wine from our rucksack and placed it on the table between us. Was a *gris* a rosé?

Gilles picked the bottle up and shifted it casually between his hands, not knowing that if he dropped it, we'd have to go back to Corsica to get another.

'There's no actual definition for a rosé,' said Gilles. 'Your Corsican *gris* is a wine made from a direct pressing. It looks like it's been oxidised, which would explain the slightly yellow colour.'

We looked perplexed. Did that mean that Gilles, a man who had made his career from rosé, thought our wine was a white wine?

'And?' I hung the question in the air, hoping he'd continue with his explanation.

'And, yes, it's a rosé like any other.'

Before we had time to celebrate Gilles fetched his colour chart and sat back down. His blue eyes fixed us with an intense stare, and he swung back on his chair shaking his head. Then his face cracked into a wide grin.

'You know, the perfect rosé is supposed to be the pink of a

baby's skin. And this, this definitely isn't,' he paused. 'But it is the palest rosé I have ever seen.'

21

The Boules Tournament

The hood of the car was down and the sun was shining. We had a bottle of the palest rosé in France in the boot and we were singing 'Do you know the way to Saint Tropez?' In preparation for her arrival at Brigitte Bardot's spiritual home, around her head Tanya had wrapped a white silk scarf, which whipped in the wind. Peter sat in the back, with a massive smile on his face, desperately clutching his hat to his head. According to France's pre-eminent rosé scientist, we'd succeeded in our quest. All we had to do now was relax for a couple of days in the south of France and then drive to the Etiennes' for the celebration.

We were booked in for lunch at Nikki Beach, one of Saint Tropez's newest and trendiest beach bars. The guidebook described it as a wannabe's heaven. The only problem was that we couldn't find it. Tanya called three times and asked for directions. On the third occasion our pay-as-you-go mobile ran out of money.

'Presumably wannabes would rather die than admit they don't know where the in place is,' I added helpfully.

'I guess that makes us wannabe wannabes,' said Peter. His face was entirely obliterated by his sunglasses and so I couldn't tell whether he was joking or not.

We drove through the thick pines of Ramatuelle, passed the gated villas of the rich and famous and finally turned down the hill to Pampelonne beach. Two catamarans sat at anchor in the golden sweep of the bay, and the bright sun flashed off their bobbing hulls. Stretched in colourful lines across the sand were the beach clubs where the jet set had been coming to play since the 1930s. La Voile Rouge, host to naked boxing matches and innocent table-dancing long before the world had heard of Spearmint Rhino, was renowned as the wildest. Over the years it had lured Hollywood's hottest stars – Stallone, De Niro, Nicholson and Eastwood. And while Ivana Trump and Elton John might have preferred Coco Beach, we'd chosen the newest club – Nikki. Every wannabe in town wanted to emulate the high priest of cool, Bono, and have lunch there. Our only problem was getting in.

The entrance to Nikki was at the end of a long dusty track. A white flag fluttered against the cloudless blue sky, but between us and the most exclusive beach club in the world stood a high fence and a gated entrance that was guarded by a bald man in a karate suit. He wore wraparound shades, clearly visited the gym twice a day and stood with his heavy arms crossed, barring the way.

'A wannabe would know just what to do now,' said Peter. Our options were to run over the karate-suited bouncer or get out of the car and see what happened. We chose the latter. Peter left the car running, and with some disdain it was valet-parked between a Maserati and a Bentley. 'Start thinking about an appropriate tip,' said Peter, as we were given a ticket for our keys by the testosterone-charged bouncer.

We were in. Under the blue sky and the bright sun everything was dazzling white. Row upon row of sunloungers the size of double beds stretched across the sand in front of us. Beautiful people lounged indolently in the shade of umbrellas, and staff members flashed perfect teeth and perfect breasts (or biceps, depending on their sex). Acid jazz played in surround sound from speakers concealed in palm trees, and the pool area doubled as a catwalk, with topless women periodically rising from their beds and strutting up and down.

Propped on an elbow at one end of the pool was a dark-haired, dark-skinned twenty-something man, who sipped Coke, flicked through magazines and barely glanced up as the parade of women continued around him. I thought he was a study of wannabe coolness from whom I had a lot to learn. In fact, he was a total exhibitionist just waiting for the arrival of his partner.

While Tanya disappeared for a massage, the Coke-sipping, magazine-reading pool-side Adonis and his newly arrived elastic-limbed girlfriend began to perform. The more we averted our eyes, the more we wanted to know just how far things would go. It began with a bit of ear nibbling and moved on to movie kissing – all trembling lips, gaping mouths and restless tongues. They spread their hands wide like stars, shooting them from thigh to cheek to breast, moving a stray lock of hair here, pinching an errant nipple there. Then it got totally out of control.

Thankfully, it was at this point that Tanya limped back from her hour with the masseur, Fabian.

'He's invited me to his winter clinic in Saint Bart's,' she said as she slumped on to a sunlounger. 'I don't think I'll be going,' she groaned.

Shielding ourselves from the pool-side X-rated scene, we lunched under umbrella pines on such Nikki delicacies as fruit soup infused with menthol ice cream and – apart from Tanya – lobster spring rolls. A ward of surgically enhanced beauty joined us, sucking on sushi, sipping champagne and blowing air kisses to all the other tables apart from ours. The jazz played on, the sun beat hotter, and the four-poster beds that fringed the restaurant began to look attractive places to spend the afternoon.

We toasted the success of our quest with a bottle of Château

Minuty rosé. In other circumstances we'd have visited the vineyard, which was only a couple of minutes up the road, but we were at Nikki and no one seemed to want to leave, ever.

I was supposed to hate Saint Tropez. People had warned us of two-hour-long traffic jams to enter the town. They'd told us of a hideously pretentious harbour where large gin palace after large gin palace slipped into berth. Of a town where dressing down for the evening meant wearing jewels valuable enough to clear Third World debt and where women were reduced to the status of show ponies to be paraded by decrepit millionaires.

And it was all true. And yet somehow I still loved the place. We crawled towards the town centre behind a flotilla of Ferraris parked next to an array of Aston Martins and ambled past the mega-yachts. On each boat there were enough crew members to staff a small hotel, but there were rarely more than two guests. The owners sat at the rear of their gilded boats revelling in the attention of mere mortals like us, who gawped at them like children discovering exotic animals at a zoo.

And as for the harbour-side women, the show ponies we'd heard about – they were the stars of the show. The first we encountered was a statuesque black woman. She was tall and thin and hooked on to the arm of a lover who was surely no more than five minutes from the morgue. Her flowing blonde hair extensions swung like a pendulum behind her bottom as her head twitched this way and that. She wore a tight black catsuit which clung to her curves as she led her octogenarian lover up and down the harbour. Presumably she believed that some strenuous exercise might hasten his final moment. She could then dab a tear from her eye and sign the deeds for the diamond mine.

Just along the street another woman – or young girl to be more accurate – was attached to a proudly proffered wrinkled arm. In the middle of the port, in the middle of the day, she wore nothing but stilettos, a G-string and a totally transparent dress. The couple were asking directions from a policeman, who was doing his best to forget whatever public decency laws existed in France. The girl had short cropped blonde hair and an arrogant pout straight from the catwalk. Her cleavage jutted into the policeman's chin, and he couldn't so much as twitch, let alone point out the right way, without brushing her breasts.

Even in the bar of the more relaxed Hôtel Sube overlooking the port, we couldn't escape from the mammary-fixated rich. Two middle-aged couples on the next table were discussing their misfortune. The women were platinum blonde and over made-up, and their surgically enhanced chests projected at right angles like DIY shelves. The men were short with round potbellies and gold signet rings on their chubby fingers. Their voices were pompous, and to mask their background, they enunciated each syllable with the care of a surgeon.

'The boat is dry docked in Tahiti for repair so we had to come here for the summer.'

'Well, if you are missing being on board, you can join us for supper. She's a hundred footer, you know?'

'Delighted.'

'More champagne?'

We should have envied the super rich and their inconsequential obsessions, such as teaming the right sunglasses with this season's handbag or finding stuffed leopards to mount on the prow of their boat. Instead, we found them amusing. The whole place was like some grotesque Hollywood comedy. It was so far from reality that just walking through the port was like a holiday from life. And miraculously, amid all the excessive wealth, the warped values, the egos and the G-strings, the beauty of Saint Tropez remained.

It was there in the moment when the light of the dying sun lifted the pastel pinks and ochre oranges of the harbour-side houses. In the playful smiles of the waiters, and the exasperation of an old man re-fixing bait to the end of his rod. It was there in the canvases of the artists capturing the retreating sunrays in the ripples around the yachts. And in the bustling cobbled alleys crammed with cafés, which sloped steeply away towards the sea.

So that by the time we walked towards Place des Lices, far away from the entertaining madness of the harbour, I'd understood why Bardot fell in love with the town all those years ago. Its soul was still there in the gentle light, hanging in the pine-scented air.

According to the purists, the finest place to play boules in the world is a swathe of gravel in the shade of Saint Paul de Vence's ramparts. It's the game's Wembley or Lords. But, for us, there was nowhere better than the Place des Lices in Saint Tropez. A legion of cicadas called to us from the rows of plane trees which shaded the dusty gravel square stretching out from the terrace of Le Café restaurant. There was a line of benches for spectators, and the ground was uneven enough to introduce an element of chance into every throw. And it was a relief to find that there wasn't a designer heel in sight.

At 2 p.m., as we wandered through the square, there was an incessant clacking of metal upon metal as a crowd of maybe fifty men anxiously waited for the beginning of a two-day *tournoi*. At a small table in the centre of the Place, a man with a lopsided face was taking the competitors' money. His nose slanted away from his lazy left eye and immobile pock-marked left cheek, and his right eye twitched from the face of each new entrant to his notebook. As they paid their money he made a note of their name and flipped a small counter into a cloth bag.

Peter edged closer and closer. Since his first visit to France over fifty years ago, he'd been fascinated by the game. And on our last holiday he'd even invented his own version – extreme boules. Rather than play within a restricted area, extreme boules was a rambling game, played over small trees, down precipitous paths, through vines and even under water. The object, as in the more traditional format, was to get as close as possible to the small target ball, or *cochonnet*, except that when you played the game Peter's way, you could end up miles from the nearest town, pitching your boules off the side of the mountain. For a while he toyed with the idea of creating the Extreme Boules Federation of France and using a picture of Rosie clutching a bottle of rosé in one hand and a boule in the other as the game's mascot. Unfortunately it never caught on.

As well as getting the Extreme Boules Federation off the ground, Peter had always dreamt of playing in a tournament. So he paid his money and waited patiently as the man with the lopsided face looked him up and down. 'Where are your boules? No boules, no play.'

The nearest shop that might sell a set was way down the hill by the harbour. But as I was preparing to run and fetch some, the organiser who'd just refused Peter's money put a whistle in the corner of his mouth and blew one shrill blast. The metallic clacking stopped, and all the men gathered around the central table. No more entries were allowed because the draw for partners was about to commence.

Boules could be played individually, *à deux* or in three-men teams. There were three different versions of the game: *pétanque* – which the English typically called boules – played with a standing start over a distance of between six and ten metres; Provençal, played with one stride between fifteen and twenty metres; and finally Lyonnais, played with larger boules and a run-up over distances greater than twenty metres. The event we were witnessing was the town's annual *à deux pétanque* competition. It began as a round robin and moved into the knock-out phase on the second day. The counters were placed one by one into the cloth bag and given a good shake. Just as the organiser put his right hand into the bag, someone nudged Peter on the shoulder. Turning around, Peter found a diminutive man with spindly legs, scuffed sandals and a baseball cap pulled low over his eyes.

'Here, quickly, pay him and you can use my spare set.'

Tanya and I left a delighted Peter to be paired off and browsed among the designer shops that proliferated in the streets behind the square. Chanel, Gucci, Versace, Ralph Lauren, Tod's, it seemed we couldn't buy a T-shirt for under €100. We entered Pucci – a niche Italian designer – attracted by the psychedelic prints on the bags, dresses, skirts and boots. Foolishly, Tanya reached out towards a pair of shoes in the window display. As the tip of her finger touched the heel, we froze.

From behind us came an ear-splitting shriek of horror emitted by a young male shop assistant. He came running towards us in a blur of peroxide hair and glinting diamond earrings, and as he darted across the shop his Pucci shirt, which was tucked into his tight black pants, inflated like a hot-air balloon. The emotional trauma of seeing flip-flop-wearing heathens touch his display was clearly too much for him, and so he screamed at us like he'd been sucking on helium.

After we'd left, Tanya was in shock. She sat and mumbled, 'All I did was reach out. Maybe I didn't even touch them. It was as if I'd stabbed his pet chihuahua through the heart.'

I put a consoling arm around her shoulder. 'Come on, let's find out how Peter's getting on,' hoping that by watching the boules I'd be able to forget a guilty feeling that was creeping into the pit of my stomach.

Peter had had the good luck to be paired with last year's champion, the same person who had lent him the boules. They made an unlikely couple – Peter, with his hair flying every-where, repeatedly tossing his favourite French phrases into the air, and the silent Frenchman standing barely as high as Peter's shoulders, with his features shrouded by a baseball cap.

Peter was appointed the point man, while his partner played

the key role of the thrower. Each game started with Peter and the opposition's point man taking it in turns to see who could get closer to the *cochonnet*. The moment either of them was too successful, the throwers would take over, pitching the heavy metal balls high into the air and trying to land them like a bomb on top of the opposition's boules.

It had taken Peter a couple of games to learn these tactics, and at one stage his team was within one point of being knocked out of the tournament. Then his partner, Jules, took over, scattering the opposition's boules with an arcing lob shot.

Before the next match Jules took Peter to one side and explained exactly how he wanted him to throw. The motion began with Peter standing up straight with a boule resting in the palm of his upturned hand. Next he had to bend his knees and reverse his hand so that his fingers formed the shape of a claw. Then, with one swing of the arm and a twist of the wrist to impart spin, he was taught to send the boule scuttling along the gravel towards the *cochonnet*. It worked so well that they won through to the second day.

And there began our problems. I'd finally realised why I'd begun to feel guilty. Madame Etienne's harvest party was just two days away, but since visiting the rosé laboratory, we hadn't been to a single vineyard. All summer we'd pursued our goal with the fervour of zealots, and then at the last moment, over-confident of victory, we'd stopped. According to Gilles, the ideal rosé was the pink of a baby's skin, but the more I looked at it, the more our Corsican wine appeared a jaundiced yellow. After all our efforts, shouldn't we at least try to find the perfect pink rosé? I was assailed by last-minute doubts. If our *gris* was disqualified on a technicality, how would I find an importer for the Etiennes' rosé? The longer we frittered away time in Saint Tropez, the worse I felt.

For Rosie, for all our shared experiences and for our future bank balance, we had to win. There were only forty-eight hours left of a summer-long bet and yet we were hanging around beach clubs and playing boules. There was also still one lead we hadn't followed up. Back in the Dordogne, when we had visited Château de Parenchère, the vigneron, Jean Gazaniol, had told us about a fantastic pink wine. He'd described the vineyard that produced it as the most beautiful in France. Surely we had to visit?

The next morning, as we watched Peter and his partner triumph in the first round of the knock-out stage, I suggested we resume the quest.

'You mean we haven't won?' said Tanya.

'Maybe, maybe not. But we've got time to find this perfect pale rosé.'

'Fine by me,' said Tanya, 'but what about him?' She pointed at Peter who stood, as rapt as a small boy, as his partner, Jules, demonstrated the correct amount of spin to impart on the boules.

'Well, somebody's got to knock them out soon,' I said confidently.

But Peter had been practising in his hotel room overnight. He'd shattered a couple of glasses, chipped the furniture and in the process become rather good at the game. He greeted each point that he and Jules won with a great roar of delight, and the smile on his face grew broader and broader as the number of competitors diminished. He even turned down wine at lunch-time because he wanted to have a steady hand for the afternoon's play. 'It's not darts, you know,' he said proudly.

In between games he restlessly prowled the square, jangling his boules together in his hands as he watched the other competitors. 'The young lad's the one we've got to watch out for; he imparts more spin than the Labour party. Oh, and have you seen how the tournament organiser is playing? Everyone's saying he's got the easiest draw. There's nothing but us between him and the final.'

As the semi-finals started I glanced anxiously at my watch. If

Peter won through to the final, we'd have to put off our trip to the vineyard until the next day. 'We could always leave him here and come back and get him,' I suggested.

'I think he needs our support,' said Tanya. 'Anyway, apparently the organiser used to be a professional, so unless his partner's rubbish, they should beat Peter and Jules quite easily.'

They nearly did, racing to a 10–5 lead. The tournament organiser walked with a pronounced limp, which matched his lazy left eye, and whereas everyone else played with shiny silver boules, his were jet black. Whenever Peter landed a boule close, it was immediately cannoned out of the way by one of these deadly black balls. There seemed no way back for Peter and Jules against this onslaught. Time after time they came close to winning an end only for the opposition's final shot to sidle up next to the *cochonnet*. Throughout the first ten points the organiser's lopsided face had remained stern, but as the lead lengthened, he cast little smiles at Peter and his partner. Secretly I was relieved and I slipped away to fetch the car.

Ten minutes later I gave a hoot from the edge of the square to attract Tanya's attention. She held one finger to her lips, and with her other hand beckoned me across.

'It's twelve all, and they both need one more point to win,' she whispered. 'The opposition has the two closest balls, and Peter's side have used their turns. This is the final throw.'

Inexplicably, rather than play safe, the tournament organiser went for one final dramatic shot. Perhaps it was a desire to show off. He pitched his boule into the air, twisting his wrist to impart the right amount of check on the ball. It was the perfect throw. A dark shadow passed over all the other boules and grew in size as it plummeted to earth plunging the target ball into the shade. Peter's dream of winning a boules tournament was apparently over.

But the shot was too good. The black boule landed directly on top of the *cochonnet*, sending it flying towards the back of the playing area, where one of Peter's errant shots waited. Peter let out a whoop of delight and hugged his partner. Somehow they were through.

The final didn't go so well. Their opponents were the young boy Peter had singled out earlier and his father. The boy was maybe twelve years old but he had all the mannerisms of the old men around him. Between shots he removed a cloth from his back pocket and polished his boules. He carried a tape measure which he produced for contentious decisions, and rather than bend to pick up his boules, he flicked them into the air with the aid of a magnet suspended on a piece of string.

It seemed the whole town had gathered to watch. Staff from the yachts in matching blue uniforms, women wearing sunglasses that obscured their faces, old men in collapsible chairs who commentated like experts and even a TV crew who were in Saint Tropez to cover a movie festival. Whether it was the crowds or the pressure of trying to help last year's champion regain his title, Peter just didn't perform. In previous games he'd hit upon a smooth throwing rhythm, pitching each of his shots an identical distance, but when he needed it most his form deserted him. And the young boy was simply fantastic, prancing quickly between the ends, he wrapped up the final in under half an hour, with very little assistance from his father.

Tanya handed Peter a glass of wine and gave him a hug. 'Never mind, you did very well to get this far.'

'Did you see what they did?' said Peter.

We both looked quizzically at him.

'It was gamesmanship, pure gamesmanship.'

Still confused, we both nodded sympathetically.

'You remember the girl with the see-through dress from the port?'

'With the G-string and the bare breasts?' I asked all too quickly, earning myself a dirty look from Tanya.

Peter nodded. 'She stood directly in my line of vision. I was throwing blind out there.'

Peter was still complaining about gamesmanship the next day when we arrived at Château Sainte Marguerite. This was the vineyard that Jean Gazaniol called the most beautiful in France, and in my head I'd created a picture of an imposing castle set amid a kingdom of vines. It had peaked towers at either end of the façade, floor-to-ceiling windows and rows of ornate shutters. I'd stopped short of sketching in a moat and drawbridge, but the stones were as thick as the length of my arm, and the cellar the largest in France. Outside there was an extensive garden filled with umbrella pines and great bushes of wild lavender, rosemary and thyme. Surely nothing could compete with this mental image, could it?

But rather than a castle, Château Sainte Marguerite was a small Provençal mas nestling behind bright-pink bougainvillea. Two tall thin palm trees formed a natural arch at the foot of the gravel road, and cacti and prickly pears sprouted from the baked orange earth. Rows of vines fanned out from the small courtyard, drawing the eye across the wide bay to the glistening sea. Looking back down the drive, through the centre of the two palm trees, the island of Porquerolles filled the view, basking in the middle of the Mediterranean. It was quite simply idyllic.

As was the girl who greeted us. She had a deep tan, a coy smile and long blonde hair that tumbled to her waist. At last I had a chance for a little revenge for Tanya's flirting with the Champenois vignerons. We were shown into a small tasting room with a large window at the far end, framing the view of the Med. If ever there was a place to drink pale rosé, this was it.

Our pretty hostess produced three glasses and reached under the counter for the wine. None of us could speak as we waited for the colour to be revealed. After six months and over three hundred visits to vineyards, it had all come down to this final tasting. Tomorrow was 15 September, the predicted date of the *fête de vendange* at Château Etienne, and we were still several hours' drive away. We were also out of leads. Popping into more vineyards on our way would be like looking for a needle in a haystack.

As the rosé filled the glasses, coating the sides with a deep viscous film, Peter let out a deep sigh, and I turned to Tanya and gave her a hug. I hadn't realised how much I'd wanted the perfect ending.

And I hadn't realised how much it would hurt when it didn't arrive. I felt strangely hollow as I looked at the wine. We'd encountered hundreds of paler bottles, and at a time when we'd been expecting the natural climax to our quest, the dark rosé we were drinking tasted bitter-sweet.

Despite the colour, I bought a couple of bottles. At least the arched palm trees on the label would remind us of the beauty of the place. Our friendly hostess tossed her blonde hair and cast a smile over her shoulder as she disappeared to box the wine, leaving us to our thoughts. I studied the road map, and Tanya flicked anxiously through our wine books, hoping for some last-minute inspiration. We both ignored Peter, who was poking around in the corner of the room. At least we had the Corsican *gris* in the car. I gave Tanya a consolation hug and hunted in my wallet for the right change. Then from the corner of the room I heard a cough. Looking over, I saw that Peter had disappeared. From out of nowhere there was another cough, this time a deep hacking noise. Then Peter stumbled back into the room appearing from a recessed alcove covered in dust. As he brushed dirt from his clothes and hair, the coughing fit gradually subsided.

'I think you're going to like this,' he called, with a massive grin on his face.

In his right hand he held a bottle of rosé, which he wiped vigorously clean with his handkerchief. Putting it up to the window, he let out a dramatic low whistle as it caught the light.

Peter balanced the rosé on the window sill, and we stood back in a line to admire his find. I thought back to all the vignerons we'd visited to get this far – the enthusiasm of Nicolas Reverdy in Sancerre, the kindness of Bauduin Parmentier in the Luberon, Jean Gazaniol, and his enormous nose, in the Dordogne and the morning in the garden with Guy de Saint Victor and François Boujol. We were grateful to them all.

And somehow at the last minute we had succeeded. If there was such a thing as a perfect rosé, we were looking at it now. Was it as pale as the Corsican *gris*? Perhaps, but significantly, rather than tint everything yellow, the sky, the sea and the palm trees all took on the gentlest pink colour.

'Marvellous,' said Peter, 'it's as pink as a baby's skin and as pale as anything.'

'I think you mean, absolutely marvellous,' said Tanya and I together, triumphantly beating Peter to his favourite phrase.

'I am afraid that's not for sale.' Our pretty hostess had returned with our boxed-up rosé. 'It's our special *cru classé* and comes from a select parcel of land. We sell all our available production in the first two months of the summer.'

It seemed so unfair. We'd gone from disappointment to elation back to disappointment again in the space of minutes. I just wanted to grab the bottle and run. The same thought must have crossed Peter and Tanya's minds as well because for a guilty second our eyes met. Maybe it was the memory of Sancerre, where we'd failed in similar circumstances, maybe it was just a refusal to accept defeat, or maybe it was really revenge for Champagne, but in any event I decided to flirt rather than flee.

I winked, I ran my hands through my hair, and I generally made a fool of myself. I played on our hostess's vanity, her conscience and, if I'm honest, her patience. I explained in my pidgin French how we'd been travelling throughout the country looking for pale rosé. And how, after six months, we'd finally found what we were looking for right here. 'You simply must sell us this bottle,' I pleaded.

In response, probably to shut me up, she said, 'Do you know what the saying "*Aujourd'hui, c'est Noël*" means?'

I looked bemused. She took our box of wine away and began to open it. I was just about to start a fresh wave of flattery when Tanya whispered under her breath, 'Today, it's Christmas.'

'Don't tell my boss,' she said as she slipped the *cru classé* rosé inside the box and waved goodbye.

'I didn't even get a chance to ask her name,' I muttered as we got back into the car.

'Just call her Cameron,' said Peter, playing with Tanya's hair and beaming naughtily at her. 'We've found our Diaz, so you'd better look out for Brad.'

22

The *Fête de Vendange*

The following morning we arrived at Château Etienne. As we drove up to the vineyard, the sun rose, blood red, behind the house and a line of cypress trees cast angular shadows over the sweeping drive. To the left was a copse of olive trees, and in front of the château were two large fields of lavender, overlooked by a large terrace. The purple flowers had long since been harvested, but Peter insisted he could still smell their perfume in the air.

The rest of the valley was filled with vines. They broke like a wave over the hillside, rolling down towards us. They were planted in close rows and tightly trained to supporting wires. In front of each row was a small blackboard denoting the grape variety and a single flowering rose – if it withered, the vigneron knew a disease was about to attack the vines. Madame Etienne's were blooming a deep pink, and the soil was sandy – perfect for pale rosé. It was 7.45 a.m. but already the workers were harvesting, trying to get as much done as possible before the sun settled over the valley.

We'd volunteered to help with the harvest before attending the *fête de vendange* that evening when our quest would reach its conclusion. Bernard and Miriam Etienne were busy with their oenologist and interrupting an oenologist in full flow was just not done, so we collected our secateurs and headed for the fields.

The air was still cool as we trudged in single file between the rows of vines. A dusting of dew lay on the ground, and already there was a faint hum of sound as the birds and insects awoke to the promise of a new day. Our summer was swollen with experiences. We'd followed the vines from first bud to their current grape-laden splendour. In the next hours we would pluck hundreds of bunches from their stems, and however much we'd enjoy the experience, I felt a personal sadness. Despite Tanya and I discussing it for hours and trying to invent a new life in the country we'd both come to love so much, there was nowhere else to go but home.

As we caught up with the other harvesters a cry went up: 'Look, the English have arrived.'

'There's always some mad English who do this for fun.'

'They think this is fun?'

The fifteen or so workers descended into laughter. They were a strange mixture of people – old women in their cleaning pinnies, men with rickety faces more at home clutching a pastis than secateurs, and students with ear and nose piercings who appeared to smoke more roll-ups than they picked grapes.

And they were right. Harvesting was no fun at all. Château Etienne was one of the few remaining Provençal vineyards that did it by hand. Most now used large machines that straddled the rows of vines, pulled back the leaves and stripped the grapes away. Arguably, however, the machines bruised the crop and picking by hand added an extra element of quality control because the workers would discard grapes which, for example, the wild boar had nibbled on.

To begin with, just getting at the grapes, let alone discarding them, was difficult. I rummaged gently among the leaves like a child looking for a prize in the lucky dip. But I quickly decided that I had to be more brutal. I copied Dominic, a young man in a baseball cap who was working on the same vines as me but from the opposite side of the row. He yanked the intertwined stems apart and stripped off the leaves to expose the grapes.

The next problem was to determine where to cut with the secateurs. I snipped away at bunches, but only four or five grapes fell into my hand at a time. I also had to ensure I didn't snick Dominic, whose hands were moving rapidly amid the leaves. Eventually I learnt to prise apart the stems of the interlocking bunches, but it could be as frustrating as untangling a line of fairy lights. After ten minutes my back was aching; after an hour it had settled down into a monotonous throb; after two hours I was resigned to a lifetime of osteopathy.

Peter and Tanya had been allocated a row to themselves. They'd yet to discover that the French take a cigarette break at every opportunity and were forging ahead of everybody else. 'Look, the English are beating us,' the workers called out in mock horror as they took another puff. 'First they work for nothing, then they don't even take a break. They are fools.'

At lunchtime we sat in the shade of a tree and had a picnic of local cheese, bread and red wine. By now I was coated in grape juice. When I had pulled away the leaves, the swollen grapes had exploded in my face and eyes. My hair was gelled together, and flies swarmed around my head. All the French sensibly wore caps.

As we ate, we explained our quest. Most of our audience nodded encouragingly as we told them of the Corsican *gris* and our last-minute trip to Château Sainte Marguerite, but one of the older *vendangeurs* looked up from sharpening his secateurs. 'Why did you bother?' He shrugged his shoulders. 'Everybody knows that Bernard Etienne produces the palest rosé in France.' He went back to his sharpening with a slightly perplexed look. He would never understand the English.

Looking across the fields to the château, I noticed that the terrace was being prepared for the fête. A line of silver lights was strung from tree to tree, and a long table was dressed for dinner. I could smell the deep-red-wine sauce of the *daube* bubbling away. 'It's your hair you can smell, not the stew,' laughed Tanya, as we returned to work.

The afternoon passed slowly. The adrenalin at reaching the conclusion of our quest had been replaced by a simple desire for the exacting labour of harvesting grapes to end, and as I picked I became hungrier and hungrier. The heat and the flies were incessant, and the rows of vines seemed to stretch for ever. I'd ceased to feel my back, but my hands had started to cramp from the repetitive snipping action. At times I was so desperate for a break that I nearly took up smoking. Through the shredded leaves of the vines I could glimpse the pine-crested hills and the toasted-green copses of olive trees, but temporarily the landscape had lost all romance for me. I began to dream of the moment when Madame Etienne would appear on the terrace and wave her hands in the air, signalling that the *cuves* were full. By early evening I'd visualised it so often that when it actually happened I assumed I was hallucinating in the heat.

But then Dominic grasped me by the shoulder and declared, '*C'est tout.*' Château Etienne's harvest was over for another year, and I collapsed to the ground a broken man. In that moment I didn't give a thought to pale rosé or the consequences of losing our bet, I was just thankful that within the hour I would be able to slip into a warm bath. Our fellow *vendangeurs* kissed us on both cheeks. '*A ce soir*,' they said as we limped back to our car for a quick trip back to the hotel to rest our limbs and change into the last of our clean clothes.

'Remember, English, don't jump in the swimming pool or you'll turn it pink,' called Dominic from the back of the tractor.

'*A ce soir, Dominic, à ce soir*,' I shouted.

'I can't believe the summer has gone so quickly,' said Tanya.

'Yes, but hasn't it been marvellous?' said Peter. 'Absolutely marvellous.'

★

At eight o'clock that evening we drove back up the drive to Château Etienne. The terrace was illuminated by the tiny silver lights, which hung in waves between the trees. They blinked in the half-light, as the olive grove, the lavender fields and the vines faded into shadow.

I felt nervously confident of winning the competition. Tanya, Peter and I had lined our Corsican *gris*, the *cru classé* rosé from Château Sainte Marguerite and Madame Etienne's wine up against various different backgrounds in various different lights. We'd even taken photos and asked the opinion of complete strangers, and the universal conclusion was that our rosés were the palest. Which was lucky because I had no idea what I'd do if we lost.

By the time we arrived all the *vendangeurs*, except Dominic, were gathered around the table. It stretched the length of the terrace and was laid with a red paper tablecloth, paper plates and plastic knives and forks. Interspersed along the table, almost like a defensive line of forts, were tall thick candles and magnums of red, white and rosé. At either end tea lights floated in glass bowls of water next to huge trays full of cured meat and pâté.

'Isn't it romantic?' said Tanya.

Everyone sat down next to the person they'd been harvesting with. A space was left next to me for the inexplicably absent Dominic. There was also no sign of either Miriam or Bernard. The bottles of wine were passed down the table, and I was on the point of pouring us all some rosé when the elderly *vendangeur* who'd spent most of the day sharpening people's secateurs called across to me, 'Don't drink that unless you want to be ill.' He rubbed his stomach and his head and handed me a bottle of red instead.

As I accepted the bottle I heard a high-pitched whoop of joy from behind the house, and seconds later what appeared to be a pantomine dame emerged. Beneath the smudged red lipstick and the heavily applied blusher I thought I could make out Dominic.

A multicoloured dress billowed like a parachute around his body, revealing tights riddled with holes and a pair of black stilettos, which he wobbled on like stilts.

People laughed, smoked and drank as Dominic paraded up and down, blowing kisses and talking furiously quickly. After about ten minutes of the skit I finally understood that he was impersonating Madame Etienne scolding Bernard for all manner of things – not cleaning the vats properly from last year's harvest, starting this year's harvest too early, stopping it too late and, rather ominously, always reserving the best grapes for his personal rosé. 'After all,' said Dominic, at the climax of his sketch, 'no self-respecting vigneron makes rosé with his best grapes.'

Everyone banged the table with their hands and cheered raucously as Dominic left the impromptu stage, nearly turning over on his stilettos as he did so. He returned, in trousers rather than a skirt, holding hands with Bernard and Miriam Etienne. Since last summer Miriam had had her hair chopped short and little blonde ringlets curled across her forehead. Her hands and neck were still covered in gold, but instead of the black dress we'd seen her in previously, she wore a pair of jeans and an open-necked shirt. Rather than the formidable figure I'd built her up to be in my mind, she seemed slight and fragile before the assembled crowd.

It was the first time we'd met her husband, Bernard. And whereas Miriam appeared much younger than I'd remembered, Bernard was older than I had expected. His grey hair was swept back over a deep forehead, and his skin was a deep walnut brown. He walked with a straight back and a slight limp, periodically tapping the pocket on the breast of his shirt, as if to check something was still there. He raised his hand, and the table fell obligingly silent.

'Miriam and I would like to thank you for working so hard on the harvest. Our wines keep on getting better and better and are now known throughout France. For this we thank you.'

Everyone gently applauded.

'And, as always, let's thank Dominic for his lamentable attempt at imitating my wife.'

Catcalls, whistles and more table banging followed.

'We should also welcome our English friends. As many of you know, my wife and I have a little bet which will be settled this evening.'

Our fellow *vendangeurs* grinned at us. It was as if they knew the secret to a terribly funny joke.

'And finally I would like to invite you all to enjoy the food and raise a glass to another successful harvest.'

The trays were ferried down the table, pâté and cold meat was heaped on to plates, and glasses filled with wine. The first course was quickly finished and cleared away, and steaming hot plates of *daube* accompanied by fresh tagliatelle were passed along. We'd spent a summer journeying through France sampling some of the best food that the country had to offer, but nothing even came close to this stew. The hours in the field under the hot sun and the ache in my back seemed worth it. I'd smelt the *daube* cooking all afternoon, and it was as thick and rich as I'd imagined, with the slight taste of anchovy which was so typical of Provençal cooking.

Plates of cheese and more glasses of wine followed. Looking across, I could see that Peter was drawing a map of France on the paper tablecloth and marking the locations of the vineyards we'd visited. Tanya was also chatting happily away, but I couldn't relax, not until we'd resolved the bet. As I became increasingly nervous, the idea of just telling them it had all been a dreadful misunderstanding began to appeal. We could still call the whole thing off, couldn't we?

Once the cheese had been removed, Bernard stood up, and the table fell silent. I looked anxiously at Tanya and squeezed her hand under the table. Win or lose, our summer had been the most enjoyable of our lives. Bernard cleared his throat, but rather than call us to the head of the table, he began to sing. It was a soft, melodic song, but I couldn't understand any of the words, and from the confused expression on Tanya's face I could see that she couldn't either. Dominic whispered into my ear, 'It's called "And Also Happiness". It's a famous French song, only he's singing it in Provençal.'

Once Bernard had finished and received a round of applause, one of the women *vendangeurs* stood up and sang in the harsh guttural Provençal dialect. She was so completely out of tune it was painful to listen to, and the song went on for verse after verse, but when she finished she too received rapturous applause. As she sat down, and another *vendangeur* stood up to sing, I felt a tap on my shoulder. It was Miriam. 'I think Bernard's waiting for you in the cave.'

We felt the customary chill as we entered the cave, and an acrid smell filled our nostrils. Throughout our trip Tanya had commented on a musty aroma which the vines seemed to give off. As the summer had progressed so this smell had become stronger and stronger. Until, during the harvest, it had become almost overpowering. Eventually we recognised it as the smell of fermenting wine.

Stalks lay scattered on the concrete floor, which was stained red with juice. A metal walkway was suspended from the ceiling, and thick hosepipes were draped from it and attached to each *cuve*. It was like a life-sized snakes and ladders board, and Bernard's voice echoed down from somewhere near the top of it, which I guessed meant he was poised to win. All we could see were his legs dangling over the edge of a stainless-steel vat. Then an arm holding a large pipette emerged and finally his grey hair.

'Just testing this year's rosé,' he said, as he descended a ladder and led us through to another corner of the cave. A white screen had been set up against the wall, and a freestanding light, with four darkened shutters around each side of the bulb, cast a focused bright beam. It was like entering a photographer's studio. Intriguingly, a camp bed was tucked underneath the screen and, seeing my curious glance, Bernard explained, 'I won't be sleeping much tonight. I'll rest here and every hour I'll test this year's rosé. Once it's the perfect colour, I'll end the *macération*.'

As we'd previously agreed, we handed over the Château Sainte Marguerite rosé, and Miriam produced two tulip-shaped glasses. After endless hours on the road, countless visits to vignerons and a summer steeped in the scent of lavender and spent in the shade of plane trees, we'd reached the end. Bernard and Miriam were polite and courteous, but at the same time they resembled a couple of scientists about to demonstrate the truth of their theory. They methodically checked the light was at the right angle and lined up the glasses at precisely the same height before pouring the wine. Peter was too nervous to say 'marvellous' and just rubbed his hands together in anticipation as we waited for the wine to settle.

According to our colour experiments, our rosé should have emerged as the narrow winner. I expected a little harmless argument, to have to squat down on my haunches and examine the wines from different angles, perhaps even to have to adjust the light slightly to prove that at whatever angle it hit the glasses, our wine was the winner. But instead we stood in shocked silence.

The colour of the Etiennes' rosé was the most beautiful translucent pink which seemed to wink in and out of existence. At one moment the wine would appear totally colourless, like the lightest of crisp whites, but as the liquid was swished around the glass a gentle ripple of pink would catch the light. Late at night, in the cool of the cave, it held us captivated.

'How on earth did you make that?' said Peter finally.

★

Once he'd re-established his credentials as the producer of France's palest rosé Bernard relaxed. He was only too willing to show us how his rosé was made, and we drew up chairs and sat around his camp bed as the noise from the party outside gradually died away.

The rosé that the Etiennes sent to England was from the bulk of the vineyard's production. But this evening's winner was instead taken from the small *cuve* which Bernard always made for himself and some select clients on the last night of the harvest. This year, with our help, he was keen to start selling this wine more widely. He'd opened the final bottle of last year's special *cuve* to win the bet, and it was now time to make some more. 'Much, much more,' he proudly declared. 'This year our production is doubling.'

I tried to visualise just how much rosé he could produce. The cave was no bigger than a typical farmyard barn. But time and time again on our trip I'd been surprised by just how many bottles a small producer could make. I guessed that Château Etienne could turn out up to 30,000 bottles of rosé – more than enough to bankrupt Tanya and me for the foreseeable future.

I popped outside to the car for a little air and also to fetch some of our collection of rosé. Once I'd calmed down I returned with a selection of wines – Rosé de Ricey, a clairet from Bordeaux, a sand wine from the Camargue, our Corsican *gris* and some pink Sancerre. Peter, Tanya and Bernard chatted happily away, reliving our experiences, but all I could think of was how I was going to fulfil my promise to provide a UK importer for his wine.

As we talked, it became apparent that we'd challenged the wrong Frenchman. Bernard's knowledge of rosé was encyclopaedic; he recognised half the producers we'd visited and recommended alternative vignerons to try in each region. Our quest appeared to him to be the most natural thing in the world, and he became so carried away with the conversation that for the first hour he forgot to check the colour of his rosé. Miriam poked her head into the cave, but she seemed unwilling to interrupt when her husband was looking so happy and gave a little wink and shut the door.

Eventually Bernard remembered to take a sample from his *cuve*. The liquid in the first few pipettes looked like muddy water and tasted like grape juice, but after just a little while it began to take on the faintest pink hue.

'There, it's done,' said Bernard, giving a broad smile and turning off the spotlight.

'Now, let's discuss how many bottles you're going to want for England.'

It was now or never. I could explain the misunderstanding with Rosie and try to talk our way out of it. Bernard took a little notebook from his shirt pocket and began making various calculations. I hoped he was working out a generous discount for us, but the numbers looked alarmingly large. He also wrote down the names and addresses of a couple of good shippers and explained that we should insure the wine while it was in transit. As each detail was agreed I felt guiltier and guiltier about raising the Rosie issue as an excuse. I just wanted to know how many bottles he wanted us to take – selling up to five hundred bottles of wine a year would be perfectly possible, any more and we'd be in trouble – but the whole process of working out the logistics seemed to take for ever. Bernard was horrified that we didn't have a cellar in London to store the wine in, and paced up and down until he'd remembered the name of a friend who could help us. And so it went on until we'd agreed everything but the number of bottles.

'How many were you thinking?' Tanya asked.

'Well, this year I'll make five thousand bottles, so say a thousand.'

I tried to smile confidently as I extended my hand to Bernard, but the reality was that we were returning to England with an agreement to import 1,000 bottles of wine a year and no income with which to pay for it. I felt like a complete fool. It was one thing enjoying the adventure of a lifetime in France, quite another to return to England with a millstone around our neck.

'There's just one thing,' a voice called from the metal walkway above our heads.

I looked quizzically upwards.

Peter was holding a pipette full of Bernard's new rosé up to one of the strip lights on the ceiling. 'There might be a problem with next year's batch,' said Peter as he climbed down the ladder with the pipette in his hand, and an ever-widening grin on his face. Squeezing the juice from the pipette into a glass, Peter flicked the spotlight back on. 'It's certainly no longer the palest rosé in France.'

Instead of bleeding off the juice, Bernard had forgotten about it and his rosé had continued to change colour. It was now a dark luscious pink, more of a clairet than a rosé. Bernard stared in disbelief at the glass in Peter's hand. His pen was frozen in the air just above his notebook and beneath it were all the calculations he'd made for the export of the rosé.

A sentence which had been haunting us all summer had suddenly become our friend. It came from Miriam's initial letter to us in February, and Tanya and I mouthed it to each other, 'A small percentage of our annual production, until you discover a paler rosé than Château Etienne.' Nearly all the rosés lined up against the wall – the Billecart-Salmon, the Marsannay, the Corsican *gris*, Château Sainte Marguerite – were now paler than Château Etienne.

'Never mind,' said Peter, giving the immobile Bernard a sympathetic hug, 'there's always the year after. And, anyway,' he added, taking a large gulp from the wine glass, 'I'm sure it will still be marvellous. Absolutely marvellous.'

Some of Peter's Favourite Rosés

'They are all bloody good.' P.T.

Bordeaux

Château de Parenchère, 33220 Sainte Foy la Grande,
Tel: 05 57 46 04 17
Château Lauduc, Maison Grandeau Lauduc, 5 Avenue de
Lauduc, F-33370 Tresses, Tel: 05 57 34 11 82

Vignoble Despagne, Naujan et Postiac, 33420 Branne,
Tel: 05 57 84 55 08

Château de Sours, 33750 Saint Quentin de Baron,
Tel: 05 57 24 10 81

Burgundy

Laurent Fournier, Domaine Jean Fournier, 29 et 34 Rue du
Château, 21160 Marsannay-la-Côte, Côte d'Or,
Tel: 03 80 51 49 42

Champagne

Vilmart & Cie, 4 Rue de la République, 51500 Rilly la
Montagne,
Tel: 03 26 03 40 01

Champagne René Geoffroy, 150 Rue du Bois des Jots, 51480
Cumières, Tel: 03 26 55 32 31

Gaston Chiquet, 912 Avenue du Général Leclerc, BP 1019,
51530 Dizy, Tel: 03 26 55 22 02

Corsica

Clos de Bernardi, 20253 Patrimonio, Corse,
Tel: 04 95 37 01 09

Mark Giovannetti, Domaine Pastricciola, 20253 Patrimonio,
Corse, Tel: 04 95 37 18 31

Languedoc

Félicie Plantation, Domaine de Sainte Marie, 34370
Maureilhan, Tel: 04 67 90 50 32

Loire

Domaine Pascal and Nicolas Reverdy, Maimbray, 18300
Sury-en-Vaux, Tel: 02 48 79 37 31

Domaine Robert and François Crochet, Marcigoué, 18300
Bué, Tel: 02 48 54 21 77

Provence

Domaine les Luquettes, 20 Chemin des Luquettes, 83740 La
Cadière d'Azur, Tel: 04 94 90 02 59

Château de Rochebelle, 400 Chemin des Luquettes, 83740
La Cadière d'Azur, Tel: 04 94 90 06 34

Domaine Tempier, 1082 Chemin des Fanges, 83330 Le Plan
du Castellet, Tel: 04 94 98 70 21

Château La Dorgonne, Domaine de la Dorgonne, 84240
La Tour d'Aigues, Tel: 04 90 07 50 18

Château Sainte Marguerite, F-83250 La Londe des Maures,
Tel: 04 94 00 44 44

Domaine Saint Jean-Baptiste, 1525 Route des Arcs, 83510 Lorgues, Tel: 04 94 73 71 11

Château La Calisse, Route D-560, 83670 Pontevès, Tel: 04 94 77 24 71

Domaine de Saint Janet, 83570 Cotignac, Tel: 04 94 04 77 69

Château Blanc, Quartier Grimaud, Route de Saint Saturnin, 84220 Roussillon, Tel: 04 90 05 64 56

Château de Roquefort, Quartier des Bastides, 13830 Roquefort la Bedoule, Tel: 04 42 73 20 84

Rhône

Domaine de la Mordorée, 30126 Tavel, Tel: 04 66 50 00 75

Some of Tanya's Favourite Places to Stay

Le Mas des Carassins,
Chemin Gaulois, 13210 Saint Rémy de Provence,
Tel: 04 90 92 15 48, Web: www.hoteldescarassins.com

We didn't even manage to stay here on this trip, but when Peter's Bermuda shorts were banned from the municipal swimming baths, Christophe kindly let us use the hotel's pool. It's a renovated Provençal mas with a garden full of olive trees, lemon trees and too many herbs to name. Beware of tripping over ZuZu the dog.

Rouvignac,
34370 Cazouls les Béziers,
Tel: 04 67 93 61 99, Web: www.chateau-de-rouvignac.com

I am not sure which is the greater attraction, Guy or his wonderful château. Enjoy the sumptuous rooms, breakfast on the terrace and make sure you laugh when Guy cracks a joke. By far and away the best place we stayed on our journey.

Auberge des Seguins,
84480 Buoux,
Tel: 04 90 74 16 37

This is where the wedding in the Luberon took place. It is in the middle of nowhere, and some of the rooms are carved from the cliff face. The swimming pool is fed from a mountain stream and it's absolutely freezing. There's a very good restaurant with a pretty terrace as well.

René's villa,
Marine de Farinole, 20253 Farinole, Corsica,
Tel: 04 95 37 10 59

An evergreen part of the island, thanks to René's constant watering. There are a number of small apartments, an immaculately kept swimming pool and two beaches within 100 metres. Patrimonio and Saint Florent are just ten minutes' drive away.

L'Ancienne Auberge,
81140 Puycelsi,
Tel: 05 63 33 65 90

All hotels should be like this. Its American owner, Dorothy, has totally refurbished the building. Each room is beautifully furnished with luxury touches, and Dorothy cooks traditional local cuisine on the small terrace. When we stayed the baker arrived in the morning with brioche still hot from the oven.

Some of My Favourite Restaurants

Nikki Beach,
Saint Tropez,
Tel: 04 94 79 82 04, Web: www.nikkibeach.com

You can almost forget the food, this is all about the experience. Dining under umbrella pines and white parasols, looking up at the blue, blue sky, listening to acid jazz and trying not to upset Tanya by staring at girls in bikinis. It's so perfect, it feels like you are in an advert.

Juveniles,
47 Rue de Richelieu, Paris
Tel: 01 42 97 46 49

Paradise for wine lovers. Tim provides some amazing wines by the glass. Smoky, noisy, ramshackle and utterly adorable small restaurant.

Demeure de Flore,
106 Route Nationale, 81240 Lacabarède, Haut Languedoc
Tel: 05 63 98 32 32, Web: www.hotelrama.com

After the meal I told the chef it was the best food we'd eaten in France and he nearly kissed me. Adventurous cooking, in the middle of nowhere, highly recommended for foodies.

Bar de la Fontaine,
Saint Rémy de Provence, 19 Boulevard Mirabeau,
Tel: 04 32 60 16 89

Salads and *steak frites*, but we go for the view. Right on the outside of the old town, it's perfect for people-watching, and if you crane your neck, you can even seen the Alpilles. Don't tell Dan it's your birthday otherwise he'll dunk you in the fountain.

La Grillade au Feu de Bois,
Flassans, 83440 Le Luc,
Tel: 04 94 69 71 20

The à la carte menu here is just for show. Instead, Madame takes a drag on an impossibly long cigarette and tells you about the dishes of the day. If you still look unsure, she brings the raw ingredients to your table and fixes you with a glare which leaves you with little choice. The food when it arrives is fantastic. It would be – Madame has been up since six in the morning preparing it.

Acknowledgements

My thanks to Peter Tate for being such an enjoyable travelling companion, my parents and Tanya's parents for their unfailing support, my agent, John Saddler, for dreaming of rosé on a rainy Monday morning, my publisher, Alan Samson, for showing such faith, and Lucinda McNeile for that wink as I walked through the revolving doors. In the US, many thanks to George Lucas at Inkwell and Michael Flamini at St Martin's for all their enthusiasm.

And to Claire, Neil (in particular for his wonderful illustrations), Tristan, Martine, Michelle, Chris, Helen, Nick, Hettie, Alexis, Emma, Amanda Doo Win, the Aarvolds, the Hawkes, Remi, Guy, Sophie, Brice, Pierre, Faiza, Libby, Deborah, Sally, Tim, Ali, Cherry, Seb, Uncle Alan and everybody we met along the way for joining us on the adventure.

And finally thanks to Rosie for being the inspiration for this book. I promise to treat you to a nice lunch when you grow up!

For more information on the travels of Jamie, Tanya and Peter, please visit www.extremelypalerose.com

Index